TAB Guide 2007

Money, Pensions and Tax

Sandra Gannon, Jill Kerby, Neil Brooks

Eagle House, 14 Wentworth, Eblana Villas, Dublin 2.

Telephone: (01) 6768633   Fax: (01) 6768641

Published by

TAB TAXATION SERVICES LTD.

Eagle House, 14 Wentworth, Eblana Villas, Dublin 2.

Telephone: (01) 6768633

E-mail: tab@eircom.net

Web Site: www.tab.ie

ISSN No: 0790 9632

ISBN No: 0-9543730-6-5

Printed by Typeform Ltd., Dublin.

Sandra Gannon

Co Author of TAB Guide

Director of TAB Taxation Services Ltd.

Jill Kerby

Personal Finance

Co Author of TAB Guide

Columnist with the Sunday Times

Neil Brooks

Co Author TAB Guide

Director of TAB Financial Services Ltd.

Over 50% higher returns than anyone else since 1989?

Some pedigree!

Table of Contents

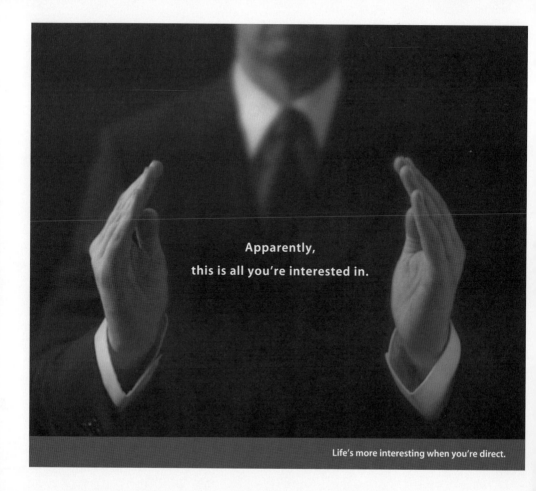

Apparently,
this is all you're interested in.

Life's more interesting when you're direct.

So you're all for giving the small guy a chance until it comes to your money. And who can blame you? We'd be the very same ourselves. Luckily for us, we're the big guys. We're AAA rated. That means safe. And not only are we Europe's largest online bank, we're also part of Rabobank, a Dutch bank that's over 100 years old and has more than €506 billion in assets. That makes us bigger than AIB and Bank of Ireland put together. Ah, bless them.

For a more interesting rate on savings
www.rabodirect.ie

MoneyMate and Investor Magazine
Award for Best Newcomer

RaboDirect.ie
The straight talking online bank   Rabobank

Turning risks into rewards

Your personal finances involve more than putting a little money aside every week, or buying a life insurance policy to ensure a decent burial. Irish people are becoming increasingly sophisticated about how their money is earned, taxed, spent, saved and invested. The huge range of financial products on the market is testimony to this general rise in spending power and awareness.

What is often lacking, however, is personal financial planning. Many people spend more time planning a summer holiday than planning for their retirement - which could last 20 years or more. The hours spent choosing a new car, would be just as well spent looking for the right education investment scheme for your children.

Proper financial planning doesn't take place in a vacuum: a young person starting their first job may not be ready to think about a pension plan, but may need to find the best finance package for a first car or the right savings account to fund the deposit for a new home. What are the most tax-efficient ways to be paid or to spend your surplus income? Does it make financial sense to work abroad for a few years?

Young married couples are always looking to the future. They may be planning a family, moving house, taking on all kinds of responsibilities. They need to make their Wills, get the best finance deal for their new home, make sure they have insured each other's lives (especially when a baby arrives) and they need to set up a viable family budget.

Children bring enormous joy - and bills! If a parent does not stay at home with the baby, someone else may have to be hired to provide childcare. Either way a significant cost is going to be incurred.

Since your child is going to have to be fed, dressed, educated and amused for the next two decades, the sooner you start planning for all these costs the better - it is best to start putting aside even a modest amount of money each week or month. Taking out a savings policy two or three years before secondary or third level school fees fall due is usually about 10 years too late. Now is also the time to consider starting a tax-efficient pension fund, PRSA or AVC (Additional Voluntary Contribution) if you don't have one at your workplace, and to review your life and health insurance policies. Debt management should also be a priority.

The financial needs of someone middle aged are very different from those of a single person or a young parent. Though your monthly outlay may be high, there is light at the end of the child rearing tunnel; ideally you are earning more and have built up some equity in your home and in other savings or investment funds. You may still have 15 or 20 years before retirement, but do you have a pension plan and if so, is it being fully funded?

For the over 60s, retirement can be a blessing or a burden. Without an adequate pension or other assets, day to day spending may have to be curtailed and outstanding debts may provoke a serious financial crisis. For the financially secure, retirement can provide exciting new opportunities to enjoy life at your own pace. Whether you work for someone else or have your own business, you need to take stock of your financial position, including your assets and debts, plus your short and long term health care provisions.

This book also takes you through a number of financial issues that must be dealt with when somebody dies: Wills, Inheritance Tax, Probate, Intestacy and the tax adjustments that come with widowhood.

Financial planning is best done with a trusted advisor, whether it be an accountant, broker or a bank manager. However, independent objective advice is by far the best option and the fee you pay such a person may be one of the best investments you will ever make.

Risks and rewards

Everyone takes chances at some time in their lives. One of the ingredients of success, aside from talent and luck, is the ability to take a few risks to achieve a difficult task or goal.

Taking risks with your money can be difficult to handle, especially if it has been hard-earned or if there is any history of poverty in your family. Yet in the long term, higher risk will give greater potential for higher rewards.

2

Financial institutions recognise this reluctance on the part of many people to take chances with their income or savings, and offer a range of interest earning products with little or no risk and thus low long term rewards.

Low growth/low risk

Deposit-based bank, building society and post office accounts carry the security of vast capital-based institutions of the State. However, since there is virtually no risk associated with the most basic deposit accounts the interest paid is minimal. Savings accounts which may require a minimum deposit amount and savings term, will pay higher interest rates, but will not much exceed the level of inflation over the long term.

Higher returns reflect risk and if you want a high reward, you need to first look at your ability to deal with risk: taking into account your age, your general financial circumstances and your ability to absorb any losses. For example, an elderly widow relying on a State pension for her income, is not a suitable candidate to invest her savings in the stock market. No matter how buoyant the performance of shares may appear to be.

A younger person with a steady rising income, or a professional with existing assets and excellent earning potential, is a good candidate to take some short or long term risks. Whether by investing directly in the stock market, buying property or international managed funds.

Living with risk

To establish your own level of risk, you need to ask yourself the following questions:

- Can I afford to lose my money? Will I be able to meet all my regular, day-to-day obligations if it disappears?

- Am I prepared for the fact that investment markets are cyclical and values are likely to go down as well as up?

- Can I wait for investment markets to recover, if they go down?

If you answer no to any of these questions, then you probably have a relatively low risk threshold. Investing directly in the stock market, or even in unitised funds or property - which all require relatively long term investment periods - may not be for you.

Risk also needs to be related to age. A young person taking out a pension plan which will mature in 40 years should take some risk with the underlying investments in the fund in the early years while someone in their 50's investing in a pension needs to be more cautious, especially if retirement is coming up in just five or ten years time. Parents of young children who want to save for their education, need to take fewer risks than a long term pension investor since time may not be on their side.

Matching the risk

Post Office Savings Certificates, Bonds, Installment Savings Plans, and high yield deposits are good options for low risk savers (like pensioners) or people with short term funding needs, but the biggest danger associated with deposit type products is that they are not always inflation proof. If you leave all your money on deposit for a long period, it could get eaten away by the inevitable rise in the prices of everyday goods and services.

Unit linked or with-profit bonds and tracker bonds are more suitable for those with low to medium risk personal profiles who wish to save on a regular or lump sum basis for up to 10 years or so. For people prepared to go for more of a roller-coaster ride, they could start with domestic or international managed equity funds, where the risk is spread. Then work their way towards direct stock market or property investments.

Independent financial advice

Unless you are a financial expert yourself, the huge variety and types of savings and investment products on the market may make it very difficult for you to know which one is suitable for your particular needs and circumstances. An independent financial advisor could be of great assistance in helping you choose which deposit account to open and which savings policy, pension or stocks and shares to buy.

Independent financial advice is not available from the Post Office, banks or building societies, stockbrokers or life assurance companies since they all want you to buy their individual products. A bank official is not going to recommend that you take out a Post Office Installment Savings Plan, even if it happens to pay more interest than the bank's equivalent scheme. The

Credit Union will not recommend that you borrow from the building society, even if the society's interest rate is lower. A life assurance company wants you to buy into their managed equity fund, not go directly to the stock market.

Commissions are paid by financial institutions as a sales reward to the broker or sales agent when you opt to buy one of their products. The size of the commission will vary in size from institution to institution and also depends on whether you are contributing a lump sum or are making regular monthly or even weekly payments.

Many people advertise themselves as 'independent' financial advisers on mortgages, general and life assurance policies, pensions, deposit accounts and investment funds. Yet nearly all of them accept commission payments from the institution. Those institutions which do not pay broker commissions - the Post Office, some banks and building societies (depending on the product), are unlikely to be recommended by a broker or salesperson who relies solely on commission for their own income.

Avoid misselling

The best way to reduce the danger of being missold an expensive financial service or product is to seek advice from a genuinely independent financial advisor, who ideally should be paid a fee. Knowing that their time and expertise is being rewarded, regardless of whether you buy a product, your wider financial situation will more likely be taken into account and the chance that you will be sold an unsuitable product should be lessened.

Such advisors may be specialist life and pensions brokers, mortgage brokers and/or investment brokers, accountants and management consultants who deal with the personal finances of their private clients.

If you prefer to deal with a commission-based advisor rather than pay a fee, make sure they explain why they are recommending one product or policy over another, and satisfy yourself that they are not being influenced by the size of the commission they are being paid.

2

What you should know about saving

There have never been so many outlets for your savings, whatever your age or financial position. Whether you're 8 or 80, choosing the right savings outlet, and the most tax-efficient one, depends on:

- Why you are saving?

- How accessible you want your money to be?

- The interest rate on offer?

  and

- Security?

An Post

Savings Bonds are a three year investment and require a minimum investment of €100. At the end of the three years, you will currently earn 8% or an annual compound rate of 2.6%. An individual is restricted to holding no more than €120,000 worth of bonds or €240,000 for joint holdings. However you can now reinvest the entire proceeds of maturing savings bonds without regard to the maximum limit. Since the interest is cumulative, and increases towards the latter part of the savings period, you should avoid encashing savings bonds early. Withdrawals are subject to seven days notice.

Savings Certificates are another very tax-efficient way to save your money, at no risk. With a minimum purchase of €50, savings certificate pay 16% interest guaranteed and tax-free over a five year and six month period. This is the equivalent of an average annual compound interest rate of 2.74% per annum.

The following table illustrates how an investment of €1,000 grows every six months:

Investment of €1,000	€
After 1 Year	€1,020
After 2 Years	€1,042
After 3 Years	€1,080

An individual can hold up to €120,000 worth of savings certificates or €240,000 for a joint account, with a minimum purchase of €100. As the interest is low in the early years and high in the later years of the Certificates, you should avoid encashing early.

Term	€	Term	€
After 6 Months	€1,008	After 3 Years & 6 Months	€1,077
After 1 Year	€1,017	After 4 Years	€1,092
After 1 Year & 6 Months	€1,027	After 4 Years & 6 Months	€1,110
After 2 Years	€1,038	After 5 Years	€1,132
After 2 Years & 6 Months	€1,050	After 5 Years & 6 Months	€1,160
After 3 Years	€1,063		

National instalment savings

To join An Post's Instalment Savings Scheme, the saver - who must be at least age seven - must make regular monthly payments for at least one year, of between €25 and €500. Left for another five years, your accumulated savings will then earn 15% tax free. Or a typical compound rate of 2.57%, including the first 12 month contribution period, when no interest is paid.

Instalment Savings are a popular - and tax free way - to watch savings grow over the medium to longer term. They are a good way to save for a child's education, and other domestic goals. Many parents take advantage of the automatic facility on offer which deposits the monthly child benefit allowance (Worth €150 a month per child for the first two children and €185 for third and subsequent children, from April 2006) directly into the Instalment Savings Scheme (as well as into Savings Certificates and other An Post accounts). An early childcare supplement of €1,000 per year is also payable to parents for each child up to the age of six.

The following table illustrates the annual growth rates of National Instalment Savings from the first to fifth years after the 12 month contribution period has been completed:

Term	%
After one year on deposit	2.0
After two years on deposit	4.0
After three years on deposit	6.6
After four years on deposit	10.0
After five years on deposit	15.0

Deposit accounts

An Post has a number of deposit accounts on offer. Similar to bank and building society demand accounts, the interest rate is very low and these are not very suitable as saving vehicles, even if all you want to do is match the rate of inflation.

Prize Bonds

Prize Bonds are a State guaranteed risk free investment. There are thousands of tax-free prizes each month with a monthly jackpot prize of €150,000. Prize Bonds are sold in units of €6.25, (there is a minimum purchase of €25, 4 units). They can be cashed in at any time after an initial period of 3 months.

Children's accounts

Most of the banking institutions have special children's saving clubs or accounts which pay modest rates of interest. Some may also supply the child with a toy savings bank to bring home and fill up, a membership card, savings book and a special joining gift. Some send out bi-annual kids club magazines or posters. Teen and student accounts can be interest bearing and include access to an ATM card for easy withdrawals.

Almost 3 out of 4 women don't have a pension

Contact your broker for further information on Irish Life's pensions

Irish Life

Fixed term accounts

These accounts require that you leave your money with them for an agreed period of time - usually from 1 to 12 months. The interest is higher than is paid on deposit or "share interest" accounts from the building society. The downside of these accounts is that you cannot access your funds until the maturity date.

Regular savings accounts

These accounts reward the regular saver with a slightly higher interest rate (usually about 0.5% more) than is paid by a share or demand deposit account. For this, you must agree to save a set amount over a set period of months.

Regular income accounts

These are ideal for someone who needs a regular income, though they usually require a minimum initial deposit. Interest rates can be quite low, but some banks/building societies offer a high rate if you agree to certain restrictions on the amounts you can withdraw at any one time. The income may vary if interest rates go up or down.

Fixed interest accounts

A sort of savings bond, these accounts are extremely popular and involve the bank or building society guaranteeing to pay a fixed amount of interest for a minimum sum over a specific period. The following table shows typical rates that were available in November 2006 for a €10,000 deposit:

Deposit Term	3 Months		6 months		12 months	
	Gross %	Net %	Gross %	Net %	Gross %	Net %
A.I.B.	1.68%	1.344%	2.25%	1.80%	1.90%	1.52%
Anglo Irish Bank	3.67%	2.945%	3.77%	3.02%	3.87%	3.10%
Bank of Ireland	2.10%	1.68%	2.15%	1.72%	2.25%	1.80%
EBS *	2.50%	2.00%	2.65%	2.12%	2.80%	2.24%
First Active	2.74%	2.19%	2.85%	2.28%	2.96%	2.37%
I.C.S.	2.10%	1.68%	2.15%	1.72%	2.25%	1.80%
Irish Nationwide	3.75%	3.00%	3.90%	3.12%	4.00%	3.20%
Rabo Direct **	n/a	n/a	3.44%	2.752%	3.56%	2.848%
Permanent TSB	2.95%	2.36%	3.25%	2.60%	3.40%	2.72%

* Based on a €25,000 Deposit

Credit Unions

The credit union movement has three million members who save regularly at over 530 different credit unions. Credit unions are essentially savers' co-ops in the community or at the saver's place of work. Members come together to save on a regular basis and to provide loans to each other from the collective savings fund.

Members can save in two ways in a Credit Union:

- Shares which pay a dividend which is determined at the end of the Credit Union financial year

- Deposits which pay interest which is determined in advance. Not all Credit Unions operate deposit accounts.

Loan protection insurance

Many people choose to take out insurance to cover outstanding loans in case of death. In a credit union the loan balances of all insurable members are automatically covered (up to certain limits) at no direct cost to the member. This means that insurable members can borrow in the full confidence that their dependents will not be obliged to repay the outstanding loan balance in the event of their death. Should a member with an outstanding loan balance die, the balance is repaid in full, subject to certain cover limits and conditions which may apply.

Share balance and your age	%
Share balance at age 55 (or lowest balance thereafter)	100%
Share balance at age 60 minus share balance at age 55 (or lowest balance thereafter)	75%
Share balance at age 65 minus share balance at age 60 (or lowest balance thereafter)	50%
Share balance at age 70 minus share balance at age 65 (or lowest balance thereafter)	25%.

Life Cover

Credit Unions can insure their members' savings up to a limit of €7,700, €10,200 or €12,700. The board of each Credit Union decide the limit that will apply to their Credit Union's members. On the death of a member, subject to the relevant limit, the amount of life cover paid is calculated on the lowest balance in your account as follows:

Any savings made after the 70th birthday are not insured. Policy terms and conditions apply.

Example

An individual has the following insurable savings in their account

At age	€
55	€2,000
60	€5,000
65	€7,000
70	€9,000

The individual died last year aged 71 – their Credit Union has an insurable saving limit of €12,700.

The total amount due on the individual's death is €14,750 i.e. €9,000 savings + €5,750 life cover calculated as follows:

	Balance	Savings	Savings Insured	% Insured	Amount Insured
A	At age 55	€2,000	€2,000	100%	€2,000
B	At age 60	€5,000	€3,000 (B less A)	75%	€2,250
C	At age 65	€7,000	€2,000 (D less C)	50%	€1,000
D	At age 70	€9,000	€2,000 (D less C)	25%	€500
Total insurance cover					€5,750

Tax

As a credit union member, you now have several options available to you for the taxation of your annual dividend. In summary, you can continue with the old taxation system for dividend or you can pay Deposit Interest Retention Tax (DIRT) @ 20% on your dividend. You can also avail of significant tax-free allowances on medium term and long term share savings accounts, subject to certain terms and conditions.

Regular Share Accounts

If you have a Regular Share Account, you are required to declare the dividend you receive on your annual tax return and are liable to pay tax on it at your marginal tax rate.

Special Share Accounts

If you opt to have a Special Share Account, your credit union will automatically deduct DIRT at 20% from any dividend you receive on your shares. You will have no further liability to tax on these dividends and you are not required to make any declaration to the Revenue Commissioners

Medium Term Share Accounts

If money invested in a Medium Term Share Account remains in the account for three years, you can earn an annual dividend on that money up to €480 without having to pay any tax. Any dividend you earn above €480 will be taxed at 20%.

Long Term Share Accounts

If money invested in a Long Term Share account remains in the account for five years, you can earn an annual dividend on that money up to €635 without having to pay any tax. Any dividend you earn above €635 will be taxed at 20%.

Each member can only have one Medium or Long Term Share Account. Also penalties apply if you withdraw your savings early.

Summing up

Deposit accounts will never be a way to get rich quick. In the current climate they are barely able to maintain the value of your assets. However, what cash deposits do offer is safety and ready access to your money. So it makes sense to use them:

- To provide cash reserves for emergencies.

- When you know you will need money for a particular purpose soon (a new car, wedding etc.).

- When you think other types of investments are particularly risky and you want to play safe.

Tax

Irish interest

DIRT at the standard rate of 20% will be deducted at source from interest earned on deposit accounts. While no further tax is payable, interest earned from a non special savings account should be included on your tax return as it may be liable to PRSI and health levies. Interest earned from a special savings account should only be on your tax return if you are entitled to a refund of DIRT.

UK interest

Where the UK tax has been deducted at source, the tax will be repaid in full from the UK Tax Authorities on completion of the appropriate form IRL/Individual/Int. If you are resident in Ireland you will only be liable to tax in Ireland on deposit interest earned in the UK. The gross interest is taxed in Ireland under Case III Schedule D.

Other interest

Other interest arising abroad for Irish residents will be taxed whether or not it is remitted to this country. Any tax paid abroad will generally be available as a credit against tax payable here.

Tax rebates

If your income is so low that you don't pay any income tax and you are either permanently incapacitated or 65 or over, you are entitled to claim back any DIRT you have paid on deposit interest. The Income Exemption Limits are listed on page 109.

Budget 2007:   Credit institutions will operate DIRT-free accounts for those aged 65 and over and the permanently disabled, where their income falls below the relevant income tax limits.

Special Savings Incentive Accounts (SSIA)

The first accounts in the Special Savings Incentive Account (SSIA) scheme matured in May 2006, with the bulk of the accounts maturing in the months before the end of April 2007. It is estimated that as much as €16 billion will be paid out during this period.

This unique Government supported saving scheme began on 1st May 2001 and closed for applications on 30th April 2002. The scheme lasts for five years. Account holders are required to save a minimum amount of at least €13 each month for the first year after which they can adjust their savings or investment up to the maximum €254 per month. The Government makes a €1 contribution for every €4 saved every month into the individuals account. Growth in the fund is subject to 23% exit tax.

Account holders can still increase their monthly contribution if they are not paying in the maximum €254. Scheme members can also transfer their funds to other providers, but should check the terms of their scheme before proceeding.

Example 1

> You open an account and decide to save €64 a month for the five year period. You will save €3,840 over the five year period and the Exchequer will contribute a further €960. If the return on investment is assumed to be 4% per annum, the return on this €4,800 saved over a period would be to the order of €495 which would be taxed at 23%. Tax will amount to approximately €114 and your net return would be €5,181.

Make the most of your SSIA nest egg

With Caledonian Life's With-profits Bond, you can use your SSIA nest egg to help plan for your future financial security.

Caledonian Life
Protection Savings & Pensions

To find out more about our With-profits Bond, Life Assurance, Business Assurance and Pension Term Assurance plans, contact your local insurance Broker.

Example 2

> You decide to open an account and save €127 per month. At the start of year two you increase your contribution to €254 per month. Over the term you will save €13,716 over the five year period and the Exchequer will contribute €3,429. Again assuming a 4% annual return, the gain on this €17,145 would be in the region of €1,742, which would be taxed at 23%. Tax will amount to approximately €400 and your net return would be €18,487.

Example 3

> You open an account and save the maximum €254 per month, this time into an investment SSIA that earns a steady 8% return per annum. Over the five year term you save €15,240 and the Exchequer contributes €3,810. The gain on this total of €19,050 is €2,566 which would be taxed at 23%. Tax will amount to approximately €590 and your net return would be €21,026.

	Example 1	Example 2	Example 3
Amount Saved	€3,840	€13,716	€6,096
Government Subsidy	€960	€3,429	€1,524
Interest Earned	€495	€1,742	€242
Total	€5,295	€18,887	€7,862
Taxable Amount	€495	€1,742	€7,862
Tax on Encashment @ 23%	€114	€400	€1,808
Net Proceeds	**€5,181**	**€18,487**	**€6,054**

Revenue Exit Rules

The Revenue Commissioners have issued their guidelines to providers of SSIA about the maturity of accounts. The following is part of the summary of the conditions that will need to be met before the proceeds of SSIAs can be released to their owners:

What is the difference between an SSIA ceasing and maturing?

Where an SSIA is "ceased", either because the account holder no longer wants to maintain an SSIA or is ceased because of a breach of one of the conditions attaching to the scheme, the account is closed and all savings in the account are taxed at 23%. All savings will include original savings as well as the 25% top up and any accrued income/gains earned by the account. Where however, an account holder stops making contributions to the SSIA, the account will remain open and will, subject to the conditions set out below, mature in the normal fashion.

An SSIA will mature either on the death of the account holder or on the fifth anniversary of the opening of the account. When an SSIA matures, only the accrued income/gains on the account will be taxed at 23%. The accrued income/gains does not include the original savings or the 25% top up.

Declaration on maturity

As part of the maturity process, all SSIA account holders must sign and return a declaration (SSIA4) to their Qualified Scheme Manager (QSM) at any time during the three month period ending on the maturity date. The declaration will involve the account holder confirming that the following conditions have been met:

- The individual has only one SSIA.

- The individual is the beneficial owner of the funds in the SSIA.

- The individual was resident or ordinarily resident in the State for the duration of the SSIA.

- The individual subscribed to the SSIA from funds available to him/her or his/her spouse without recourse to borrowings, or the deferral of repayment (whether of capital or interest) of sums borrowed.

- The individual did not assign or otherwise pledge SSIA funds as security for a loan.

Declarations will be issued by the QSM's to each account holder about three months before the account is due to mature. The signed declaration must be returned directly to the QSM. It is important to note that an SSIA cannot be matured by a QSM without a signed declaration.

What are the residency conditions referred to in the declaration?

Individuals who continued to live in the State since the commencement of their SSIA – which will be the case for the vast majority of SSIA holders - will automatically satisfy the residency requirement. However, details of the residency condition are as follows.

Each SSIA holder was required to be resident in the State (essentially living in the State) when the SSIA commenced. Thereafter, he/she is obliged to continue to be either resident or ordinarily resident until he/she makes and signs the SSIA declaration on maturity (SSIA4).

The term "ordinarily resident" as distinct from "resident" refers to an individual's pattern of residence over a number of tax years. An individual who was resident and ordinarily resident in the State does not, on going abroad, cease to be "ordinarily resident" until the individual was not resident for three consecutive tax years. Therefore, an individual who went abroad for a continuous period of not more than three years during the term of his/her SSIA will satisfy the residency condition. This can be the case even if the individual concerned is not resident in the State when he/she is issued with an SSIA4

What if one or more of the conditions have been breached and the declaration cannot be signed?

If an account holder is unable to sign a declaration because of a breach of one or more of the conditions, the account holder must notify the QSM in writing, who will then cease the account and apply tax of 23% to the full proceeds of the SSIA.

Spending your SSIA

The financial institutions offer a wide selection of savings and investment accounts, so shop around carefully before you make your final decision. Surveys undertaken show that a large proportion of account holders are prepared to re-invest their funds as well as spend some of it on travel, cars and home renovations. Whatever the value of your SSIA windfall, you might want to consider the following options:

- Pay off expensive debt, such as credit card, store card and hire purchase borrowings.

- Reduce your outstanding mortgage capital, earn a guaranteed return that is the equivalent of the interest rate and reduce the term of the loan by several years.

- If you have dependents, use this money to pay for adequate term life insurance or other protection policies.

- Open a pension. You have three months after your SSIA matures to take up the SSIA pension Incentive which allows you to transfer up to €7,500 into a pension plan. The Government will top it up with up to €2,500. See page 227 for details.

- Consider investing in low cost investment funds either for dividend and capital growth, or to produce an annual income.

- Use the SSIA fund as a downpayment for a property investment, or for property renovations that will enhance the value of your home.

- Consider using your SSIA as seed capital for a new business.

- Save or invest your fund to pay for the cost of your children's education.

Example

Mortgage interest rate 4.4%

Kate and John bought their house 16 years ago and have four years left on their mortgage. Both have SSIA's worth €22,000 as they saved the maximum amount. They re-mortgaged a few years ago to buy an overseas property and they currently owe €55,000 on their mortgage.

Kate and John have decided that they want to pay off as much of their mortgage as possible using their SSIA money. By paying €44,000 off their mortgage, they save over €4,000 in interest costs and reduce the mortgage term on their mortgage so they would be mortgage free in about 10 months.

* Source: Financial Regulator

When does your SSIA account mature

Your SSIA account will mature 5 years after it was opened. If you have a deposit based SSIA, it will mature at the end of the month following the 5th anniversary of the commencement date. For example if your SSIA was opened on May 15th 2001, it will mature on May 31st 2006.

Maturity dates for SSIA accounts

SSIA Commencement date	SSIA maturity date	SSIA4 required in period
May 2001	31 May 2006	1 Mar 2006 -31 May 2006
June 2001	30 June 2006	1 Apr 2006 - 30 Jun 2006
July 2001	31 July 2006	1 May 2006 - 31 Jul 2006
August 2001	31 August 2006	1 Jun 2006 - 31 Aug 2006
September 2001	30 September 2006	1 Jul 2006 - 30 Sept 2006
October 2001	31 October 2006	1 Aug 2006 - 31 Oct 2006
November 2001	30 November 2006	1 Sept 2006 - 30 Nov2006
December 2001	31 December 2006	1 Oct 2006 - 31 Dec 2006
January 2002	31 January 2007	1 Nov 2006 - 31 Jan 2007
February 2002	28 February 2007	1 Dec 2006 - 28 Feb 2007
March 2002	31 March 2007	1 Jan 2007 - 31 Mar 2007
April 2002	30 April 2007	1 Feb 2007 - 31 Apr 2007

For example, if you commenced your SSIA in February 2002, the maturity date is 28 February 2007. You will be obliged to complete and sign and return a SSIA4 declaration to your financial institution between 1 December 2006 and 28 February 2007.

Important Revenue Requirements

In order to correctly mature your SSIA account, Revenue have stipulated that a SSIA 4 Declaration of Maturity form **must** be completed by the SSIA account holder within the correct time frame. This will ensure that the 23% tax will only be charged on the bank interest earned on your SSIA.

Failure to complete the SSIA 4 form will incur a 23% exit tax charge on the total balance of your account.

You should receive a SSIA 4 Declaration of Maturity form from your financial institution before your SSIA maturity date. When you receive this form please read it carefully. If you are satisfied that you meet all the conditions stated on the form, please sign it and return it to your financial institution.

The declaration states that:

- you have only one SSIA

- you are the beneficial owner of the assets of the SSIA

- you are resident, or ordinarily resident, in the State since commencement of the account

- your SSIA is funded from resources available to you (or your spouse) without recourse to borrowing or by the deferral of repayment of sums already borrowed.

- you did not assign or pledge assets held in the SSIA as security for a loan.

It is an offence to falsely make these declarations.

Why is the SSIA 4 declaration of maturity form so important?

Returning the SSIA 4 declaration is very important as it determines the tax that you will pay when your SSIA finishes.

- if you return your SSIA 4 declaration form on time, a tax of 23% will apply to the interest only, earned on your account.

- if you return your SSIA4 declaration late or cannot fulfil all the conditions on form, a tax of 23% will apply to the **total balance** on your SSIA account.

3

Take advantage of your investments

If you have spare cash each week or month and want to put it away for a rainy day, there are plenty of secure, accessible savings outlets such as the post office, bank or building society and the credit union. These savings can normally be withdrawn or even borrowed against at any time.

Other people with spare cash or a windfall, whether an inheritance, a gain from the sale of a capital asset (a house, car, antique) or perhaps even a retirement or redundancy lump sum, often want more than a modest, guaranteed return. They want to see this money earn more significant returns, - they want an investment.

Investments come in three basic forms:

- Bonds
- Stocks & shares
- Property

Historically, high quality shares have on average tended to give greater returns than any other class of investment. Beating property, bonds and deposits.

WINNER OF THE
MONEYMATE/INVESTOR MAGAZINE
PROPERTY INVESTMENT COMPANY
OF THE YEAR 2005 AND 2006

For Property Investments go with number

1

As the premier innovators in the Property Investment market, Friends First are the first door you knock on if you want to invest in property without the inconvenience of actually purchasing and maintaining a property itself. Our high-performing funds are second to none and we offer unrivalled management expertise to ensure your fund performs to its highest potential. These options are available to investors with a lump sum to invest or as part of a pension plan.

Contact your Broker, Local First Active Branch or Friends First Direct on 1890 201 430.

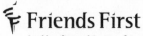

Friends First
Looking forward to your future
www.friendsfirst.ie

Bonds

Beyond the security of the bank and building society deposits, lie a whole family of fixed-income assets, which are dependent on fluctuations in the national and world economies for their day to day values.

When you understand how they work, bonds can be a very useful instrument for investment purposes.

Bonds are long-term fixed-interest debt. They are issued by companies and Governments - particularly by Governments. What happens is that companies or the Government take your money now and promise to repay you sometime in the future.

Nominal value

This is the value guaranteed to be repaid to you by a government or company at maturity. The price of a particular Bond is normally quoted in terms of €100 nominal value of the stock. For example, a price of €115.35 for the 11.75% Capital Stock 15th April 2010, means that €100 of the nominal value of the stock could be bought today for €115.35.

Maturity date

Most Bonds have a maturity date, i.e. the date at which the nominal value of the stock is guaranteed to be repaid to you by a Government or company. Remember that the guaranteed payment at maturity is not the original sum you invested, but the nominal value of the stock you hold.

There is a wide choice of Bonds available - with maturity dates that may only be a few months away or as much as 20 years or more away.

Gilts

Because they have always been regarded as being extremely safe, government bonds are often called 'gilt-edged' securities, or simply 'gilts'.

However, it is important to note that unlike bank or building society deposits, bonds are only completely safe if you are willing to hold them until they mature. If you need to get at your money earlier you can sell your holding in the 'gilts market'. Gilts are traded in much the same way as shares and, as in the case with shares, prices fluctuate daily.

Coupon

The "coupon" is the term used to describe the rate of interest payable on a gilt. It is expressed as a % of the nominal value of stock. In the case of the 11.75% Capital Stock 15th April 2008, the coupon is 11.75%. So, if you buy €100 nominal value of this stock, the annual payment guaranteed by the Government is €11.75 p.a.

Stock types

Gilts are generally categorised by reference to their maturity dates:

Short term gilts: The maturity date of the stock is within the next 5 years.

Medium term gilts: The maturity date of the stock is more than 5 and less than 15 years away.

Long term gilts: The maturity date of the stock is more than 15 years away.

Ex div/cum div

In general, interest payments are made on gilts at six monthly intervals.

To facilitate these payments, the Register of Gilt Owners is closed 31 days before a dividend is due to be paid and each registered owner on this closing date is paid the upcoming dividend.

If you buy stock before this closing date you are said to buy it "cum div" and you will be entitled to receive all of the next dividend payment when it becomes due. If you buy a stock after this closing date, you are said to buy it "ex div" and you will not receive the upcoming dividend.

Tax

If you sell a government stock "cum div", the price you receive will reflect an interest element which the purchaser will receive. This interest element can also be taxable in your hands, under Case III Schedule D.

Example

You purchased €20,000 4% Guaranteed Stocks on 7th July 2006 and resold the stock on 28th November 2006 for €21,000. The details are as follows;

Last dividend date	01/07/06
Ex dividend date	02/12/06
Next dividend date	01/01/07

You held the stock for 145 days and received no interest payment. However the following interest will be deemed to have accrued and may be taxable,

$$€20,000 \times 4\% \times \frac{145}{365} = €317.80$$

No tax may be payable on this amount if:

- The stock transfer was between you and your spouse.

or

- The stock has been held by you for a continuous period of two or more years.

If you are deemed to be trading in "gilts", the full gain will be taxed as income.

Other interest received from gilts will be taxed in the normal way under Case III Schedule D on a current year basis. If you made a capital gain on a gilt, no tax is payable unless you are deemed to be trading in gilts.

UK gilts

Where the UK tax has been deducted at source, the tax will be repaid in full from the UK tax authorities on completion of the appropriate form IRL/Individual/Int. The gross interest is taxed in Ireland under Schedule D Case III.

Stocks and shares

Suppose that at the end of 1919, one of your relatives had invested €1,000 on the London Stock Exchange. This portfolio would now be worth over

€6,695,623*. Of course, €1,000 doesn't buy what it used to in 1919 -in real terms the purchasing power of the €1,000 then would have turned into something like €222,003 now. However, the €1,000 investment on the London Stock Exchange in 1919 would have increased your real wealth by a factor of more than 30.

When you buy stocks and shares, you become a part owner of the company and are entitled to a percentage of its profits by way of a dividend. Dividends are normally paid twice a year. Unlike the income from a bank or building society, share dividends are not directly related to the money you invest but, instead, are linked to the growth in the company's profits and its dividend policy. When you invest money in shares, you may be more interested in capital growth or the increase in the relevant stock market valuation.

However, if you are going to need your money next month or next year, shares are not for you and you would be better off putting your money in a more secure place. On the other hand, if you can wait for five, ten or even twenty years for your investment to "mature" and can cope with the "crashes" along the way, then shares are likely to give you a very good return.

Buying shares is a risky business and there is always the possibility of a bad investment and of losing some, or all, of your money. This risk of loss usually diminishes over time, provided you choose wisely and spread your risks.

If you decide to invest in shares, you may want to keep an eye on their performance by reading the financial pages of your daily newspaper. At first sight these can be puzzling but they do contain a lot of useful information. A typical section of a financial page will look like this;

High	Low	Company	Share Price	+ -	Div. yld.	P/E	Times cover
14.05	8.70	ABC Ltd	10.73	-0.47	3.10	10.60	2.80
20.40	11.22	XYZ Ltd	14.70xd	0.00	1.91	9.70	5.14
11.15	6.26	Z Ltd.	7.23	+0.05	2.20	9.40	3.22

High and low

The first column usually gives the highest price paid for that individual share in the current year and the second column gives the lowest price. The idea is to buy as close as possible to the lowest price and sell as close as possible to the highest price.

Company

The next section gives the relevant company or stock name.

Share price

The share price in column four is usually the previous day's closing price.

Ex-dividend

As we said earlier, companies usually pay dividends twice a year. About six to eight weeks before a dividend is paid, the company announce what the next dividend will be. A week or two after this announcement, the company's share register is temporarily closed. Upcoming dividends will be paid to the registered shareholders on this date. The company's shares will then go ex-dividend and are marked "xd" in the paper. So, if you buy shares marked xd you will not get the upcoming dividend.

Rise or fall

Column five gives the difference between the opening and closing prices of each share in the previous day's trading.

Dividend yield

The dividend yield is the ratio of a share's annual dividend to the share price. Column six gives the gross dividend yield i.e. the dividend yield before tax.

Price earnings ratio (p/e)

Traditionally, many people related a share price to a company's net asset value. Another way of valuing a share is to relate the share price to the company's flow of profits. The price earnings ratio in column seven is calculated by dividing the company's share price by the after-tax earnings due to each share over the company's most recent financial year. This ratio can also be calculated using expected rather than historical earnings. A high P/E ratio shows that investors have a lot of confidence in that company's future prosperity. A low P/E ratio can mean an investor is getting earnings "cheap" or can imply a lack of confidence in that company's future prosperity.

Times cover

The times cover is the ratio of last year's profits to the dividends paid. In the case of XYZ Ltd., it is 5.14. In other words, if XYZ Ltd. had paid out all of its profits to shareholders, the dividend would have been 5.14 times higher.

CFD Accounts

What are CFD's?

CFD's, or Contracts For Difference, are an agreement between you and a broker to exchange, at the closing of the contract, the difference between the opening and closing prices, multiplied by the number of shares in the contract.

You predict whether the price will rise or fall and invest money on this basis. You take a long position if you think the price will rise, or take a short position if you think the price will fall. You make a profit or loss depending on whether you have correctly predicted the direction in which the price will move. This means you can make money even if the price of a share falls, if you have predicted correctly and 'gone short'. Going short means that you sell stock you don't own then buy it back later, hopefully at a lower price to realise a profit.

In CFD dealing you do not physically buy or hold the physical underlying share; you only have indirect access to the price performance. However, you would benefit from a dividend payment when going long.

Margins and gearing

CFD's are dealt with on a margin basis, and you secure the transaction by paying a deposit, also known as a Notional Trading Requirement, of around

10% of the contract value. So if you wanted to undertake a contract worth €20,000 you would need an NTR of €2,000. The understanding is that you must be able to cover the entire contract value and any associate costs if the price moves unfavourably. You must also be able to maintain the required margin, which may involve topping up the deposit if the level of exposure increases during the period of the contract.

The benefits of margin trading are that if you make a profit, you haven't had to make a full outlay of collateral. Also, you are able to take a much larger position than you would normally be able to, and there is the potential of significantly greater profits than traditional shares dealing (also known as 'gearing').

However, you should note that gearing also means that the potential for losses is equally increased. Because of this, you should be absolutely clear about how the CFD works and you should consult an independent financial adviser, if you are unsure whether CFD's are a suitable investment for you.

Pricing of CFD's

A CFD contract price is worked out using the calculation below. The unit value of the underlying shares x the percentage deposit requirement x number of shares.

Example

Commission rates apply to CFD's in the same way as traditional share dealing, although no stamp duty is charged on CFD transactions.

> If you were dealing a CFD on 600 shares of a share with a market price of 800c:
>
> 800 x 10% x 600 = (48000c) = €480

In essence:

- If you go short then you receive an interest credit to your account.

- If you go long, then you pay the interest (also known as a daily financing charge).

The best way to understand how a CFD works is to look at some examples of CFD deals.

Going long - buying a CFD

You are described as going long if you believe the price will rise, and enter into a contract for this. Like traditional share dealing, going long means a profit if the price rises, and a loss if the price falls. If the CFD is not opened and closed on the same day then a daily financing charge will apply. There will also be commission charged on the transactions.

Example

A client believes that the price of Company X will rise, so decides to buy a CFD for 10,000 shares at 193c. The deposit is 10% of the contract value. In the same day. the prices rises to 267c, and so the client decides to sell and close the position. There is no stamp duty, and no financing charge as the deal was completed in one day.

Opening position		Closing the position	
Value of shares 10,000 @ 193c	€19,300	Value of shares 10,000 @ 267c	€26,700
CFD Commission	€28.95	CFD Commission	€40.05
Deposit required	€1,930	Profit	€7,331

Going short - selling a CFD

You are described as going short if you believe the price will fall, and enter into a contract for this. Unlike traditional share dealing, going short means a profit if the price falls but a loss if the price rises. If the CFD is not opened and closed on the same day then a credit will be paid to your account. There will also be commission charged on the transactions.

Example

> A client believes that the price of Company X will fall, so decides to sell a CFD for 10,000 shares at 193c. The deposit is 10% of the contract value. In the same day. the prices falls to 100c, and so the client decides to by back and close the position. There is no stamp duty.
>
> | Opening position | | Closing the position | |
> |---|---|---|---|
> | Value of shares 10,000 @ 193c | €19,300 | Value of shares 10,000 @ 100c | €10,000 |
> | CFD Commission | €28.95 | CFD Commission | €15.00 |
> | **Deposit required** | **€1,930** | **Profit** | **€9,256.05** |

Investment clubs

Investment Clubs are another way to invest directly in stocks and shares, while at the same time spreading your risk and keeping your costs down. These clubs involve a group of like-minded people (usually no more than 20) getting together once a month to pool their cash and their respective skills to research and buy stocks.

Tax

Buying and selling shares can give rise to two taxes:

- Income tax on dividends you receive.
- Capital Gains Tax (CGT) on investment gains.

Irish resident companies

Dividend Income is liable to income tax under Schedule F.

When you receive a dividend from an Irish Resident company, withholding tax at the standard rate tax (20%) is deducted by the company. If the amount of tax withheld exceeds your total tax liability you can claim a refund. However, if you are a higher rate taxpayer you will have to pay the difference between the standard rate and the higher rate.

Example

> You receive a dividend of €1,000 in November 2006. Dividend withholding tax of €200 (20%) is withheld by the company. Assuming you have already used up your standard rate cut off point (see page 132), your tax liability will work out as follows:
>
> | | | 2006 €|
> |---|---|---|
> | | Irish Dividend Gross | €1,000 |
> | | Tax @ 42% | €420 |
> | Less: | Withholding Tax | €200 |
> | | **Additional Tax Payable** | **€220** |

UK dividends

When you obtain a dividend from a UK company it will normally show:

(a)   The net dividend; and

(b)   A tax credit which is equivalent to 1/9th of the net dividend.

Only the net dividend is taxable in Ireland, i.e. the cash amount received exclusive of any tax credit.

Example

> You get a net dividend from UK Ltd. of €180, your dividend voucher will also show a tax credit of €20 (1/9th). You pay Irish income tax as follows, assuming that your top rate of tax is 42% in 2006 (ignoring the rates of exchange).
>
> | | 2006 €|
> |---|---|
> | UK Dividend (€180 net) | €180 |
> | Irish Tax @ 42% | €76 |
>
> The UK tax credit of £20 is non-refundable even if you are a non-taxpayer.

Capital gains tax

All realised gains in excess of your annual exemption limit (€1,270) will be liable to Capital Gains Tax at 20%. (See page 285).

Property

There are three reasons why most people think property is a good investment:

- Buying property has been, for most people, the only way to borrow large amounts of money cheaply.

- Rapid increases in property values over the years.

- Tax incentives relating to property investment. Although these were severely curtailed in the 2006 Finance Act.

Borrowing money cheaply

Suppose you buy a property for €200,000 cash and its price rises by 3% in real terms each year for the next 20 years. At the end of that 20 years, the property will be worth €361,200 in real terms. You make a real profit of €161,200 (after accounting for inflation).

Now, suppose that instead of putting up the whole €200,000 yourself, you borrow €180,000, over 20 years and rent the property. We also assume that the rent you will receive from the property will be sufficient to repay the loan and also pay all interest charges, expenses and tax bills associated with the property over the next 20 years.

After 20 years, your stake in the property will have gone up from €20,000 to €361,200 and your new profit is €341,200. Now, because your original investment was low, your stake has increased by a factor of 17 in real terms (€341,200 ÷ €20,000). That's a good investment by any standards.

The ups and downs of property prices

Although property prices have steadily increased in this country over the past 30 years - these increases, as the figures below will highlight, have not always been consistent.

INVEST IN EUROPEAN PROPERTY
WITHOUT EVER LEAVING HOME.

Hibernian's new European Residential Property Fund
invests in a range of European property locations including
apartments in Prague or Warsaw. Which means you can
now combine all the convenience, transparency and tax
benefits of a Hibernian Pension with exposure to Europe's
most dynamic property markets. Talk to your financial
adviser about a Hibernian Pension today.

HIBERNIAN
an AVIVA company

Good Thinking

The following chart illustrates how the average three bedroom semi-detached house in typical Dublin has increased in price over the past 30 years.

Average price of 3 bed semi-detached house in suburban Dublin

Year	€
1977	€8,5000
1987	€47,500
1997	€104,000
2007	€325,000

Commercial property

The value of commercial property is normally directly related to the rental income it can generate. In the table below, we highlight how rental income from commercial properties has been increasing at different paces over the years. This illustration outlines the average cost per square foot of commercial properties in the Dublin area over the past 30 years.

So, when it comes to investing in property it is always wise not to lose sight of both the current and long-term potential return on your investment.

Year	Average office rental cost per sq. ft.	Average retail rental cost per sq. ft. (shopping centres)	Average industrial rental cost per sq. ft.
1977	€4.75	n/a	n/a
1987	€12.50	€26.50	€3.65
1997	€20.50	€210.00	€9.25
2007	€65.00	€325.00	€12.00

(The above figures relating to property were provided by CB Richard Ellis Research)

How to Fix Bad Habits

4: Procrastinating

Stems from fear of failure. Results in missed opportunities, missed bin collections, lots of shouting and possibly plate throwing. Remedy by introducing personal incentives for completing things. Also consider replacing this behaviour with a more beneficial habit, see below:

The Regular Saver Account: *A better habit to get into.*
Call us 8am - 8pm Monday to Friday to find out more on **1850 44 22 22** or simply free text ANGLO to **50100.**

YOUR SAVINGS SPECIALISTS

Rental Properties

Individuals who purchase rental properties normally have substantial incomes so the rate of tax on rental income will generally be high (42% tax plus 5% PRSI & levies).

The rate of Corporation Tax on rental income is 25%. Undistributed rental income in a closed company is liable to a surcharge of 20% so the effective Corporation Tax rate can be as high as 40%.

Tax on disposal

When a property is sold the taxable proceeds will normally be subject to CGT at 20%. So, if you own the property personally you retain proceeds less 20% CGT. If the property is owned by a company it also pays CGT at 20%. However, there will be a further personal tax liability if you wish to gain access to the cash within the company. If you access the cash by way of salary or dividend, the rate could be as high as 42%. The other option is to liquidate the company, this will give rise to a new 20% CGT liability or what is commonly known as the double "hit".

Example

You set up "A" Limited ten years ago with ordinary share capital of €2. "A" Limited bought a property for letting for €130,000. "A" Limited sells the building now for €500,000. Here we assume indexation of 30% for CGT purposes and that the company has no other assets or liabilities. The tax position for you is also illustrated as if you bought the property personally.

	Personal purchase €	"A" Limited €
Sale Proceeds	€500,000	€500,000
Less: Cost of property plus indexation	€130,000	€130,000
Taxable Amount	€370,000	€370,000
CGT on €370,000 @ 20%	€74,000	€74,000
Available for distribution		€426,000
CGT on liquidation of A Limited €426,000 @ 20%		€85,200
Net personal proceeds	€426,000	€340,800
Total Tax payable	**€ 74,000**	**€ 159,200**

Stamp Duty

Market Value	Houses/Apartments
Up to €127,000	Exempt
€127,001 - €190,500	3%
€190,501 - €254,000	4%
€254,001 - €317,500	5%
€317,501 - €381,000	6%
€381,001 - €635,000	7fi%
Over €635,000	9%

If you purchase a property for investment purposes stamp duty will be payable as follows;

Market Value	Non Residential Properties
Up to €10,000	Exempt
€10,001 - €20,000	1%
€20,001 - €30,000	2%
€30,001 - €40,000	3%
€40,001 - €70,000	4%
€70,001 - €80,000	5%
€80,001 - €100,000	6%
€100,001 - €120,000	7%
€120,001 - €150,000	8%
Over €150,000	9%

Where VAT is included in the cost of the property, it should be deducted before calculating the charge or rate of stamp duty.

Property tax incentives

Property Tax incentives fall into two main areas:

- Capital allowances relating to Industrial buildings.

- Tax incentive relating to designated areas.

Qualifying industrial buildings

Section 268 TCA 1997 sets out the type of industrial buildings or structures, which qualify for relief. These are, a building or structure in use:

- For the purposes of a trade carried on in a mill, factory or other similar premises, or a laboratory the sole or main function of which is the analysis of minerals in connection with exploration for or extraction of such minerals.

- For the purposes of a dock undertaking.

- For the purpose of growing fruit, vegetables in the trade of market gardening.

- For the purpose of the trade of hotel-keeping.

- For the purpose of intensive production of cattle, sheep, pigs, poultry, or eggs in the course of a trade, other than farming.

- For the purpose of a trade which consists of the operation or management of an airport and which is an airport runway or an airport apron used solely or mainly by aircraft carrying passengers or cargo for hire or reward.

- For the purpose of a trade which consists of the operation or management of a qualifying nursing home.

- For the purpose of a trade which consists of the operation or management of a qualifying convalescent home (such convalescent home must hold a certificate from the relevant Health Board) for the provision of medical and nursing care or persons recovering from a treatment in a hospital which provides treatment for acutely ill patients.

Type of allowances available

Initial allowance

An initial allowance is available in the case where a person incurred capital expenditure on the construction of an industrial building or structure which is occupied for the purpose of a trade.

The initial allowance is available to both owner occupiers and lessors. These allowances were severely restricted over the years and were eliminated for capital expenditure incurred after 31st March 1992, except in certain cases. e.g. buildings in designated areas.

Annual allowance

An annual allowance is generally available to persons holding an interest in an industrial building or structure. The rate varies between 4% and 15% depending on the type of trade for which the industrial building or structure is being used. The annual allowance is available to both owner-occupiers and lessors of buildings.

Nursing homes, **convalescent homes** and **crèche facilities** will normally qualify for a 15% annual allowance on qualifying expenditure for the first six years and 10% in year seven.

Capital Allowances on hotels and holiday camps are allowed at 4% per annum for 25 years.

1999 Urban renewal scheme

Following an in-depth consultancy study on the operation of urban renewal schemes, the Government introduced a major new urban renewal scheme in 1999. The scheme, which benefited five cities and thirty-eight towns represented a more targeted approach to urban renewal incentives, concentrating not just on areas of physical development but also on issues of local socio-economic benefits.

The termination date was extended to 31st July 2006 in respect of the 1999 Urban renewal scheme, provided 15% of the total project cost had been incurred by 30th June 2003. Application for certification must have been submitted to the local authority by 31st July 2003 and certification must have been issued by 30th September 2003.

Town Renewal Scheme

Town Renewal Schemes are based on a similar approach to that which applies in relation to the 1999 Urban Renewal Scheme. Designations are based on Town Renewal Plans (TRPs) which in turn were based on the principles of promoting the physical renewal and revitalisation of towns, enhancing their amenities and promoting sustainable development patterns. The termination date for Town renewal scheme has been extended to 31st July 2006 provided full planning application has been received by the relevant planning authority by 31st December 2004. See page 47 for changes that were announced to the scheme in the Finance Act 2006.

Rural renewal relief

This relief was introduced in the 1998 Finance Act. It designated parts of Cavan, Roscommon and Sligo and the administrative county of Leitrim and Longford.

The deadline for the Rural and Urban Renewal Schemes for tax relief for expenditure on commercial, industrial and residential projected was extended to 31st December 2004.

The termination date for Rural renewal relief was extended to 31st July 2006 provided full planning application has been received by the relevant planning authority by 31st December 2004. See page 47 for changes where were announced for the scheme in the Finance Act 2006.

Phasing out of property tax incentives

The qualifying period for Urban Renewal Scheme, Rural Renewal Scheme, Town Renewal Scheme and the special reliefs for hotels, holiday cottages, student accommodation, multi-storey car parks, third-level education buildings, sports injury clinics, developments associated with park and ride facilities is being phased out as follows;

- 100% relief where expenditure has been incurred by 31st December 2006

- 75% relief where expenditure has been incurred in the period 1st January 2007 to 31st December 2007

- 50% relief where expenditure has been incurred in the period 1st January 2008 to 31st July 2008.

The time extensions in 2006 and 2007 will only apply if 15% of the construction expenditure (excluding site cost) has been incurred by 31st December 2006.

The tax reliefs will cease for expenditure incurred after 31st July 2008.

The tax reliefs for investment in childcare facilities, private nursing homes and private hospitals are to be continued. Private psychiatric hospitals can now qualify for tax relief.

The park-and-ride (excluding the residential and commercial elements) and Living-over-the-shop scheme are being continued but in a more focused way.

Example - Residential owner occupier

You bought a new home for €375,000 in a designated area: - site cost €35,000.

		€
	Purchase Price	€375,000
Less:	Site Cost	(€35,000)
	Qualifying Expenditure	€340,000
	Annual Allowance **(5% of €340,000 over 10 years)**	**€17,000**

This annual allowance will be granted at your marginal rate of tax

Tax summary

Below, we summarise the tax incentives available to owner occupiers and investors for urban, town and rural renewal schemes.

Residential - owner occupier	• Construction: 5% deduction against total income for 10 years • Refurbishment: 10% deduction against total income for 10 years
Residential - investor	• Section 23 - type relief in respect of expenditure on the construction, conversion or refurbishment expenditure.
Non residential - owner occupier	• Free depreciation - 50% • Initial allowances - 50% • Annual allowance for 12½ years - 4%
Non residential - investor	• Initial allowance - 50% Year 1 • Annual allowance for 12½ years - 4%

Residential - Investor

Section 23/27

Section 23/27 type relief is available on the construction, conversion and refurbishment of certain residential premises in designated areas.

The minimum floor area for a house is 35 square metres and the maximum area is 125 square metres. The minimum floor area for a flat or maisonette is 30 square metres and the maximum area is 90 square metres. The property must be used solely as a dwelling and cannot be owner-occupied within ten years of the first letting. If, however, within the ten year period, the property ceases to be a qualifying premises e.g. is sold or owner-occupied, all the allowances already given will be clawed back. If a qualifying property is sold within the ten year period and is then rented, the purchaser will be entitled to the same allowance as the original owner. There is no restriction on the amount of rent which may be charged, however the property must be let under a qualifying lease. i.e.

- The lease must be a genuine rental agreement with regular payments by way of rent.

- The tenant cannot be granted an option to buy the property at less than the market value.

Qualifying expenditure

If you buy a qualifying property in a designated area, the site cost together with a portion of the builder's profit is not allowed as qualifying expenditure.

Qualifying expenditure is arrived at by applying the formula:

Purchase Price   x $\dfrac{\text{Builder's Development Cost}}{\text{Site Cost + Builder's Development Cost}}$

Example

	€
Cost of Site	€ 45,000
Development Costs	€230,000
Builder's Profit	€ 25,000
Purchase Price	**€300,000**

Qualifying expenditure is as follows:

€300,000 x $\dfrac{€230,00}{€45,000 + €230,000}$	=	€250,909

This €250,909 is available to offset against all taxable rental income.

Example

	Without Section 27 €	With Section 27 €
Taxable Rental Income	€30,000	€30,000
"Section 27" relief	-	€250,909
Tax Payable @ 42%	€12,600	Nil
Rental Loss to be carried forward to the following year	**Nil**	**€220,909**

Buying a second hand "Section 27" property

If you buy a property where the qualifying expenditure has already been claimed, all relief already granted to the original owner will be clawed back and passed on to you, provided you rent a property and the property is less than 10 years old.

Example - Non residential

You bought a site in a designated area for €1,000,000. The qualifying building expenditure at December 2005 was €600,000. Your tax rate is 42%. Your tax savings are as follows;

	€
Development Cost	€600,000
Capital Allowances 50% in Year 1	€300,000
Tax Saving @ 42%	**€126,000**

You will also get a €24,000 Annual Allowance for years 2 to 13 and an annual allowance of €12,000 in year 14. These annual allowances will be granted at your marginal rate of tax.

Double rent allowance for traders

A trader is entitled to a tax allowance of double the rent payable for an industrial or commercial building in a designated area if the lease has been negotiated during the qualifying period. The allowance is available for a period of 10 years. The relief does not apply unless the building is let on bonafide commercial terms to an unconnected person.

Restriction on capital allowances

The maximum amount of capital allowances which you can offset against your total income has been capped at €31,750 in any one year for investors. This cap does not affect owner occupiers or active partners.

Tax

Property investment can give rise to two taxes;

- Income Tax on the Rental Income.

- Capital Gains Tax on investment profits (see page 287).

Restrictions on the use of tax relief by high income taxpayers

From 1st January 2007 the amount which an individual can claim as a deduction in respect of specified reliefs will be restricted to the greater of €250,000 or 50% of the person's regrossed income. The specified reliefs include property tax incentive schemes and artists exemption. Any unused reliefs can be carried forward.

Income tax

Rents are taxed under Schedule D Case V on the basis of the actual year's income - e.g. rents arising in the year ending 31st December 2006 are assessed to tax in the income tax year 2006. The following expenses can normally be deducted from the gross rents for tax purposes.

- Interest paid on money borrowed to purchase residential property.

- Rent payable on the property.

- Rates payable on the property.

- Goods provided and services rendered in connection with the letting of the property.

- Repairs, insurance, maintenance and management fees.

- Capital allowance of 12.5% per annum on the value of the fixtures and fittings.

- Mortgage protection premiums

Be sure to keep all receipts, especially for repairs and maintenance, as your Inspector of Taxes may wish to examine these.

A typical rental income and expenditure account is shown on page 53.

Residential Property

Rental Income and Expenditure Account Y/E 31st December 2007

Name: _____   PPS No: _____

                                 Y/E: _____

€

			€
	Rents Received		€15,000
Less:	Allowable expenses		
	Rates/Ground rents payable	€ 100	
	Insurance on premises	€ 500	
	Repairs and renewals	€ 900	
	Light, heat and telephone	€ 400	
	Cleaning and maintenance	€1,000	
	Agency and advertising	€ 700	
	PRTB Registration	€ 70	
	Interest on borrowed money	€6,500	
	Mortgage protection premiums	€ 300	
	Sundry expenses	€ 300	
	Total expenses		€10,770
	Net rental income		€4,230
Less:	Capital allowances on fixtures & fittings €7,000 @ 12.5%		(€875)
	Taxable rental income after capital allowances		€3,355
	Income Tax & Levies - assuming a 42% rate of tax + 5% PRSI & Levies.		**€1,543**

Private Residential Tenancies Board

Entitlement to a deduction for interest paid on borrowed money employed in the purchase, improvement or repair of a rental residential property is now conditional on compliance with the registration requirements of the Residential Tenancies Act 2004. This change applies to interest paid by individuals during the year of assessment 2006 and subsequent years.

Persons who are required to register

The Act applies to the vast majority of private rented dwellings situated in Ireland (dwellings outside Ireland are outside the scope of the Act). Below is a list of the types of dwellings that are excluded and in respect of which there is no requirement to register tenancies.

- Business premises.

- Former rent controlled dwellings occupied by the original tenant or by his/her spouse.

- A dwelling let by a local authority or a voluntary housing body.

- A dwelling occupied under a shared ownership lease.

- A dwelling in which the landlord also resides (this would include the 'rent a room' scheme).

- A dwelling in which the spouse, parent or child of the landlord is resident and where there is no written lease or tenancy agreement.

- Holiday lettings.

A dwelling let by, or to, a public authority is also excluded. A "public authority" includes a recognised educational institution. Therefore, owners of student accommodation dwellings let to third level college for onward letting to students are excluded from the requirement to register. However, tenancies in dwellings that are let directly to students **must** be registered.

Registration requirements

Landlords are required to register details of **all** of their tenancies within one month of the commencement of those tenancies. Once a tenancy is registered it remains a registered tenancy for as long as the tenancy remains in existence. Once the tenancy is terminated, any new tenancy created in respect of the dwelling must be registered with the PRTB. If the tenancy has not previously been terminated it will be deemed to have terminated when it has lasted 4 years and a new tenancy will then be deemed to commence. This new tenancy must be registered with the PRTB and the appropriate fee paid.

The registration application form PRTB1 is available from local authority Housing Sections, or it can be downloaded from www.environ.ie.

Rent a Room Scheme

Where a room or rooms in a person's private principal residence is let as residential accommodation, gross annual rent of up to €7,620 will be exempt from income tax. Room rental coming within the scope of this scheme will not trigger a clawback of;

- Any stamp duty relief claimed.

- CGT relief on your principal private residence when you sell.

- Mortgage interest relief.

Budget 2007: From 1st January 2007, it is proposed to close off the use of the Rent a Room Scheme where the rent received is from connected person's who in turn are claiming rent relief.

Managed Funds

As the name implies "Managed Funds" are funds where investors pool their resources to create a common investment fund which is controlled by professional managers. The two main benefits of this collective approach are, more efficient and economical investment management, plus greater security to investors, as the risk is spread over a diverse range of investments. Managed Funds are normally marketed under a number of headings;

- Life Assurance Products.

- Investment Bonds / Unit Linked Funds.

- Tracker Bonds.

- Offshore Investment Funds.

QUINN-life

- UCITS

Life assurance products

With-profit investment plans also invest your money in various assets outlined above over a fixed number of years. However, instead of your money being subject to the daily movement of the investment markets, the company sets out future minimum guaranteed values, as profits are earned and annual bonuses are declared, and this will increase your overall guaranteed values. Once declared, these bonuses cannot be taken away. The aim is to pay a bonus that relates to market growth but one that can also be sustained if the market falls. Some companies pay a higher proportion of performance growth in the form of a final bonus than others. This can penalise policyholders who encash their policies early and reward those who stay the course of the contract.

The smoothing-out effect of the bonus system protects with-profit funds from the volatility that is part and parcel of the market place. However, with-profits policies cannot buck the market: The values that are paid out at maturity will reflect the overall growth achieved by these stocks, property, gilts and cash investments that have underpinned them.

Investment bonds

Aimed at the lump sum investor, bonds come in different guises, such as

- Unit-linked and with-profit bonds.
- Tracker bonds.
- Special Investment bonds.

Life assurance bonds are among the most widely sold. Nearly all require a minimum investment of €5,000 and at least a five year investment time frame. Ideally, these should be regarded as medium to long-term investments to allow a good maturity value to build-up. Entry costs are usually between 3%-5% and annual management charges are usually 0.75%.

Tracker bonds

Tracker bonds are a relatively safe way of participating in international stock markets, such as the FTSE-100, the DOW and Japanese Nikkei, without many of the associated risks. Most tracker bonds have an investment term of three to six years and normally require minimum investments of €5,000.

Tracker bond fund managers are not buying actual stocks and shares, just the options on the performance of shares represented by a particular stock market index. In order to guarantee the safety of the investor's capital - a strong selling point for tracker bonds - a large portion of your investment must be put on deposit.

A number of years ago many tracker funds guaranteed the return of virtually the entire capital so long as the investors left their money untouched. With interest rates so low, the cost of this guarantee has risen, and recent tracker bonds are not achieving the same kind of returns that were enjoyed by people in the early nineties.

Tax

The returns from life assurance products funds commenced before 1st January 2001 are paid tax-free. All taxes due on profits earned will have already been paid at source by the life assurance fund managers to the Revenue Commissioners.

For new products issued after the 1st January 2001 no tax will be imposed within funds. However, the life assurance company is obliged to deduct an exit tax on any gains or investment income generated during the currency of the product at the standard rate of income tax plus three percentage points. This tax will be a final liability tax, for Irish residents. No tax will be deducted from payments to a person who is neither resident nor ordinarily resident here provided they have complied with the Revenue declaration requirements.

Tax on death or disability

From 15th February 2001, the proceeds payable on death or disability are liable to the same level of exit tax as if the product had been surrendered at that date. Prior to this such payments were exempt from exit tax.

Example - Lump Sum Investment

An individual invests €100,000 in an Investment Bond on 4th January 2006. They die on 13th March 2010 when the gross value of their bond is €150,000. They made no withdrawals from the investment over the term. The "taxable gain" is the reduction in the surrender value of the bond as a result of the payout i.e. €150,000 less allowable premiums paid.

Chargeable amount = €150,000 - €100,000 = €50,000

Exit Tax @ 23% = €50,000 x 23% = €11,500

Example 2 - Protection Plan

You took out a long term savings/protection plan on 5th March 2006. Annual Premuims €1,000, Life Cover €30,000. This gross surrender value after 15 years is €20,000 (at 5th March 2021).

In the event of a full encashment, exit tax is charged on the difference between the surrender value (€20,000) and the total premium paid (€15,000). Assuming an exit tax rate of 23%, this would amount to €1,150. So, the net encashment value payable is €18,850.

Death

Using the above example and assuming the individual dies on 5th March 2021, the Life Company would pay the life cover sum (€30,000) less the appropriate exit tax. This tax would be calculated as follows - the surrender value of the plan after the payout is nil. Therefore, the reduction in surrender value as a result of the payout is € 20,000. So, exit tax is calculated on the difference between total premiums paid and the reduction in the surrender value after the payment of the sum assured is agreed (€20,000 less €15,000 = €5,000). Assuming a tax rate of 23%, the tax payable on the individual's death would also be €1,150.

Offshore policies

Irish investment managers are as competent, professional and lucky (or unlucky) as their counterparts in the UK, America or Japan. Some concentrate solely on the Irish market. Others buy and sell equities and other assets in far flung parts of the world. Certainly all the larger investment companies here offer a selection of domestic and international equity funds (such as UK, American, Japanese, European, Developing Economies and Sectoral Funds) to their clients as well as fixed asset funds such as government gilts or currency funds.

One of the perceived advantages of buying an investment from a larger player is that it will usually have considerably greater access to research and analytical resources, often directly on the ground in the country where the investments are directed. This in-depth knowledge has produced consistently good results for many of the big international players familiar to Irish investors, such as Fidelity, Gartmore, HKSB, Invesco and others.

UCITS

'Undertakings for Collective Investments in Transferable Securities' are very popular and tax efficient with investment mainly in equity funds. UCITs are highly regulated by EU authorities, the unit prices are highly transparent, as are charges. The tax treatment of UCITs means that there can be greater overall potential for growth.

Tax

Every person acquiring an offshore policy or fund is obliged to make a tax return to the Revenue Commissioners no later than the 31st October following the end of the relevant tax year. This return will detail;

When and how the policy or investment was acquired.

The description of the product including premiums payable.

Name and address of the person through whom the offshore product was acquired e.g. an intermediary.

Prior to 1st January 2001

Returns from offshore products, were normally subject to CGT at a flat rate of 40%, without indexation relief.

Post Finance Act 2001

The 2001 Finance Act introduced a new tax treatment for certain offshore products with effect from 1st January 2001, regardless of when the product was effected. Generally the new arrangement can be summarised as follows:

Nature of payment	Tax if payment included in tax return	Tax if payment not included in tax return
Annual income payment.	Income Tax @ standard rate, plus Health Levy.	Income Tax at marginal rate, plus Health Levy.
Other payments, e.g. partial or total encashment of the product.	Income Tax @ standard rate + 3% plus Health Levy.	Income Tax at marginal rate plus Health Levy.
Gain on disposal of product.	Income Tax on gain @ standard rate + 3%. This tax may also be offset against Inheritance Tax	CGT @ 40%. This tax may not be offset against Inheritance Tax.

4

Borrowing wisely

"Neither a borrower nor a lender be" may be sound advice, but few of us can afford to be so virtuous. Yet borrowing money can be a perilous activity, since there are so many things that can go wrong when it comes to repaying the loan - illness, unemployment, other unexpected events, even happy ones like having a baby and having to interrupt a career.

Before you take out a loan, whether it be a term loan from the bank, a mortgage or even a credit card limit, you need to consider the following:

- The amount.

- The type of loan.

- The interest charge.

- The duration of the loan.

- Your ability to pay, especially should interest rates rise.

- Your personal circumstances.

- Borrowing outlets.

Loans

Banks, building societies, credit unions, finance houses and money lenders are all willing to lend you money, if you meet their criteria which is usually based on your age, income and credit record.

Borrowing money for a long term purpose, such as a mortgage or to finance a business is very different from borrowing to buy a car, household goods or even a holiday. For one thing, the interest rate you pay and the repayment period are going to be very different. So, try and match the loan with the right lender from the start.

If you want to borrow money for a home, go to a building society or bank. If you want an overdraft that you dip in and out of, you must stick with the bank or building society with which you have your current account. The lending pool for personal loans widens to include finance houses, credit unions and even life assurance companies if you happen to hold a valuable with-profits policy. But money lenders, who are the keenest of all to lend, should be avoided by all but the most desperate because of the crippling interest rates they charge.

The cheapest interest rates are provided by mortgage lenders, who are counting on you borrowing over a period of many years. The most expensive interest rates are charged by credit card providers and money lenders whose lines of credit are designed to be paid off - ideally in a short amount of time. Credit card "loans" are ideal for people who can pay off the amount borrowed each month since they will incur no interest at all.

An upward change in interest rates will not normally change the amount most people pay back each month for personal short term loans, even if the rate is a variable one. However any adjustments that have worked against you over the period will have to be settled up at the end - usually with a final balance payment(s).

Variable rate mortgages don't work this way. Any rate hike or fall is usually applied to the homeowners next repayment. If rates go up by a half per cent, you will have to pay more each month until they go down again. Fixing your personal loan or mortgage interest rate is one way to avoid this kind of volatility, but it is difficult to predict interest rate movements: if you fix your rate and interest rates fall, you must continue to pay the fixed rate for the agreed term or incur penalties to break the contract.

Many term loan borrowers are keen to stretch their repayments over a longer number of years because the monthly repayment is smaller. But they sometimes forget that ultimately they will pay more interest on this loan.

Example

> If you borrow €10,000 for three years and the interest rate is 10%, you will pay back nearly €322 a month or a total of €11,592. If you borrow the same amount for five years, however, the repayments drop to €212 a month, but you will have paid back €12,720.
>
> The effect is more dramatic with a mortgage. Borrow €250,000 at 4.25% over 20 years and the monthly repayment will be €1,548 per month. The total repayment is €371,520. Extend the loan by five years and your monthly repayment drops to €1,354 a month but total repayments rise to €406,200, a difference of over €34,680 in just five years, money that you could put to a better use.

Term loans

Before you take out a term loan with a bank or building society you need to determine the real cost of the loan, the Average Percentage Rate (APR) and the total repayments. The APR is the true interest rate and is calculated based on the duration of the loan and any fees that may fall due. The APR is inevitably higher than the published flat rate. Along with the APR rate you should also ask for the cost per thousand per month which will tell you how much every €1,000 borrowed will cost. You then multiply this amount by however many thousands of euro you borrow and by the number of months over which you are repaying the loan. This figure represents your total repayments.

Overdrafts

Arranged on your current account, overdrafts are a cheap and simple way to arrange extra credit as you need it. Interest rates are usually the same as the personal lending rate and payable only as you use the facility. If you exceed your overdraft limit, without permission, the bank is entitled to charge extra interest and a "referral charge".

Revolving credit

Also known as a budget account, this is a type of overdraft which smoothes out the annual cost of running your current account. It allows you to borrow a multiple of your monthly pay cheque (paid directly into the account) to cover large once-off outgoings like school expenses in

September, Christmas spending in December or the cost of a summer holiday. Interest is charged only as you draw down the facility.

Credit Unions

Credit Unions do not seek collateral before lending money - your record as a regular saver and whether you are employed or not, is how they judge your ability to repay. The loan amount is usually a multiple of the value of shares you hold. Credit unions tend to show more flexibility regarding repayment schedules than conventional lenders and calculate the interest on the diminishing balance basis.

Life assurance

Life assurance companies may seem like an unusual source from which to borrow money, but there is provision for lending up to 80% of the cash value of a with-profits policy. Interest rates are usually quite competitive and borrowing against the fund value is nearly always better than encashing the policy. Investment policies like this should always be allowed to run their course - since a significant part of the total value of the policy may be paid in the form of a final bonus which only comes into effect on the maturity of the policy.

Life assurance policies are frequently used as security against conventional loans - if you renege on your debt the bank will simply encash the policy.

Credit and charge cards

These are among the most expensive but convenient forms of borrowing. Designed for short-term purchases, the APR can be as high as 18% for those card holders who don't clear their monthly balances in full. Disciplined cardholders can take full advantage of the 50 plus days of free credit available, but those who don't, can run up large balances very quickly. The most popular credit cards are VISA and Mastercard which now come in different guises - such as affinity cards for professional groups who can benefit from a slightly lower interest rate and a donation to their college or charity or in the form of a loyalty card with which you can build up cash discounts with a series of retailers. With charges, conditions and interest rates varying so much, it is a good idea to shop around for the best rate and conditions.

Credit Card Charges

As at November 2006

Financial institution	Card type	Interest rate payable	Minimum fee on cash withdrawals	Interest charged from [1]
AIB [2]	[2] 'Be' Visa / Mastercard	16.9%/13.9%	€1.90	25 days from statement date
	[3] Platinum Visa	10.5%	€1.90	25 days from statement date
Bank of Ireland	Standard Advantage Mastercard/Visa	16.8%	€2.54 / 1.5%	Purchase date
	Gold Advantage Mastercard	14.5%	€2.54 / 1.5%	Purchase date
	Platinum Advantage Mastercard	14.9%	€2.54 / 1.5%	Purchase date
First Active [5]	Mastercard	15.9%	€2.54 / 1.5%	Transaction date
National Irish Bank	Mastercard Standard	10.2%	€2.00	Statement date
	Mastercard Gold	9.4%	€2.00	Statement date
	Mastercard Platinum	8.8%	€2.00	Statement date
	Visa Standard	10.5%	€2.00	Statement date
Permanent TSB	Visa	9.9%	€2.00 / 1.5%	Purchases - Transaction date Cash - Statement date
Ulster Bank [4]	Mastercard/Visa card	18.3%	€2.54 / 1.5%	Transaction date
	Zinc card	13.4%	€2.54 / 1.5%	Transaction date

(1)   If the full amount is not paid by due date.

(2)   13.9%/16.9% APR depending on spend. Introductory rate of 6.9% for first 12 months.

(3)   Introductory rate of 6.9% , & 0.5% cashback on purchases on purchases over €5,000 (maximum €50,000) for first 12 months

(4)   Introduction offer of 0% for 6 months on balance transfers from date of account opening

Charge/Store cards

These include the likes of American Express and Diners Club as well as popular store cards like Arnotts, Clery's, Debenhams or Marks and Spencer. Charge cards may involve an annual membership and require that you clear your balance off monthly within a set time frame or face hefty interest penalties. Unlike store cards, however, American Express and Diners club do not have spending limits. The store cards are handy and convenient but interest rates can be very high (sometimes higher than ordinary credit cards) if you do not clear your balance monthly.

5

Control your finances -make a family budget

Whether you are single, married or a parent with family responsibilities, most of us need some help controlling our finances. A good way to do this is to create an annual budget, which sets out the household's income and outgoings and allows you to plan your immediate and longer term financial needs in an ordered and stress-free way.

So where do you start?

Begin by setting aside a couple of uninterrupted hours for yourself or with your partner for the review. The time you spend sorting out all your bills, accounts and receipts will pay dividends for the rest of the year.

Step 1:   Buy a large copybook or ledger.

Step 2:   Gather all your financial documents together, such as pay slips and P60s, social welfare books, bank and credit card statements, loan statements, utility bills, insurance policies, savings books, investment and pension accounts/statements. Copies of weekly grocery bills, for example, will also be useful to get a picture of how much you spend on food.

Step 3:   On one page, under the heading, "Income" itemise all gross annual earnings and income coming into the household and then calculate the monthly, after-tax, figure. In addition to salaries and wages and/or pension income, this should include commissions and bonuses, share dividends, anticipated capital gains, rental income, etc.

Don't forget to include any social welfare payments, such as monthly child benefit. On the opposite page, under the heading "Essential Spending", list your annual outgoings, beginning with the amount of tax you pay and any automatic deductions from salary or direct debits for pension/PHI contributions. Prioritise the rest of your spending according to value, usually beginning with mortgage or rent payments and childcare costs if they apply. Leave two spaces for the annual amount, and the monthly average. Next, mark down your annual/monthly food bill, not forgetting to include the amount spent in addition to the large weekly shopping visit to convenience stores. Your food bill may be higher during the Christmas season and perhaps a bit lower over the summer if you are away on holidays. Utilities - gas, electricity, telephone/mobiles, television and solid fuel - are often the next largest outgoing, followed by on-going transport, essential clothing and insurance costs, annual education fees/costs. Bank charges on current accounts should also be included.

Step 4:   Underneath your list of "Essential Spending", mark down another heading, "Non-essential Spending" or "Discretionary Spending". This category should include occasional savings, personal loans, credit card balances, entertainment and hobbies, holidays and travel, miscellaneous shopping.

Discretionary Spending

While most of us have a pretty good idea of the size of our essential outgoings, too often we underestimate how much we spend for discretionary purposes. The best way to get a clear picture of exactly how much you are overspending is to keep a spending diary for one month.

This diary should be small enough to fit into a handbag or inside jacket pocket so that your daily purchases – from newspapers and magazines, cigarettes and coffee, milk and bread, petrol and flowers, evening drinks at your local pub, can all be marked down. Bigger spontaneous items can also be recorded in your ledger: that must-have CD or top, the lunch out with a friend you've met in the street, the no-frills weekend flight to somewhere warm.

Keeping a spending ledger will be an eye-opener. It will point out exactly why your income is not stretching as far as it should; it will probably reveal your spending patterns and triggers, especially concerning indiscriminate credit card or laser card usage. Ideally, it will make you more conscious of just how much you can afford for discretionary purchases.

Prepare your budget

You are now ready to create a budget for yourself or your family, to which you can refer to as the year progresses. By knowing how much you spend for housing, utilities, food and transport, clothing and insurance, entertainment and holidays, you can try and make some savings by eliminating waste or unnecessary purchases.

For example; are you paying the keenest interest rate on your mortgage or personal loans? Is there any cheaper credit card on offer? Are your savings enjoying the highest deposit rate on the market? Are you paying over the odds for motor, home, life or health insurance. A good broker should be able to find some savings – after all, that's their job.

Is there room to cut your food and waste charges bill, either by eliminating wastage or by switching to a better value grocery store? By only shopping with a list, and avoiding any impulse purchases, you could reduce your weekly bill. Are you and your family paying too much for telephone, internet and mobile phone bills. This is one area of expenditure that has exploded in recent years and deserves being carefully scrutinised. If you have children in the family a spending and time limit should be placed on internet usage.

What about bank charges and interest repayments? Is your bank providing good value for its services? Would something like a current account mortgage, which automatically helps to reduce the cost of your home loan provide long term interest savings to your family?

Once you have trimmed your expenditure page of wasteful and unnecessary spending you can now allocate your budget to all the different categories of spending events and purchases. Some will be pretty immutable: the mortgage, car loans, utilities and insurance. Others will be a moveable feast, depending on the month or season. For example, you may need to budget for higher spending in August and September to accommodate the children going back to school and in December for Christmas. The month in which a summer holiday is booked will eat into your (usually) fixed income more than ones in which the family stay home.

A good way to tackle this is to set up a payment plan scheme at your bank, in which all your major outgoings are estimated. The bank then averages this expenditure over a year and arranges for an overdraft facility to cover those months when your expenses are higher than usual – but which have been budgeted for. Over the course of the year, your income and expenditure usually balance out, with only a small drawdown on the overdraft. Costs are kept to a minimum, and there are no monthly money crises to deal with.

Savings and Investments

An important part of any personal budget exercise is the review of your savings and investments. Everyone needs a good savings account, into which you hold sufficient cash reserves to see you over any short-term financial emergency, such as illness, temporary unemployment. Ideally, such a fund should amount to between three and six months net income. It might take you some time to build up this fund, so start making steady contributions as soon as you can, ideally, from the moment you start drawing your first pay cheque.

If you have achieved any spending savings over the year, you should prioritise how it can be allocated: expensive debt like credit card, store card balances should be paid off first. Paying off a higher portion of your mortgage each month will have a disproportionate, positive impact on the capital sum because of the effect of compound interest on long term debt.

If debt is not an issue you can use your budget savings to increase your life insurance, if need be, build up your emergency fund, or to start a longer term investment fund or to even buy individual stocks and shares.

An investment fund is aimed at longer term financial goals – the purchase of a house, to cover education costs for your children, early retirement. The best way to arrange such an investment is to speak to a good financial advisor about your financial goals and to establish your risk profile and how much you are willing to set aside. The advisor can then produce a list of appropriate options. Once you choose one, the amount you contribute can automatically be deducted every month and you can adjust your budget accordingly.

Money that isn't there, isn't necessarily missed as the tens of thousands of Special Savings Investment Account have discovered over the past few years.

Every year, on your personal Budget Day, you should review the state of your savings/investments and occupational pension fund. If you are unhappy with its performance, find out why it has underperformed and research the affordable alternatives.

Once your Budget is in place, you can now rest more easily. Your income and expenditure is under control. You have reviewed the important financial contracts – mortgages, loans, insurance policies – and have made savings on other essential purchases like food, clothing, utilities and transport costs. Now that the family holiday and Christmas has been budgeted for, there is less chance for mad overspending.

Children, of course, learn by example. When they see how you keep control of your spending, and having a responsible attitude towards debt and savings, chances are they will develop the same good habits. Their own savings account and a spending ledger could be the best gifts you give them this year.

What goes into your Personal Budget?	
Annual Income	**€**
Salary/Wages Commissions Bonuses Pensions Part-time earnings Social welfare benefits **Total Income**	
Annual Expenditure - Essential Spending	**€**

Income tax/PRSI
Mortgage/rent
Childcare costs
Utilities: Gas/oil
               Electricity
               Telephone
               Mobile
               Internet (ISDN/Broadband)
               TV and cable
Insurance: Life insurance
               Health
               Home and contents
               Motor
               Travel / pet
Food: Grocery (weekly/daily)
Clothing: Essential purchases and uniforms
Transport: Bus or train tickets,
               Car tax, petrol and maintanence
Bank account charges & loan repayments
Charitable donations
Christmas: Gifts
               Food
               Alcohol
               Entertainment
Savings and investments
 	
Total expenditure	

Annual Expenditure - Non-essential or discretionary spending	€
Private education fees/expenses/donations	
Holidays: Transport Accommodation and food Travel insurance Entertainment Souvenirs Kennel fees	
Hobbies & Entertainment: Eating and drinking Entertainment Memberships and equipment Video's, DVD's, CD's Books, cinema, theatre, sports tickets Collector's items Pets Gifts - birthday, weddings anniversary, etc.	
Consumables: Clothing Jewellery Personal grooming products & services Electrical equipment Gadgets Newspapers & magazines Snacks, food, drink	

Specialising in Independent Professional Advice on Money, Pensions and Mortgages

tab
financial services ltd

	Yes	No
Want to continue your SSIA savings habit?	☐	☐
Unsure about your pension arrangements?	☐	☐
Want to maximise your investments?	☐	☐
Do you need advice on your mortgage options?	☐	☐
Want to know more about PRSA's?	☐	☐
Concerned your Life/Health Insurance is inadequate?	☐	☐
Want to finance your child's education?	☐	☐
Planning on buying a house or apartment?	☐	☐

If you tick even one "YES" to the questions above you'll find this
TAB Guide a very useful aid to managing your finances.
But if you'd like a private consultation with an independent professional
TAB Financial Services advisor to discuss what options are available
and to get the most from your finances …

… we have some very good news for you.
For readers of the TAB Guide,
TAB Financial Services Ltd has a fixed

private consultation
fee of only
€150

contact

**Claire Burtenshaw in TAB Financial Services
to arrange an appointment on**

01 – 6768633

Fax: 01 - 6768641   email: claire@tab.ie   web: www.tab.ie

TAB Financial Services Ltd. is regulated by the Financial Regulator
as a Multi Agency Intermediary and as a Mortgage Intermediary

6

Protecting your lifestyle

Everyone has something to protect – your wealth, your health, your life and those dearest to you. Insuring your own life against sudden serious illness or unexpected death relieves the financial burden on your dependents. Insuring your car, home and contents is yet another way for you to avoid financial disaster should anything unexpected ever happen to you.

The variety of insurance products available to you has increased considerably in recent years with the result that prices have now become very competitive. There are a number of different ways for you to arrange your insurance. You can either contact an insurance company of your choice directly or you can arrange insurance through your bank, building society or a service provider like a motor association. Alternatively, you can contact an independent financial advisor who can offer you independent advice on the type of insurance protection that best suits your needs and your budget.

Life assurance

The purpose of life insurance is to make sure that your dependents are financially secure in the event of your death. As a general rule, the younger you are, the better your health and the safer your lifestyle, the cheaper the cost of your insurance. You may not be able to obtain any life assurance cover at all if you are suffering from a serious illness. Alternatively, you could be offered insurance at a premium price – which, in insurance jargon, is called 'loading'. For example, a 50% loading could mean you pay 50% more than the average insured person of your age for the same amount of life cover. Since women live longer than men, the cost of insurance cover for women is cheaper.

How much cover do you need?

Ten times the size of your net, after-tax, salary is a standard gauge for the amount of life insurance cover you should have. A good rule of thumb when trying to decide your total level of cover - is to aim to provide a fund to adequately replace your income in the event of your premature death. This means that your income, the number and ages of your dependents, your assets and outstanding loan commitments etc. all have to be carefully considered. You may find that you don't need as much 'stand-alone' life cover as you might initially think if your employment benefits package includes a "death-in-service" benefit and a spouse's/dependent's pension, or if your mortgage is covered by mortgage protection insurance. This is something that an independent financial advisor will be able to offer you invaluable advice about.

When you meet an independent financial advisor they will tell you that basic life assurance is arranged for a fixed number of years and comes in a number of forms:

Level term cover

This type of cover is relatively inexpensive. But it only pays out at death and has no underlying investment value. Quite simply, when you take out a term assurance plan, you agree to pay a specific or level premium over a pre-agreed number of years. Every year, as you get older, your risk of death increases so your level premium is based on the average risk of death.

'Averaging' means that in the early years of your plan you'll pay too much in proportion to the actual risk of death involved, and this extra premium in the early years is used to "subsidise" the cost of your life assurance benefit in later years. If your plan is discontinued, or in the event of an early claim, before your pre-agreed number of years have elapsed, this surplus will not be repaid.

Convertible term cover

This is slightly more expensive than Level Term Cover but it gives you the flexibility, without any further medical test or examination and regardless of any change in your health circumstances, to convert into another type of policy at any future date in your contract. This could include converting to a 'whole of life assurance plan' which could be a very valuable option for you to have because, regardless of any changes in your health, no unexpected 'loadings' are applied to your premium payable at conversion. Like all 'term' covers, this is a protection policy only and it will never acquire a cash value.

Decreasing term cover

This is a variation on the basic 'term' cover, which means that it is a protection policy only. Decreasing Term cover is often taken out as a mortgage protection policy where both the requirement and the amount of cover decreases as your mortgage is repaid and your need for protection recedes.

Guaranteed 'Whole of Life' cover

Effectively 'whole of life' is a term cover protection policy which guarantees to pay a specific sum of money whenever you die, provided of course, that you continue to pay the premiums. Because of 'averaging', your premiums are relatively high at the outset, but they remain unchanged for the entire duration of your life. As you might expect, these policies do not have any residual or investment value but the cost is relatively cheap, particularly when you are young and healthy. They are very suitable if, for example, you are self-employed and don't have a pension plan but you want to provide long term financial protection to a dependent spouse or partner in the event of your death. They are also very useful if you have a disabled child or relative who will need financial protection after your death.

Monthly cost of a male, non-smoker, obtaining €350,000 life assurance cover (Different plan types)

	Age next birthday	25	35	45	55
A	Decreasing Term over 20 yrs	€12.00	€21.73	€51.35	€131.06
B	Level Term over 20 yrs	€18.39	€31.07	€73.03	€187.25
C	Convertible Term over 20 yrs	€19.71	€33.62	€80.33	€205.45
D	Whole of life	€168.59	€258.28	€423.25	€730.02

Guaranteed whole of life

Although the name sounds rather long and complicated, this policy is actually very straightforward. The 'whole of life' aspect means that your plan has a level premium payable from the time you take out the policy up to a specific age, normally 75 or 85. The 'guaranteed' aspect means that it will pay out the cash value of the plan or a guaranteed sum assured, whichever is the greater, whenever you die. So, in the event of your death, a minimum amount of money is always guaranteed. These plans normally acquire a cash value after approximately two years and, as illustrated in the example above, the amount of cash can be quite substantial.

There is a saying among Life Assurance professionals that 'a little life assurance can be a dangerous thing'. Effectively, what this saying means is that, all too often, the very fact that you know you have 'some kind' of a life assurance cover, lulls you into a false sense of security. The years slip by without you ever feeling the need to check and make sure that your 'fixed' level of protection is still sufficient for your 'changing' requirements. It's always good advice to discuss your changing requirements with an independent financial advisor on a regular basis.

Own Life / Joint Life Policies

If the policy is an "own life" plan, effectively you are both the "life assured" and "the assured". This means that the lump sum that is payable from the policy upon your death will form part of your estate and may be subject to inheritance tax. In the case of a joint-life policy, usually taken out by spouses, the death benefit is normally paid to the surviving spouse.

If your policy is arranged on an "own life" basis, your legal representatives, (i.e. your "executor" if you have made a Will) may be required to produce a grant of probate and proof of title before the insurance company can pay out the sum assured. However, if no Will exists, the policy benefits will be subject to the law of intestacy and the payments of the proceeds of the life assurance policy will be as set out in the legislation (see page 365) which may not be in accordance with your wishes.

If your life assurance policy is arranged on a "life of another" basis, then, when you die, that other person becomes the owner of the policy. They can claim the encashment value of the policy from the insurance company by simply producing the policy document, together with your death certificate.

This is a very good idea for couples who are not legally married. However, you can lose control of the policy if your personal circumstances change i.e. if you separate.

Life assurance under trust

Setting up a life assurance policy under trust is an increasingly popular way of making sure that your policy proceeds will not become part of your estate when you die. In addition, a Trust ensures:

● Quick and easy payment of the death benefit. The insurance company will pay the surviving trustee(s), usually your spouse or children, on proof of death and the production of the policy document.

● By being a trustee of the policy yourself you can maintain a degree of control over the policy during your lifetime. The Trust must be set up, by completing a standard trust form and nominating trustee(s) and the beneficiaries, before you commence the policy

Tax

No tax relief is available for life assurance premiums unless it is set up as part of your pension scheme. The returns from life assurance products funds commenced before 1st January 2001 are paid tax-free. All taxes which were due on profits earned will have already been paid at source by the life assurance fund managers to the Revenue Commissioners.

For new products issued after the 1st January 2001 no tax will be imposed within funds, however the life assurance company is obliged to deduct exit tax on any gains or investment income generated during the term of the product at the standard rate of income tax plus three percentage points. This tax will be a final liability tax, for Irish residents. No tax will be deducted from payments to a person who is neither resident nor ordinarily resident here provided they have complied with the Revenue declaration requirements.

Tax on death or disability

Prior to 15th February 2001 no exit tax was payable in respect of payment made on death or disability. Under the new rules the proceeds payable on death or disability are liable to the same level of exit tax as if the product had been surrendered at that date.

Income protection insurance

Unlike life assurance, which only pays out benefits on death, disability or Permanent Health Insurance (PHI) pays benefits if you become ill or injured and cannot work. Its aim is to replace your current income - up to retirement age if necessary. It may also be included as part of your pension scheme.

If it is not provided as a benefit of your tax efficient pension scheme – there is no obligation for employers to provide this benefit, though many workers think they do - you can buy PHI (or Income Protection Insurance as it is also known)

How much does it cost?

The cost varies with age, sex, occupation and with the 'deferment period', which is explained in more detail below. Women on average suffer more ill health than men and consequently pay more for this type of insurance. Occupation is also a crucial factor in determining the cost of the risk involved and people who work in higher risk jobs and more likely to have an accident or illness and less likely to return to work than those in more sedentary jobs normally have to pay more.

Case Study

Brian, 45, is an accountant with his own practice earning €80,000 a year. Unfortunately as a result of severe depression he was hospitalised and unable to work. His income protection policy, which cost €92.59 per month, after tax relief (€159.63 gross) pays him €988 per week.*

If Brian cannot return to work (benefits are typically paid for five and a half years) his income protection policy will continue to pay him until he reaches retirement. However, should Brian decide he is ready to return to work, but not as an accountant, some PHI policies will pay him to retrain. If he only went back to work part-time, he would still receive partial benefits.

(Source: Friends First Income Protection)

Deferment period

Most disability plans will not pay you any benefit until you have been out of work for at least thirteen weeks - the deferment period. The longer the deferment period, which normally ranges from 13 to 52 weeks, the cheaper the premiums. At the outset of your plan you can decide on the length of the deferment period that best suits your budget and financial protection requirements.

To ensure that you don't actually end up financially better off claiming benefit, which could leave these plans open to abuse, many disability contracts put a limit on the amount of benefit payable and this limit applies regardless of your maximum level of benefit insured. Normally, you will not be able to receive a benefit that is more than 75% of your average annual earnings in the year prior to your disablement. Many plans also include the value of State disability benefits within this 75% rule.

Tax relief

Disability or PHI premiums are eligible for tax relief at your highest rate of income tax. However, the amount of relief granted cannot exceed 10% of your total income. All disability and PHI benefits are taxed under PAYE.

Tax relief for PHI contributions made by PAYE tax payers is given on a net pay basis i.e. the contributions are deducted from your gross salary prior to the application of income tax and PRSI.

Loan protection insurance

If you ever lose your job, become ill and are unable to work, any outstanding personal loans that you are committed to will still have to be repaid. This is why most lenders offer you the option of taking out Payment Protection Insurance with any personal loans or mortgages that they advance to you.

This important protection option is normally only available to you at the time of taking out the loan or mortgage and it covers your monthly loan repayments if you ever become redundant, sick or disabled. Payment Protection Insurance usually costs only a few euro extra per month and is included as part of your monthly loan repayments. Although it generally provides only 12 months of benefits per claim, the financial security and peace of mind that it brings can be very valuable and reassuring.

Optional Payment Protection Insurance should not be confused with compulsory Mortgage Protection Insurance. Mortgage Protection Insurance repays the mortgage in the event of death only.

If you already have adequate PHI cover, you may feel that it is unnecessary for you to take out Payment Protection Insurance as well. After all, the whole purpose of PHI is to provide you with a replacement income so that you can meet your regular outgoings and other financial commitments. Keep in mind, however, that most PHI policies only pay benefits after an average of 26 weeks have elapsed, while many Payment Protection plans pay out benefits after just one month of redundancy, illness or disability.

Serious illness insurance

Serious illness insurance pays your entire loan if you contract any one of defined number of serious illnesses.

It is designed to alleviate the financial burdens of anyone who suffers a serious life threatening illness or condition. It does this by paying you a tax-free lump sum on official diagnosis of a serious illness. The average amount of cover provided is €127,000 and this lump sum can be used to meet your day-to-day living requirements, pay off your mortgage or even meet the cost of health care.

Illnesses and conditions

The main illnesses and conditions include cancer, heart attack, stroke, kidney disease, multiple sclerosis. However most policies will also pay out for organ transplants, rare ailments like motor neurone disease and CJD, and in the rare chance that you contract HIV by accident or injury. The better policies also pay out benefits in the event of Permanent and Total Disability (PTD) (including loss of limbs, hearing or speech, Alzheimer's Disease, etc.), and offer cash benefit options if you are hospitalised.

Every insurer includes a slightly different list of conditions so it is always prudent for you to check these in advance with an independent financial advisor. The cost of cover varies with age and sex. Older women pay the highest premiums since it is calculated that women suffer more illnesses. Although the lump sum benefit is tax-free, there is no tax relief available on serious illness policy premiums.

More recent hybrid serious illness policies now offer other options which can be added to serious illness insurance, such as hospital cash. This is a daily amount that will be paid to you for each complete period of 24 hours you are hospitalised. This limit is usually capped at approximately €200 per day.

Also accident benefit may be an option offered to you by the insurer at an extra cost. Accident benefit is similar to Income Protection but is only payable if you are temporarily disabled as a result of an accident and are unable to carry out your occupation. It is a weekly amount that is tax free and usually capped at approximately €400 p.w. The deferred period before the benefit is payable, is shorter than Income Protection, usually about 2 weeks but the benefit will only be payable for a maximum of 52 weeks.

Protecting your mortgage

Serious illness cover is becoming an increasingly popular part of mortgage protection policies, and both the level of cover and the premium payments can be arranged either on a level or decreasing premium basis.

In the latter case, your cover decreases in value with the decreasing value of your outstanding mortgage. The drawback to this, however, is that although your benefits will clear your outstanding mortgage, there will be no extra cash available to ease any other financial burdens you may face. By arranging your cover on a term basis, you will be guaranteed a lump sum (the size of the original mortgage) throughout the entire duration of your loan.

Serious illness policies are often arranged by companies for key members of staff or directors. In this context they are known as "keyman" insurance and the benefits are paid, not to the individual but to the company or partners, to lessen any financial burden that they may face because of the absence of that key employee or director.

Health and medical insurance

Over two million people now have private health insurance in Ireland, mainly in response to their concerns about delays in accessing specialist consultants for diagnosis and long hospital waiting lists. Health insurance still attracts standard rate tax relief, credited at source by the insurer.

There are now three main health insurers, the VHI, BUPA Ireland and Vivas Health, that all offer a selection of plans that include not just access to out-patient and in-hospital benefits, but a growing range of other services and insurance cover.

The VHI, the largest provider, now offers five basic plans (A - E), plus five enhanced plans and Lifestage Choices - First Plan, Family Plan and Forward Plan - each tailored to a particular life stage. As well as providing hospital cover all Lifestage Choices Plans offer cover for day-to-day expenses, a range of three additional cash benefit healthcare plans that cover a range of day to day outpatient treatments and expenses.

BUPA Ireland has three plans, Essential, Essential Plus and BUPA Gold plus two 'HealthManager' plans which combine in-hospital benefits and payment of cash benefits for a range of outpatient treatments.

The most recent entrant to the Irish private insurance market, Vivas Health have three plans, the 'I' Plan, 'Me' Plan and 'We' Plan are aimed at age groups who are interested in a specific set of cost effective benefits that are more suitable to their age group and health, rather than a combined package of benefits, which younger customers may feel are age inappropriate.

Hospital cover is included as the core benefit in each of the Vivas packages, but certain other treatment or benefits, such as maternity care, for example, is not available under all the plans. Day to day out-patient treatments and benefits are purchased separately for the 'I' and 'Me' Plans but the 'We' Plan, for example, which is appropriate for families, includes core hospital and day to day benefits.

All Irish health insurance plans are "community rated" and policyholders cannot be discriminated against, either on a cost or benefits level, because of their age. However, cover may be withheld for certain periods where pre-existing medical conditions exist.

There are no penalties for switching health providers, and the age restriction, which excluded anyone age over 65 from joining a private insurance scheme has been revoked. However, pre-existing conditions will not be covered for at least 10 years.

Hospital cash benefit plan

Sold by non-profit, charitable-status, companies like The Hospital Saturday Fund (HSF) and Health Services Association (HSA), these schemes pay tax-free cash payments to members who need hospitalisation or a range of out-patient treatments.

Premiums, which can be as low as a few euro a week, are age related, but they provide reduced benefits for dependents at no extra cost. Benefits are also paid for routine optical, dental and alternative medical treatments that are not covered by VHI and BUPA. Daily cash benefits are not paid for routine maternity in-patient stays, but new mothers are paid upon delivery.

Hospital cash schemes are usually arranged on a group or company basis, but can also be purchased by individuals. There is no tax relief available on these premiums.

Insuring your home and its contents

Your home and it contents are among your most valuable possessions. Insuring them against fire, theft and other damage should be an important priority. If you have a mortgage you will have been required to take out compulsory buildings insurance, which varies in price depending on the value of your mortgage, the size, location and rebuilding cost of your property. Your lender requires this insurance, not for your benefit, but for theirs. Their major concern is to protect their financial interest vested in your property. You should take great care, therefore - especially once your mortgage is paid off - to ensure that your building and contents are properly valued and insured.

Proper valuation

The minimum insurance you require is the cost of rebuilding your home in the event of its destruction. Your rebuilding costs are not the same as your mortgage amount, or the market value of your property. If you have any doubt about the rebuilding cost of your property you should arrange for an independent valuation or survey. Take care not to underinsure your home or contents because most home insurance policies include what is known as an "averaging" clause which determines that if you underinsure your property, for example, by 50%, the insurer is only obliged to pay you 50% of your claim.

Nowadays, the cost and the scope of benefits available in home and contents insurance policies vary widely. It pays to shop around to make sure that you get the best available value in terms of level of claim excesses, exclusions, discounts and risk cover. A good general insurance broker can help you assess the value of your buildings and possessions and carefully choose the right policy for your needs and budget.

If in doubt – seek out the best professional advice available

As we said at the outset of this chapter, your wealth, your health, your life and those nearest to you are important priorities when it comes to financial protection. Likewise, your home and its contents are among your most valuable possessions. That's why it makes such good sense for you to seek out the best available independent professional advice before making your final decision about what policies and protection arrangements suit your requirements best. Keep in mind that as you get older, get married, or your family commitments change, your protection requirements will change too. So you should regularly check your existing arrangements to ensure that they are still adequate to meet your changing needs and, indeed, to ensure that you are not 'over protecting' yourself in any areas, for example, as your children grow up and become financially independent.

permanent tsb

banking only better

100% Mortgage

for first time buyers - giving you an up front **deposit.**

Drop into any branch
LoCall **1890 500 156**

visit www.**permanenttsb**.ie or alternatively contact your **broker.**

7

Home buyers options

For most people, buying a home is their single biggest investment and it can be an anxious time, especially if the property market is experiencing a boom, as it has done in Ireland in the last number of years. To buy a home, you need some capital, usually around 8% of the purchase price. Banks and building societies are prepared to lend up to 92% mortgages, but better interest rates may be available to buyers who have more than 20% of the purchase price. Some have now started offering 100% mortgages to first time buyers.

Start saving

If an average new home costs €350,000, you would typically need a minimum of €28,000 - €35,000 as starting capital. Many savers choose a good interest-yielding account in the Post Office, bank or building society to start the process, though you do not need to be saving with any particular institution in order to secure a mortgage from them at a later date. Lenders do extend 100% loans, but you risk falling into negative equity.

Choosing a lender

Once you have the appropriate minimum capital and have found the home of your choice, you need to start shopping around for the best mortgage. The property supplements in the major newspapers publish updated mortgage interest rates from all the leading lenders. These lists also include a column which shows the cost per thousand euro borrowed so that you can quickly calculate the monthly repayment of the mortgage you have in mind.

Income conditions

All lenders require certain income conditions before they will give you a mortgage. The old rule of thumb was that the loan must not exceed up to four and half times your income, and if you are joint applicants, up to three and three quarter times the combined income, depending on your income level. A self-employed individual will usually need to provide proof of average taxable earnings over the past three years. A couple earning €60,000 and €35,000 respectively can under those terms expect to borrow up to €356,250 in total. The high cost of property now means that lending practices vary between lenders with some offering higher multiples and far longer repayment terms.

House purchase related costs

Other costs which may be connected with home purchase include: application or arrangement fees, legal and valuation fees, administration fees, indemnity bonds and stamp duty as well as the cost of furnishing your new home.

Stamp duty

For first-time buyers, owner occupiers and investors, the stamp duty rates for second-hand residential property are as follows:

Rates of Stamp Duty for second hand residential property

Value	First Time Buyers	Owner Occupiers	Investors
Up to 127,000	Nil	Nil	Nil
127,001 - €190,500	Nil	3.00%	3.00%
€190,501 - €254,000	Nil	4.00%	4.00%
€254,001 - €317,500	Nil	5.00%	5.00%
€317,501 - €381,000	3.00%	6.00%	6.00%
€381,001 - €635,000	6.00%	7.50%	7.50%
Over €635,000	9.00%	9.00%	9.00%

New houses or apartments not exceeding 125sq metres in floor size are exempt from stamp duty provided the purchase is made by or on behalf of a person who will occupy the property as their Principal Private Residence for a 5 year period and no rent (other than rent under the rent-a-room scheme) is derived from the property during this period.

If the property ceases to be your principal private residence within these five years, e.g. if you move and rent the existing property then a clawback of the full amount of the stamp duty will arise. (see below)

If you purchase a property in excess of 125 sq. metres and the property is occupied by or on behalf of a person as their Principal Private Residence for 5 years and no rent (other than rent under the rent-a-room scheme) is derived from the property during this period, stamp duty will be payable on the higher of:

- The site cost, **or**,

- 25% of the total cost

Where a new house or apartment is purchased by an investor, stamp duty is payable on the entire amount paid for the property. (see page 43)

To qualify as a first time buyer (FTB) the following conditions must be met:

- The purchaser, either individually or jointly, must not have previously purchased or built on their own behalf a house or apartment, in Ireland or abroad;

- The property purchased must be occupied by the purchaser, or a person on their behalf, as their only principal place of residence;

- No rent (other than rent under the rent-a-room scheme) is derived from the property for five years after completion of the current purchase.

If you are buying a property in joint names it will be necessary for both individuals to qualify as first time buyers in order to qualify for the reduced rate of stamp duty.

Clawback of Stamp duty

A clawback of Stamp duty arises if rent is obtained from the letting of the house or apartment for a period of 5 years from the date of the conveyance or transfer, other than under the rent-a-room scheme. The clawback amounts to the difference between the higher stamp duty rates and the duty paid and it becomes payable on the date that rent is first received from the property. A clawback will not arise where the property is sold to an unrelated third party during the 5-year period.

Transfer of site to child

A site transferred from a parent to a child, for the purpose of the construction of the child's principal private residence, is exempt from stamp duty (limited to one site with a value of €254,000 per child).

Fees

Home Buyers can expect to pay up to 1.5% of the purchase price of the property plus VAT. But competitive rates can be found with solicitors reducing their fees for this type of business so you should shop around.

Lenders vary considerably in the way they apply charges. Some, for example, insist on charging you their legal costs, calculated as a percentage of the loan up to a maximum amount. It could amount to as much as €250 to €350. If a lender's fees seem low in comparison to another, take a good look at the interest rates being charged. Both in the first year when a discount of half to one percent may usually apply and over the longer term, when you will revert to the normal interest rate.

Mortgage interest relief

Mortgage interest relief is now available at source at the standard 20% rate of tax only. This means that your mortgage provider will reduce your monthly mortgage repayments by the amount of tax relief you are entitled to.

From 1st January 2007 first time mortgage holders, for the first seven years can claim 100% tax relief on the interest paid within the following limits;

- €16,000 for a married couple, who are jointly assessed for tax (tax credit of €3,200 p.a.)

- €16,000 for a widow(er) (tax credit of €3,200 p.a.)

- €8,000 for a single person (tax credit of €1,600 p.a.)

Non first time buyers can receive 100% tax relief on interest paid within the following limits;

- €6,000 for a married couple who are jointly assessed or a widowed person. (tax credit of €1,200 p.a.)

- €3,000 for a single person. (tax credit of €600 p.a.)

Bridging loan interest

Additional tax relief is allowed for interest on bridging loans obtained to finance the disposal of your main residence and the acquisition of another residence. This relief is confined to a period of 12 months from the date the loan is obtained. It is subject to the same restrictions as mortgage interest. However, both reliefs may be claimed at the same time.

Interest rates and the cost of borrowing

The cost of borrowing for a mortgage is now at historically low rates. However; recently the rates have risen slightly, but interest rates are cyclical and are likely to vary by a few percentage points either way over the 20 or 25 years. The important thing now is to take account of as many unforeseen circumstances as possible.

Although many couples are both earning incomes, an unexpected event, like illness, redundancy or even the arrival of a new baby, can put considerable strain on a family budget. A typical €250,000 mortgage being repaid at 4.25% interest will result in monthly repayments of €1,343 over 25 years.

A 1% rise in interest rates to 5.25% will increase the payment to €1,480 a month, an additional €137 per month, or an additional €1,644 a year.

Home Equity Release Loans and Annuities

The interest in equity release loans, especially amongst older, retired homeowners whose properties may be worth a great deal, but whose pensions are not, has grown in recent years.

Two branded products now exist on the Irish market, a non-repayable fixed rate mortgage which is only repaid after the death of the borrower or if the house is sold or is left uninhabited by its owner for six months or more, and a product which purchases a portion of the house in exchange for a cash payment or regular, guaranteed income.

Fixed Rate

The fixed rate home equity loan is only available to people who are aged 65 and over and who own their home. The 15 year fixed interest rate of c.6.9% currently carries a hefty premium over and above the variable interest rate, although this gap could narrow if mortgage interest rates were to increase.

The amount that can be borrowed depends on the borrowers age and the value of the property:

Aged	%
60 - 64	Up to 15%
65 - 69	Up to 20%
70 - 74	Up to 25%
75 - 79	Up to 27.5%
Over 80	Up to 30%

Annuity Based

The annuity-based product is not a loan, but involves the outright sale of a portion of the person's home in exchange for a payment that is based, not on the market value of the property, but on an actuarial formula which takes into account the borrower's age, sex and longevity risk.

The older you are – and sellers must be at least 70 and own the property outright – the higher the exchange price. There is no repayment involved in this product, but the seller must agree to exchange at least 50% ownership of the property to the buyer, remaining the legal owner of the balance of the property.

Borrowing against the equity value of your home can be a suitable way to enhance your income, but the compounding effect of the deferred interest on the outstanding capital – both of which must be paid eventually – means that your home will be worth less should you need to sell it, say, to pay for long term care. The exchange of a substantial part of the equity value of your home in the form of an annuity or cash, for much less than market value, also results in you having a much diminished asset, unless there is considerable capital growth in the property to make good your loss.

Always seek professional legal and financial advice before opting for either type of equity release product and carefully check terms and conditions and charges.

Choose lender carefully

Choosing a lender that offers the best, long-term interest rates, is very important. By carefully shopping around, you may be able to save yourself a considerable sum of money over the term of your loan. No lender will guarantee that their rate will always be the most competitive, but certain lenders have better track records than others for offering consistently lower rates and charges. Check them out.

Below we illustrate the typical monthly repayments on a €250,000 loan, assuming annual interest rates of 4,25%, 5.25%, and 6.25% p.a. over four lending periods:

Monthly repayments - €250,000 loan [*]				
Rate	20 yrs	25 yrs	30 yrs	35 yrs
4.25%	€1,537	€1,343	€1,218	€1,133
5.25%	€1,668	€1,480	€1,362	€1,282
6.25%	€1,802	€1,623	€1,511	€1,439

[*] Repayments do not include mortgage interest relief

The longer your mortgage term, the cheaper the monthly repayment will be. But when the total cost of interest and capital repayments are added up, an extra five or ten years will cost you thousands of extra euro over the entire term.

Example

A €250,000 loan arranged over 25 years at 4.25% interest will cost €1,343 per month, the same loan stretched out five years will cost €1,218 a month, a "saving" of €125. The extra five year lending term, however, will amount to an extra €35,580 in mortgage payments overall.

Anyone who arranges a 30 or 35 year mortgage should try to accelerate their payments after a few years, when their income has increased and the high early costs associated with home ownership have diminished.

Designated areas

If you buy, build or restore a dwelling in a designated area, you are entitled to offset part of the development cost against your income for tax purposes. An annual deduction of 5% in the case of construction expenditure and 10% in the case of refurbishment expenditure may be claimed each year for 10 years. To claim this relief, you must be the first owner-occupier of the dwelling after its construction or refurbishment. You will not be entitled to this relief for any year in which the dwelling is not your sole or main residence.

Example

You are single and bought a new home for €300,000 in a designated area; - site cost €40,000, mortgage was €225,000, your income was €75,000 p.a.

Purchase Price	€300,000
Less: Site Cost	€40,000
Qualifying Expenditure	€260,000
Annual Relief (5% of €260,000 over 10 years)	€13,000
Tax Relief @ 42% (41% in 2007)	**€5,460**

Mortgage repayment methods

Annuity mortgage

The annuity method, also known as a repayment mortgage, is the most common way to pay off a mortgage. Annuity mortgages involve the payment each month of interest and some of the principal of the loan. In the early years, the bulk of the payment is interest, which will be the subject of mortgage interest tax relief at source.

As the years progress, you will pay less interest and more capital until eventually your entire loan will be cleared. A typical repayment mortgage will be repaid as illustrated on page 101, over a 30 year term.

Endowment mortgage

The other way a mortgage can be arranged is by the endowment method, which combines a home loan with a life assurance policy. Under this method the borrower pays the lender, interest for the entire term, while at the same time paying monthly premiums into a life assurance investment policy. (Since it is also a life assurance policy, you will not have to take out a separate mortgage protection policy.) If all goes well with the investment markets, there will be sufficient growth to create an investment fund to pay off the original capital sum at the end of the loan term.

Unlike conventional annuity mortgages with which you repay both interest and capital each month, an endowment mortgage involves only the repayment of interest and this interest can qualify for full mortgage interest relief for the full duration of the loan. This was a major selling point of endowment mortgages in the early 1990s, but is of little merit now as mortgage interest relief has been clawed back significantly in recent years.

You should be aware that unless you take out a life assurance policy which guarantees to repay the mortgage amount at the end of the policy term, you may end up increasing your premiums during the term of the policy to ensure you have an adequate investment fund at that end of the term to repay the mortgage.

Pension mortgage

A pension mortgage is similar to an endowment one, in that only interest is paid on the loan during the term of the contract. In this case, the investment vehicle which is used to pay off the capital is the homeowner's personal pension plan. Under Revenue rules, a quarter of the final pension fund value can be paid out as a tax-free lump sum, and it is this sum which is used to repay the mortgage capital.

Variable or fixed rate?

Should you arrange your mortgage on a variable interest rate basis or fix the interest for a period of years? Nearly all new borrowers are offered a discounted fixed rate for the first year of their loan, which usually amounts to a saving of a couple of hundred euro. In year two, you immediately revert to the variable rate of interest, which can go up and down over the term of the mortgage.

A fixed interest rate can provide considerable peace of mind and protect the borrower from the volatility of world money markets, but you can also suffer financially - if rates fall and your rate is fixed at a higher level for a few more years. The cost of breaking a fixed rate mortgage can be very high. Some banks charge nearly the entire interest balance that they could have expected to earn if you had seen out the contract.

Mortgage and home insurance

The monthly mortgage repayment is not the only one you have to make. Mortgage protection and buildings insurance are compulsory in most cases and can cost up to 10% of your gross monthly mortgage repayments.

Mortgage protection insurance is a life assurance policy that covers the value of the mortgage and ensures that your debt to the bank or building society is repaid in the event of your death or that of your spouse. Rates are based on age and sex and the premiums can be paid monthly or annually. You are not obliged to purchase the policy from the lender and you should shop around for the best market rate, especially if you are a smoker.

An increasing number of new home owners are arranging serious illness cover as part of their mortgage protection policy in order that the loan can be paid off not only if they die but also in the event of a life-threatening illness. The cost is higher, but can be mitigated by arranging the policy on a decreasing term basis.

The chart on page 101 shows the capital and interest payments associated with a €250,000 mortgage at 4.5% interest over 30 years. Mortgage interest relief is explained on page 114.

End of Year	Annual repayments	Capital repaid	Cumulative capital repaid	Interest paid	Cumulative interest paid	Loan outstanding at end of year
€	€	€	€	€	€	€
1	15,200	4,033	4,033	11,167	11,167	245,967
2	15,200	4,218	8,251	10,982	22,149	241,749
3	15,200	4,412	12,663	10,788	32,937	237,337
4	15,200	4,615	17,278	10,587	43,524	232,722
5	15,200	4,827	22,105	10,374	53,898	227,895
6	15,200	5,047	27,154	10,152	64,050	222,846
7	15,200	5,280	32,434	9,920	73,970	217,566
8	15,200	5,523	37,957	9,677	83,647	212,043
9	15,200	5,777	43,734	9,424	93,071	206,266
10	15,200	6,042	49,776	9,158	102,229	200,224
11	15,200	6,320	56,096	8,881	111,110	193,904
12	15,200	6,610	62,706	8,590	119,700	187,294
13	15,200	6,914	69,620	8,287	127,987	180,380
14	15,200	7,231	76,851	7,969	135,956	173,149
15	15,200	7,564	84,415	7,637	143,593	165,585
16	15,200	7,911	92,326	7,290	150,883	157,674
17	15,200	8,274	100,600	6,926	157,809	149,400
18	15,200	8,655	109,255	6,546	164,355	140,745
19	15,200	9,052	118,307	6,148	170,503	131,693
20	15,200	9,468	127,775	5,732	176,236	122,225
21	15,200	9,903	137,678	5,298	181,533	112,322
22	15,200	10,358	148,036	4,843	186,376	101,964
23	15,200	10,834	158,870	4,367	190,742	91,130
24	15,200	11,332	170,201	3,869	194,611	79,799
25	15,200	11,85	182,053	3,348	197,960	67,947
26	15,200	12,397	194,450	2,804	200,764	55,550
27	15,200	12,966	207,416	2,234	202,998	42,584
28	15,200	13,562	220,978	1,639	204,637	29,022
29	15,200	14,185	253,162	1,016	205,653	14,838
30	15,200	14,838	250,000	364	206,017	0

Repaying a €250,000 annuity mortgage

Assumptions

Interest Rate	4.5%
Gross Repayments	€1,266.71 p.m or €15,200.52 p.a.

REA
MORTGAGE CHOICE

Mortgage Broker of the Year

as awarded by Moneymate and Investor Magazine 2006

Pictured receiving the 2006 Residential Mortgage Broker of the Year Award
Back row: Brian Byrne, Sean Doherty, Pat Macgrath, Liasa Hickey, Neill Delahaye, Jon Wood.
Front row: Liz Cloonan, Richard Eberle, Sarah Wellband, Deirdre Leonard

For the best mortgage dea
Call REA Now!
Lo Call 1890 663 663

Dublin, Swords, Newbridge, Bray, Gorey and Waterford

Example

Plan type	Monthly cost
Conventional Mortgage Protection Plan	€13.23
Mortgage Protection Plan plus Serious Illness Cover	€45.34

You and your spouse have a mortgage of €175,000 over 20 years. You are both age 29 and non-smokers. The monthly cost of a Conventional Mortgage Protection Plan and a Mortgage Protection Plan, which included Serious Illness Cover for you, will work out approximately as follows:

Protect your mortgage repayments

If you are concerned about how your mortgage would be paid if you became ill or were made redundant, even for a short period of time, you may want to take out Mortgage Payment Protection cover. Available from all the major lenders, this insurance costs about €4.50 for every €100 cover required per month and pays out benefits if you become ill or disabled and are unable to work, or have been made redundant. You need to have been out of work for about 30 days before your first claim can be made and there is generally a 12 month payment limit per claim. Payment protection insurance like this is not cheap, and if you already have Permanent Health Insurance or serious illness cover, it may be unnecessary.

Protect the building

Building insurance is also compulsory if you take out a mortgage. Again, the lender wants to protect their share of the property in the event of a fire or another disaster. The premiums are based not on the market value of the property, but on the cost of rebuilding. It is important that you have the property surveyed to ensure the rebuilding cost is correct and any increases in the cost of materials and labour are taken into account.

Most general insurance companies offer combined buildings and contents policies. Some automatically provide contents cover worth up to half the value of the building cover. Engage an independent financial advisor to help you find the right policy for you and to ensure you put a correct value on your fittings and personal belongings. Premium discounts may be available, which will depend on your age, whether the house is occupied during the daytime and if it is fitted with approved locks, fire and burglar alarms etc.

Local authority loans

Shared ownership loans are available from Dublin City Council and other county councils to those on a single income who earned no more than €40,000 in the previous tax year (subject to applicants eligibility for inclusion in the scheme). In the case of a two-income household, two and a half times the principal income and once the second income must be less than €100,000. The variable interest rate charged is currently 4.3% which includes mortgage protection cover of 0.598% The maximum price you can pay for a home under the shared ownership scheme varies between local authority lenders.

Shared Ownership Schemes are operated by local authorities and for many they offer the first step in purchasing a home of their choice. In effect the local authority buys the home for the applicant. The applicant then acquires or takes out a mortgage from the local authority - minimum 40% / maximum 75% - of the property and pays rent to the local authority in respect of the remainder. The local authority's share or the rental element must be bought out within 25 years and can be bought out after a minimum of three years.

Affordable Housing Schemes

This scheme allows lower-income buyers a chance to buy newly constructed homes and apartments in areas where an affordability gap has arisen. The prices are significantly lower than their actual market value.

The houses are bought with Local Authority loans which can be up to 97% of the house price, subject to repayments of no more than 35% of household net income. Income cannot exceed €40,000, or €100,000 for two income households.

8

Making the income tax system work for you

The day to day control of the tax system is exercised by the Revenue Commissioners, who operate under the guidance of the Minister for Finance. The country is divided into tax districts to which Tax Inspectors are appointed. Tax Inspectors have responsibility for issuing annual tax returns and agreeing annual tax liabilities.

Annual returns

PAYE taxpayers are obliged to make a return when requested to do so by their Tax Inspector. Individuals liable to self assessment and proprietary company directors are obliged to make a Return of Income on or before the 31st October for the tax year ending the previous 31st December, whether they are requested to do so or not.

Surcharge

If you miss the due date you are subject to a surcharge. This surcharge applies to the full tax payable for the year, regardless of PAYE or any other tax already paid. If your tax return is submitted before the 31st of December, the surcharge is 5%, subject to a maximum of €12,700. Where it is submitted after that date, the surcharge is 10%, subject to a maximum of €63,500.

Taxpayers who file their tax returns and pay the tax due, using the Revenue online service (ROS), normally receive an extension to the 31st October deadline. In 2006, this deadline was extended to 16th November 2006, for individuals who pay and file over ROS.

If you are in doubt about what should be included on your returns, your obligations will be fulfilled if you draw your Inspector's attention to the matter in question. This provision will not apply if the Inspector or the Appeal Commissioners believe that the doubt was not genuine and you were trying to avoid or evade paying the tax.

Classification of income

Income is classified under a number of headings. These headings are known as schedules and the income falling under each is as follows:

Schedule C:

Those who have deducted income tax from certain payments are assessed under this schedule e.g. Banks.

Schedule D:

Case I:	Profits from a trade.
Case II:	Profits from a profession.
Case III:	Interest not taxed at source and all foreign income.
Case IV:	Taxed interest income not falling under any other case or schedule.
Case V:	Rental income from properties in Ireland.

Schedule E:

Income from offices or employments together with pensions, benefits-in-kind and certain lump sum payments arising from an office or employment.

Schedule F:

Dividends and other distributions from Irish-resident companies.

Tax Credits

	2005	2006	2007
Single Person	€1,580	€1,630	€1,760
Married Couple	€3,160	€3,260	€3,520
Widowed Person			
Without dependent children	€1,980	€2,130	€2,310
Widowed Person (in year of bereavement)	€3,160	€3,260	€3,520
One-Parent Family			
Widowed Person (Except in Year of Bereavement)	€1,580	€1,630	€1,760
Other Person (Deserted, Separated or Unmarried)	€1,580	€1,630	€1,760
Widowed Parent			
First Year After Bereavement	€2,800	€3,100	€3,750
Second Year After Bereavement	€2,300	€2,600	€3,250
Third Year After Bereavement	€1,800	€2,100	€2,750
Fourth Year After Bereavement	€1,300	€1,600	€2,250
Fifth Year After Bereavement	€800	€1,100	€1,750
Home Carer's Credit - Max.	€770	€770	€770
PAYE Credit	€1,270	€1,490	€1,760
Age Credit			
Single/Widowed	€205	€250	€275
Married	€410	€500	€550
Incapacitated Child Credit	€1,000	€1,500	€3,000
Dependent Relative Credit	€60	€80	€80
(Income Limit)	(€10,997)	(€11,912)	(€12,744)
Blind Credit			
Single person	€1,000	€1,500	€1,760
One spouse blind	€1,000	€1,500	€1,760
Both spouses blind	€2,000	€3,000	€3,520
Trade union subscription	€40	€60	€60

Computation of your income tax liability

Income tax is payable on your taxable income, i.e. your total assessable income for a tax year, less deductions for any, non standard rate allowances (not tax credits) to which you may be entitled.

Tax bands and rates

2006	2007
Single/Widow(er)	**Single/Widow(er)**
First €32,000 @ 20% Balance @ 42%	First €34,000 @ 20% Balance @ 41%
One Parent Family	**One Parent Family**
First €36,000 @ 20% Balance @ 42%	First €38,000 @ 20% Balance @ 41%
Married Couple - Both Spouses Working Note 1 + 2	**Married Couple - Both Spouses Working** Note 1 + 2
First €64,000 @ 20% Balance @ 42%	First €68,000 @ 20% Balance @ 41%
Married Couple - Only One Spouses Working	**Married Couple - Only One Spouses Working**
First €41,000 @ 20% Balance @ 42%	First €43,000 @ 20% Balance @ 41%

1.   Transferable between spouses up to a maximum of €41,000 in 2006 and €43,000 in 2007 for any one spouse.

2.   Subject to the lower earning spouse having income of at least €23,000 in 2006 and €25,000 in 2007.

Individualisation

Prior to the introduction of individualisation the married rate tax band was double that of a single person. This applied regardless of whether one or both spouses worked. From 1st January 2007 (see above for 2006 rates) the standard rate tax band for a married couple, where both spouses have income, can be increased by the lower of;

- €25,000

    or

- the income of the lower earning spouse.

The maximum standard rate band available to either spouse is €43,000.

Income exemptions limits

A person whose income does not exceed the following limits, is completely exempt from income tax.

	2005 €	2006 €	2007 €
Single/Widowed Person	€5,210	€5,210	€5,210
Married	€10,420	€10,420	€10,420
Person 65 years:			
- Single / Widow(er)	€16,500	€17,000	€19,000
- Married	€33,000	€34,000	€38,000
Additional allowance per child	€575	€575	€575
Additional allowance for third and subsequent child	€830	€830	€830

Marginal relief

Marginal relief is available for those whose total income exceeds the exemptions limits, but is less than twice the relevant limit. It restricts the tax payable to 40% of the difference between your income and the appropriate exemption limit.

Example

A married man aged 70, his total income for 2006 is €35,000. His tax liability would normally work out as follows:

		€
	Total Income	€35,000
	Taxable	€35,000
	€35,000 @ 20%	€7,000
Less:	Tax Credits	
	Personal	(€3,260)
	PAYE	(€1,490)
	Age	(€500)
		€1,750

However, marginal relief will restrict the overall tax liability to €1,600.
(€35,000 - €34,000) x 40% = €400

Increased exemption/dependent children

If you have dependent children, the general exemption limit can be increased, by €575 for the first and second child and €830 for the third and subsequent qualifying children.

Personal credits

Single credit

This credit is granted to the following

- Individuals who are single

- Married couples who opt for single/separate assessment - both partners receive a single tax credit

- Separated couples who have not opted for joint assessment.

Married credit

This credit, which is double the single credit is granted to married couples who;

- Are assessed to tax under joint assessment (See Chapter 17 - Marriage Matters on page 311)

    or

- Are living apart but one partner is maintaining the other and is not entitled to claim tax relief on the maintenance paid (for more details on this see Chapter 18 - Separation and Divorce on page 319).

Single parent credit

This credit is granted to a parent or guardian, of a qualifying child who is not entitled to the married person's credit. However, it is not available to an unmarried couple who are living together as man and wife.

For a single/widowed person, the credit is €1,630 for 2006 and €1,760 for 2007.

Qualifying child

To qualify a child must:

- Have been born in the tax year

    or

- Be under the age of 16 years at the commencement of the tax year.

or

- If over 16 years of age be receiving full-time education or be permanently incapacitated by reason of mental or physical infirmity and if over 21 years of age, be incapacitated before reaching that age.

Widowed parent credit

An additional credit is granted to widowed parents for the five tax years following the year of bereavement. The credit in 2006 is €3,100 in year one, €2,600 in year two, €2,100 in year three, €1,600 in year four and €1,100 in year five. See page 107 for 2007 rates.

Home carer's credit

The Home carer's credit may be claimed by a married couple where one spouse cares for one or more dependent people.

If the Home carer has income in their own right of less than €5,080 the full home carer's credit may still be claimed. If they have income between €5,080 and €6,620 for the tax year they may claim a reduced credit. Only one credit is due irrespective of the number of dependents.

In order to qualify for the credit the following conditions apply;

- The married couple must be jointly assessed to tax - it does not apply where married couples are taxed as single persons.

- The Home Carer must care for one or more dependent persons. A dependent person is:

    - A child for whom child benefit is payable.

      or

    - A person aged 65 years or over;

      or

    - A person who is permanently incapacitated by reasons of mental or physical infirmity.

A dependent person does not include a spouse.

- The dependent person(s) must normally reside with the married couple for the tax year.

You can also claim the carer's credit for a dependent relative who is cared for outside the home provided they live in a neighbouring residence or within two kilometres of the carer.

If your income exceeds €6,620 in the tax year you can still claim the Home Carer's Credit, provided, the allowance was granted for the immediately preceding tax year.

A married couple cannot claim both the Home Carer's Credit and the increased standard rate cut off point for dual income couples. However, they can claim whichever of the two is more beneficial. In practice, the tax office will grant the more beneficial treatment.

Incapacitated child credit

Incapacitated child credit is granted where a child is:

- Under 18 years of age during the tax year and is permanently incapacitated by reason of mental or physical infirmity;

  or,

- If over the age of 18 years and had become permanently incapacitated before they reached the age of 21 years of age, for 2006 tax year the credit is €1,500 p.a. (€3,000 p.a. in 2007) or the amount spent on the maintenance of the child aged over 18 years, if this amount is less than €1,500.

Age credit

A credit is available if you or your spouse are over 65 years of age in the relevant tax year. In the case of a married couple the credit for 2006 is €500 (€550 in 2007) and for a single or widowed person it is €250 (€275 in 2007).

Dependent relative credit

This credit is granted to claimants who prove that they maintain at their own expense any person who is:

A relative of themselves or their spouse, who is incapacitated by old age or infirmity from maintaining themselves.

Their or their spouse's widowed mother, whether incapacitated or not.

A son or daughter who resides with them and whose services they depend on by reason of old age or infirmity.

The credit of €80 p.a., is reduced by the amount by which the income of the person whom the claim is made for exceeds the maximum rate of old age contributory pension payable to a single person (€11,912 in 2006 and €12,744 in 2007). If two or more people help maintain the relative the credit is divided between them in proportion to the amounts contributed by each.

Incapacitated person (employing a carer)

This allowance of €50,000 is claimable where you employ a person to take care of a family member who is totally incapacitated, owing to old age or infirmity.

This allowance is granted at your marginal rate of tax.

Blind person's credit

A credit of €1,500 (€1,760 from 1st January 2007), is available during the tax year if you are blind. If both you and your spouse are blind, a credit of €3,000 in 2006 (€3,520 from 1st January 2007) may be claimed.

Mortgage interest relief

Interest payments are divided into two categories:

- Loans on Main Residence.
- Other Loans.

Loans on main residence

Mortgage interest relief in respect of interest on money borrowed for the purchase, repair, development or improvement of your sole or main residence is now granted at source. Your monthly repayments are reduced by the amount of your tax credit. This relief may also be claimed for interest paid on a loan to purchase a residence for a former or separated spouse or a dependent relative if this accommodation is provided by you rent-free. Your dependent relative must be one in respect of whom you claim the Dependent Relative Credit of €80 - i.e. their income must not exceed €11,912 in the 2006 tax year.

First time mortgage holders, for the first seven years can claim 100% tax relief at the standard rate of tax (20%) on the interest paid within the following limits;

- €8,000 for a married couple, who are jointly assessed for tax (tax credit of €1,600)

- €8,000 for a widow(er) (tax credit of €1,600)

- €4,000 for a single person (tax credit of €800)

Other buyers can claim 100% tax relief on interest paid within the following limits;

- €5,080 for a married couple who are jointly assessed or a widowed person. (tax credit of €1,016)

- €2,540 for a single person. (tax credit of €508)

Budget 2007: From 1st January 2007 Mortgage interest relief for first time buyers is increased to €16,000 (tax credit of €3,200) for a married couple / widowed person, and €8,000 (tax credit of €1,600) for a single person. For non first time buyers mortgage interest relief for a single person is €3,000 (tax credit €600) and for a married couple / widowed person €6,000 (tax credit €1,200)

Example

A married couple are 42% tax-payers and pay mortgage interest of €8,000 in the 2006 tax year. Their mortgage interest relief will work out as follows;

A Assumes they are first time buyers.

B Assumes they are not first time buyers.

	2006	
	A	**B**
	Less than 7 years mortgage holders	**More than 7 years mortgage holders**
Mortgage interest paid	€8,000	€8,000
Maximum interest allowed for tax purposes	€6,350	€5,080
Tax credit €6,350/€5,080 @ 20%	€1,270	€1,016

Note: This tax relief will be granted at source by your bank or building society.

Bridging loan interest

Additional relief is available on bridging loan interest. A bridging loan is a loan to finance the disposal of your sole or main residence and the acquisition of another residence for use as a sole or main residence. The position on bridging loan interest is as follows:

- It is subject to the same restrictions as mortgage interest. However, both reliefs may be claimed for the relevant period.

- The additional allowance is for a period of 12 months only from the date on which the loan was granted. If the bridging period falls partly in one tax year and partly in another, the allowance is apportioned on a time basis according to the number of months falling into the respective years.

- No tax relief is granted for bridging loan interest which exceeds the limit of 12 months.

If after the end of the 12 month period the old home is still unsold, interest will continue to be allowed in the normal way if it is occupied as the sole or main residence. If the old residence is unoccupied, no interest deduction is allowed after the end of the 12 month period.

Other loans

There are no restrictions on the amount of interest on which tax relief may be claimed in the following circumstances.

- Interest paid out for business purposes under Case I and II of Schedule D.

- Interest on money borrowed to pay death duties.

- Interest on money borrowed to acquire an interest in a company or partnership or in granting a loan to a company or partnership. However from 7th December 2005 no tax relief is available on interest on loans taken out to acquire an interest in property rental companies.

Payments made under Deeds of Covenant

Tax relief on covenants is available only in the following circumstances;

- Covenant to people over 65 up to a maximum of 5% of the coventor's total income;

- Covenant to permanently incapacitated individuals.

Payments by a parent to a son or daughter under 18 do not qualify for tax relief.

If you pay tax at the higher rate you may reduce your tax liability and increase the disposable income of the covenantee. In addition, if the covenantee pays tax at a lower rate or is exempt from tax, a tax advantage may be gained.

Example

> You have an income of €58,000 in the 2006 tax year and pay tax at 42%. Your spouse has no income. In 2006 you wish to supplement your widowed mother's (aged 76) income by €2,000 p.a. Your mother's income is a pension of €11,912 p.a.
>
> You can do this in one of two ways:
>
> • Hand over €2,000 to your mother each year.
>
> or
>
> • Complete a Deed of Covenant for €2,500 - it gets a little complicated here! You deduct tax at the standard rate (20%) from this gross amount and pay the balance of €2,000 to your mother.
>
> We have illustrated both positions on the pages 119 and 120. When all the paperwork is completed, under a Deed of Covenant you will be better off by €550 p.a. and your widowed mother is better off by €500 p.a.
>
> A note of caution; if your mother's pension is a non-contributory pension, the covenant income will be taken into account for means-test purposes and may affect the amount of pension she will receive.

Your Position

		2006 Tax Year	
		Without Covenant €	With Convenant €
A	Total Income	€58,000	€58,000
B	Less: Deed of Covenant	₌	€ 2,500)
	Taxable	€58,000	€55,500
	Tax payable		
	€41,000 @ 20%	€ 8,200	€ 8,200
	€17,000/ €14,500 @ 42%	€ 7,140	€ 6,090
		€15,340	€14,290
	Tax on Covenant		
	€2,500 @ 20%	n/a	€500
	Total Tax	€15,340	€14,790
	Less: Tax Credits	(€ 3,260)	(€ 3,260)
	Personal	(€ 1,490)	(€ 1,490)
	PAYE		
		€10,590	€10,040
C	Net Tax Payable		
D	Direct payment to Mother	€2,000	€2,000
	Net Income	**€45,410**	**€45,960**
		A-(C+D)	A-(C+D)

Your Mother's position

		2006 Tax Year	
		Without Covenant €	With Convenant €
A	Deed of Covenant	Nil	€2,500
B	Pension	€12,000	€12,000
	Total Income	€12,000	€14,500
	Taxable Income (Income Under Exemption Limit)	Nil	Nil
	Tax Payable	Nil	Nil
C	Tax Refund Due (tax paid by you)	Nil	€500
D	Payment from you	€2,000	€2,000
	Disposable Income	€14,000	€14,500
		(B+D)	(B+C+D)

Retirement annuity pension contributions

Income tax relief is available for premiums paid to an approved personal pension scheme, to provide income in your retirement between the ages of 60 and 75 on non-pensionable earnings.

Relief is restricted as a percentage of net relevant earnings (NRE) as follows;

Up to 29 years	15%
30 to 39 years	20%
40 to 49 years	25%
50 to 54 years	30%
55 to 59 years	35%
60 and over	40%

Notes:

- The above rates apply to the 2006 tax year and thereafter.

- Net relevant earnings are limited to €254,000 per annum. This figure will be increased annually in line with an earnings index from 2007.

- **Relevant earnings** consist of income from non-pensionable employment or from self-employment. A husband and wife have separate relevant earnings, which cannot be aggregated for retirement saving purposes. Income from a claim under a Permanent Health Insurance (PHI) policy is considered to be relevant earnings for retirement saving purposes. Investment earnings are not treated as relevant earnings and cannot be taken into consideration in calculating your maximum allowable pension contributions. Net relevant earnings consist of relevant earning less capital allowances, trading losses and certain other charges e.g. covenants and mortgage interest, for which you can claim tax relief.

PAYE credit

The PAYE credit is €1,490 for 2006 tax year (€1,760 for 2007). If you are married and both spouses pay PAYE, each is entitled to a PAYE credit of €1,490.

The following PAYE income does not qualify for a PAYE credit:

- Income paid to a proprietary director or a spouse of a proprietary director.

- Income paid by an individual or a partner to their spouse.

A proprietary director is a director who controls, either directly or indirectly, 15% or more of the ordinary share capital of the company.

The PAYE credit is available to children of proprietary directors and the self employed, provided they work full-time in their parent's business and their salary exceeds €4,571.

Medical insurance

Tax Relief is granted at source at the standard rate of tax on the full amount of the subscription paid for medical insurance.

Tax relief is also available at the standard rate for insurance premiums paid to cover the cost of non-routine dental care.

Medical expenses

Relief is available for unreimbursed health expenses incurred in the provision of health care in respect of yourself, your spouse and your dependents including dependent relatives. You cannot claim relief for any expenditure that has been or will be re-imbursed for example by VHI, BUPA, VIVA's Health, HSE, or where a compensation payment is made or will be made.

Health expenses include the following:

- Services of a practitioner.

- Drugs and medicines.

- Hearing aids.

- Physiotherapy or similar treatment.

- Wheelchair/wheelchair lift.

- Orthopaedic bed/chair.

- Home nursing and special nursing.

- Kidney patients expenses, including a mileage allowance where the patient attends hospital for dialysis. For home dialysis patients tax relief is allowed for electricity, laundry, telephone and travel to and from the hospital.

- Maternity care.

- Child oncology patients (certain items of expenditure).

- Educational psychological assessments and speech and language therapy for children.

- In vitro fertilisation.

- Glucometer machine for a diabetic.

- Coeliacs.
Cost of gluten free food for coeliacs. As this condition is generally ongoing, a letter, instead of prescriptions, from a doctor stating that the taxpayer is a coeliac sufferer is acceptable. Receipts from supermarkets in addition to receipts from a chemist are acceptable.

- Nursing care and, in certain circumstances, maintenance paid to a nursing home, for a dependent relative.

To qualify, the nursing home must be approved by the relevant health authority and provide regular nursing services and the dependent relative must be in need of and avail of these nursing services.

Where qualifying care is only available outside Ireland, reasonable travelling and accommodation expenses can also be claimed. In such cases the expenses of one person accompanying the patient may also be allowed where the condition of the patient requires it.

Dental treatment will qualify for tax relief as follows;
Crowns which are permanently cemented to the existing tooth tissue.

- Crowns which form part of a bridge do not qualify for relief.

- Veneers/rembrant type etched fillings.

- Tip replacing where a large part of the tooth needs to be replaced and the replacement is made outside the mouth.

- Gold posts which are inserted in the nerve canal of a tooth to hold a crown.

- Gold inlays which are smaller versions of a gold crown. Relief will only be available if they were fabricated outside the mouth.

- Endodontics - root canal treatment: This involves the filling of the nerve canal and not the filling of teeth.

- Periodontal treatment which includes, root planing, curettage and debridement, gum flaps and chrome cobalt splint.

- Bridgework consisting of an enamel retained bridge or a tooth supported bridge.

- Orthodontic treatment which involves the provision of braces and other similar treatments.

- Surgical extraction of impacted wisdom teeth when undertaken in a hospital. In order to obtain tax relief certification from the hospital will be required.

Health expenses carried out outside the State also qualify for tax relief provided the Practitioner is qualified to practice in the county.

Exclusions

Health care specifically excludes expenses relating to

- Routine ophthalmic treatment.

- Routine dental treatment.

Routine ophthalmic treatment

This means sight testing and advice as to the use of spectacles or contact lenses and the provision and repair of spectacles or contact lenses.

Routine dental treatment

This means the extraction, scaling and filling of teeth, bridgework and the provision and repairing of artificial teeth and dentures.

The first €125 for an individual and €250 for a family is excluded from any claim made.

Relief for any Income Tax year is given by repayment i.e. a refund after the relevant 31st December. A condition for eligibility is that your return of income has been made for the year and all tax paid as due.

Medical expenses incurred, which are not in respect of routine health care or not covered by medical insurance, should be claimed on Form Med 1.

A claim for relief for the cost of dental treatment other than routine dental treatment must be accompanied by a certificate (Form Med 2 Dental) signed by a qualified practitioner.

Guide dog

A standard €826 per annum is allowed as medical expenses where a blind person maintains a trained guide dog and is the registered owner with the Irish Guide Dog Association.

Permanent Health Insurance (PHI)

Permanent health insurance (PHI) protects your income against accidents or illness for up to 75% of your normal earnings. After a specific period has expired, the benefits are paid for the duration of your incapacity or to a specific age, whichever is the earlier. Income tax relief may be claimed on the contributions made to a PHI scheme.

Contributions to a PHI scheme by PAYE tax payers are on a "Net Pay" basis i.e. the contribution is deducted from your gross salary prior to the application of tax and PRSI.

The amount of relief granted cannot exceed 10% of your total income for the year of assessment in which the premiums are paid. All receipts from a PHI plan are taxable, regardless of whether or not the relief is claimed on premiums paid.

Rent relief for private rented accommodation

A tax credit is available to tenants paying rent for private rental accommodation. The amount of this credit in the 2006 tax year for a single person is €330 (€360 from 1st January 2007) and for a married couple or widowed person the credit is €660 (€720 from 1st January 2007). If you are over 55 and paying rent for private rental accommodation, the credit in

2006 is €660 (€720 from 1st January 2007) for a single person, €1,320 (€1,440 from 1st January 2007) for a married couple or a widowed person.

Long term unemployed

An additional allowance is available to any person who has been long term unemployed and who is returning to work.

You can opt to claim the allowances in the tax year you commence work, or if you prefer, you can commence your claim in the year of assessment following your return to work.

Long term unemployed means that you have been continuously unemployed and in receipt of Jobseekers Benefit, Jobseekers Allowance or Lone Parents Allowance for the 12 months prior to taking up employment.

People with disabilities who have been in receipt of Disability Allowance or Blind Persons Payment for at least 12 months can also claim this allowance.

	Year 1 €	Year 2 €	Year 3 €
Additional Personal Allowance	€3,810	€2,540	€1,270
Child Tax Allowance	€1,270	€850	€425

Fees paid to private colleges

Tax credit is available at the standard rate of tax on college fees paid for yourself or a dependent relative. The following courses apply;

- Tuition fees paid for certain full time and part time undergraduate courses of at least 2 years duration.

- Tuition fees paid for certain training courses in the area of Information Technology and Foreign Languages.

- Tax relief is also available on certain postgraduate courses.

Donation/gifts

Tax relief is available in respect of donations/gifts made to certain approved bodies/charities as follows:

- Donations made to an "approved body" to teach "approved subjects".

- Gifts for education in the Arts.

- Gifts to, or for the benefit of, designated schools. Relief is granted at the standard rate on aggregate gifts in a single year of assessment.

- Gifts made to third level institutes.

- Donations to designated charities - If you are paying PAYE you are not entitled to claim tax relief on donations made to charities. However, if you make a donation to a designated Third World Charity, the payment will be treated as having been made net of tax. The charity can then reclaim the tax from the revenue. The minimum donation is €254. If you are self-employed you are entitled to claim a tax credit on charitable donations.

- Donation of heritage items.

- Donation of gifts or money to the State which are used for any purpose or towards the cost of which public moneys are provided.

- Donation made to the Scientific and Technological Education (Investment) Fund.

Relief for investment in corporate trades (BES)

The maximum BES allowance you may claim in any tax year is €31,750. The minimum allowance is €254. A married couple can obtain a total allowance of €63,500 in a single tax year, provided each has income of €31,750 in their own right.

Where amounts in excess of €31,750 are invested in any tax year, or if the tax deduction is greater than the total income, the excess can be carried forward to future years. BES relief will cease on 31st December 2006.

Budget 2007:   The BES scheme is being renewed from 1st January 2007 for a seven year period to 31st December 2013. The investor limit of €31,750 is also increased to €150,000.

Relief for investment in the Film Industry /Section 35

Special tax incentives are available for investment in the film industry - known as Section 35 investments. In order for a film to qualify as a "Section

35 investment", the film must be given a certificate by the Minister for the Arts, Sports and Tourism and it is also necessary that a certain amount of the production work be carried out in Ireland.

Tax relief is available at your highest rate of tax, on 80% of your investment up to a maximum investment of €31,750 per annum. A married couple can claim tax relief on 80% of their investment up to a maximum investment of €31,750 provided each has sufficient income.

Film Industry relief will cease on 31st December 2008.

Seafarer's allowance

In the 2006 tax year an allowance of €6,350 is available for seafarers. This allowance can be offset against the seafaring employment. It is conditional on the seafarer being at sea on a voyage for a least 161 days in a tax year.

Service Charges

Tax relief is available on service charges paid to local authorities. A tax credit is given for service charges paid in the preceding calendar year.

From the 1st January 2007:

- The total tax relief that can be claimed for both fixed charge payments made (including lift charges and pay by weight) and bin tags purchased in 2006 will be subject to an overall limit of €400.

Transitional Arrangements for the tax year 2006

- Where Local Authority fixed charge exceeds €400 in 2005 then the full amount of that fixed charge will be allowed.

- Relief claimed in respect of bin tags purchased in 2005 will be the lesser of the amount paid in 2005 or €400.

- Where an individual purchased bin tags and made fixed charge payments of less than €400 in 2005, a limit of €400 will apply in respect of the total amount paid on both.

Trade Unions

Tax relief is available at the standard rate of tax on subscriptions paid to trade unions up to a maximum of €200 resulting in a tax credit of €60.

Childminding tax relief

Where an individual minds up to three children in their own home, no tax will be payable on the childminding earnings received provided the amount is less than €10,000 per annum. If the childminding income exceeds this amount the total amount will be taxable, as normal, under self assessment. An individual will be obliged to return their childminding income on their annual tax return.

Budget 2007: This relief was increased to €15,000 with effect from 1st January 2007

9

PAYE made easy

The Pay As You Earn (PAYE) system applies to you if you have income from employment or pension directly assessed.

Tax Credits

Prior to the introduction of tax credits, tax allowances were granted at your marginal rate of tax, therefore if you paid tax at the higher rate you could claim tax relief at your highest rate of tax. However, with the introduction of tax credits, allowances are allowed at the standard rate of tax only, regardless of whether you are a higher rate tax payer or not. This means that tax allowances benefit each individual by the same amount.

Tax credit system

Tax is calculated at the appropriate tax rates on gross pay and this tax is then reduced by any tax credits due, in order to arrive at the net tax payable.

Before the start of the new tax year, around December your tax office will issue a Notification of Determination of Tax Credits and standard rate cut off point.

The Notification of Determination of tax credit and standard rate cut off point will show the following information;

- Standard rate cut off point

- Tax credit due to you

- Your rate(s) of tax

Standard rate cut off point

This is the amount of income you can earn at the standard rate. The amount will depend on whether you are married, single or widowed. Also if you have any allowances which are allowed at the higher rate of tax e.g. pension contribution, this will increase your "standard rate cut off point".

Standard rate band

	2007 €
Single person	€34,000
Married couple(one spouse working)	€43,000
Married couple(*both spouse working - maximum)	€68,000
One parent family	€38,000

*   Subject to lower earning spouse having an income of at least €25,000.

The tax credits and standard rate cut off point will vary depending on the circumstances of each individual.

Income tax is calculated for each pay period by applying the information supplied by the notification against the gross pay as follows;

The standard rate of tax (20% in 2007) is applied to your gross pay up to the standard rate cut off point for that week or month. Any balance of income over that amount in the pay period is taxed at the higher rate (41% in 2007). This gives the gross tax payable. The gross tax payable is reduced by a tax credit as per the notification sent by your tax office, to arrive at the net tax payable.

Example

A married individual has gross earnings of €50,000, their spouse has no income. For 2007 a Notice of Determination of tax credits and standard rate cut off point issues showing;

Standard rate cut off point of €43,000 per annum of €826.92 per week.	Based on a standard rate band of €43,000 for a married couple - one spouse working.
Standard rate of tax is 20%	Based on standard rate of tax of 20% and a higher rate of 41%
Higher rate of tax is 41%	
Tax credits of €5,280 per annum or €101.54 per week	Personal €3,520
	PAYE credit €1,760
	€5,280

Income tax would be calculated as follows for the first week

Gross Pay	€961.52	(€50,000/52)
Tax on €826.92 @ 20%	€165.38	(Standard rate up to a maximum of €826.92 which is the standard rate cut off point as advised by the tax office)
Tax on €134.62 @ 41%	€55.19	(Higher rate of tax in excess of income over the standard rate cut off point).
Gross Tax	€220.57	Total of higher and standard rate tax.
Less: Tax Credits	€101.54	Tax credit as advised by the tax office.
Total Tax due for this week	€119.03	Total tax less tax credit

Non Standard rated reliefs

If you have deductions from income tax which qualify for tax relief at the higher rate of income tax, your tax credits will be increased by the amount of the relief at the standard rate of income tax and the standard rate tax band will also be increased by the amount of the relief in order to arrive at the standard rate cut off point.

Example

A married individual has a gross income of €50,000. Their spouse has no income. Personal and PAYE tax credits amount to €5,280. They have a standard rate tax cut off point of €43,000 and their rates of tax are 20% and 41%. They also pay €2,000 into a personal pension scheme, tax relief on which is allowed at the higher rate of tax. Their tax credit will increase by €400 (€2,000 @ 20%) . Their standard rate tax band will also increase by €2,000 in order to arrive at the standard rate cut off point.

Calculation of tax credits	
	2007 €
Married	€3,520
PAYE	€1,760
Total	€5,280
Increased by pension	€400
Net tax Credits	**€5,680**

Calculation of standard rate cut off point	
	2007 €
Standard rate band (married couple one spouse working)	€43,000
Increased by Pension	€2,000
Standard Rate Cut Off Point	**€45,000**

Summary

Tax Credit System

- Gross pay is taxed at the appropriate tax rate(s) to give the gross tax.

- The tax office will advise you of the standard rate cut off point for each pay period. The standard rate of tax is applied to pay up to that limit. Any balance of pay over that amount in any pay period is taxed at the higher rate.

- The gross tax is reduced by a tax credit as advised by the Tax Office to arrive at the tax payable.

PAYE emergency tax

The emergency tax operates when:

- Your employer has not received a Notification of Determination of tax credits and standard rate cut off point for you for the current year or your Form P45 for the current tax year.

    or

- You have given your employer a completed form P45 with "E"written on it.

For the year 2006 the PAYE emergency tax credit for the initial period of employment and the rates at which tax will be deductible are set out on the next page.

If paid weekly:

	2006	
	Tax credit **€**	**Rate** **%**
Weeks 1 - 4	€34	20% up to €654 Balance @ 41%
Weeks 5 - 8	Nil	20% up to €654 Balance @ 41%
Week 9 onwards	Nil	41%

If you do not supply your employer with your PPS Number, your employer must deduct tax at the higher rate on your gross pay (less Superannuation and Permanent Health contribution if applicable). No tax credits are due.

Tax refund during unemployment

Any refund due to you when you become unemployed will be made by the Revenue Commissioners on application by you to your Inspector of Taxes on Form P50 accompanied by Parts 2 and 3 of your Form P45.

PAYE refund after the year end

The tax year ends on 31st December and sometime after this date your employer will give you a form P60 which is a certificate of your gross pay and tax deducted in the tax year. You have a legal right to this document.

If there are any additional allowances or deductions not claimed during this year, these should be documented and forwarded with your tax return and P60 to your Inspector of Taxes requesting a refund.

The Inspector will in due course send you a balancing statement (Form P21). If a repayment is due a cheque will be attached.

Example

| An employee's pay is €600 per week. Tax credits for the year are €3,520 (€67.69 per week). Tax rate is 20%. |

Position at	Cumulative taxable pay	Cumulative gross tax	Cumulative tax credits	Cumulative net tax
Week 10	€6,000	€1,200	€676	€524

Following a claim, your Tax Inspector issues you with a new Notice of Determination of tax credits and standard rate cut off point in week 11 for €3,880 or €74.61 per week. Your position at week 11 is as follows:

Position at	Cumulative taxable pay	Cumulative gross tax	Cumulative tax credits	Cumulative net tax
Week 11	€6,600	€1,320	€820	€500

Since tax of €524 has already been deducted you will be given a tax refund by your employer of €24.

Where the Week1/Month 1, Emergency or Temporary basis applies, no refund of tax may be made by the employer as cumulative tax credits or cumulative pay are not taken into account.

Allowable deductions incurred for your employment

For expenses to be allowable for tax purposes they must be incurred for your employment and must be "wholly, exclusively and necessary" for the purpose of performing the duties of your employment. This rule is very strictly interpreted.

Motor and travelling expenses

A mileage allowance agreed between you and your employer for the use of your car for business purposes is not taxable provided it does not exceed the civil service mileage rate. However, you are not entitled to claim the cost of getting to or from work but only expenses incurred in the actual performance of your occupation.

For employers who use their cars in the normal course of their duties the rates are as follows;

Cars

	Rates per kilometre		
	€ Under 1,200 cc	€ 1,201 to 1,500 cc	€ 1,501 cc and over
Up to 6,437	52.16c	61.66c	78.32c
6,437 and over	26.97c	30.96c	36.65c

Motorcycles

Rates per kilometre		
€ 150 cc or less	€ 151cc to 250cc	€ 251cc and over
15.35cc	21.46cc	28.33cc

Flat rate expenses

Special flat rate allowances are allowed to certain categories of workers such as teachers, nurses, journalists and building workers for expenses. The amounts are agreed from time to time between trade unions and professional bodies and the Revenue Commissioners.

Round sum expenses

If you get round sum expenses from your employer they will be regarded as part of your salary and taxed accordingly, unless you can demonstrate that the expenses were incurred "wholly, exclusively and necessarily" in the performance of your duties. If your expenses actually exceed the sums reimbursed, you are entitled to an expense allowance for the excess.

Employee tax-efficient benefits

Here we list benefits which may be paid to you tax-free or tax efficiently by your employer:

1. If an employee is working away from normal base, **daily and overnight allowances** to cover the cost of lunch, evening meal, bed & breakfast etc. may be paid tax free provided it does not exceed the following limits.

    Salary levels corresponding to above classes;
    A - salary exceeds €63,109 (full PRSI)
    €59,956 (modified PRSI)
    B - salary exceeds €33,177 (full PRSI)
    €31,159 (modified PRSI)

    Normal rate - up to 14 nights

    Reduced rate - next 14 nights

    Detention rate - next 28 nights

    Special Rules apply to absences over 56 nights

2. **Canteen meals and refreshments**, provided these are available to all employees or luncheon vouchers up to 19c per working day.

3. **Rent-free or low rent accommodation** provided this is necessitated by the job.

Class of allowances	Night Allowances			Day Allowances	
	Normal Rate	Reduced Rate	Detention Rate	10 hours or more	5 hours but less than 10 hours
	€	€	€	€	€
A - Rate	€140.44	€129.48	€70.21	€41.55	€16.95
B - Rate	€132.18	€113.05	€66.12	€41.55	€16.95

4. **Non-cash personal gifts** for reasons not connected with work but including retirement presents.

5. Share in an employer's **Revenue-approved profit sharing scheme** (subject to certain limits). (see page 255).

6. **Staff entertainment** and outgoings at a reasonable cost.

7. **Pool transport** to place of work.

8. **Mileage allowance** agreed between the employer and employee for the use of the employee's car for business purposes. The rate cannot exceed the Civil Service Mileage Rate. (see page 249)

9. **Scholarship** income and bursaries.

10. **Lump sum payment** on retirement or removal from an employment within certain limits. (see page 268).

11. Payments under the **Redundancy Payment** Act 1967. (see page 265).

12. Payments made on account of **injury or disability**.

13 **Working clothes**, overalls and tools provided by the employer.

14. Employer's contributions to a statutory or **Revenue-approved pension scheme.** (see page 214)

15. Cost to the employer of providing **life assurance** cover of up to eight times the employee's salary.

16. Employees can receive an annual benefit of up to a value of €250 tax free.

17. Cost of providing sick pay/**permanent health insurance**.

18. Cost of providing contributions to V.H.I./BUPA/VIVA's (higher rate tax payers will suffer BIK penalties)

19. **Monthly/Annual Bus/Rail Travel Passes** provided by employers to their employees.

20. **Childcare Facilities** provided by employers on a free or subsidised basis, provided;

    The childcare facility is either provided on the employer's premises,

    or

    The employer provides the childcare facility jointly with other participants, for example, with other employers, on premises made jointly available by one of the employers in the joint scheme. However, the employer must be wholly or partly responsible for both financing and managing the childcare facility provided for employees.

21. Strictly, the cost of relocating your home is a personal expense. However , if it is a requirement of your job to move home and certain procedures are followed, your employer may compensate you for these costs without attracting tax.

The types of expenses covered are:

- Auctioneer's fees, solicitor's fees and stamp duty arising from moving home.

- Furniture removal costs.

- Storage charges.

- Insurance of furniture and items in transit.

- Cleaning stored furniture.

- Travelling expenses on removal.

- Temporary subsistence allowance while looking for new accommodation.

Requirements

- The cost must be borne directly by the employer in respect of actual expenses incurred by you.

- The expenses are reasonable.

- The payments are properly controlled.

Receipts must be provided (apart from temporary subsistence), and Revenue must be satisfied that moving home is necessary.

10

Social welfare benefits at a glance

Pay-related social insurance

The main PRSI legislation comprises the Social Welfare (Consolidation) Act, 1993, together with subsequent amendments. The subject is a wide one, and here we outline:

- How much you pay.

- Your benefit entitlements.

Contribution years

The contribution year for PRSI purposes is the same as the tax year. Contribution years are normally referred to as tax years.

Benefit years

The benefit year begins on the first Monday in January each year. Your entitlement to short-term PRSI benefits is normally based on your paid and/or credited contributions in the relevant tax year, which is the second last complete tax year before the benefit year in which you claim.

Example

For a claim made in	The relevant tax year is
2006	2004
2007	2005

If you cease to pay PRSI contributions, your entitlement to benefits will normally last for the remainder of that calendar year and the following calendar year.

PRSI contributions are calculated as a percentage of your gross pay, less any payments to an approved pension scheme, and permanent health benefit scheme which are deducted at source by the employer and approved by the Revenue Commissioners. PRSI contribution costs are normally shared by the employee and employer. For the majority of employees, PRSI contributions are collected through the PAYE tax system.

The following chart shows how the Class A1 rate, which is the PRSI Class most employees pay, is calculated in the 2006 and 2007 tax year.

Class A 2007

Income €	Employer	Employee
Up to €48,800	10.75%	6% (includes 2% Health levy contribution)
From €48,800 to €100,100	10.75%	2% (Health Levy Contribution)
Over €100,100	10.75%	2½% (Health Levy Contribution)

Employees earing €339 p.w. or less, will be exempt from PRSI and those earning €480 p.w. or less, will be exempt from the Health Contribution of 2%.

Class A 2006

Income €	Employer	Employee
Up to €46,600	10.75%	6% (includes 2% Health levy contribution)
Over €46,600	10.75%	2% (Health Levy Contribution)

In 2006 and 2007 employees earning in excess of €300 p.w. will not be liable to PRSI on the first €127 p.w. of earnings.

2006

Employees earning €300 or less are exempt from PRSI and those earning €440 p.w. or less are exempt from the health levy contribution of 2%

The employer rate for employees earning less than €356 is 8.5% in 2006 and 2007.

Claiming social insurance benefits

Normally, to claim a social insurance benefit it is necessary to have a minimum number of PRSI contributions. PRSI contributions are normally classified as follows:

* PRSI Paid

  and

* PRSI Credits.

PRSI contributions are payable each week you are working in insurable employment. There is no charge for PRSI credits, but for many benefits they can be as valuable as PRSI contributions paid.

First PRSI paid

When you become insured for the first time under the Social Welfare Acts you are automatically given PRSI credits for the earlier part of that tax year, in addition to credits for the previous two tax years. For example, if you commenced employment for the first time on the 5th of October you would be entitled to credits from the 1st January to the 4th of October plus the two previous tax years. These credits can help you qualify for Disability and Unemployment Benefit as soon as you have worked and paid PRSI contributions for 52 weeks.

Credits after you have become insured

If you stop paying PRSI contributions, PRSI credits are normally awarded for the weeks you receive Illness Benefit, Jobseekers Benefit, Maternity Benefit, Adoptive Benefit, Health & Safety Benefit, Carer's Benefit, Invalidity Pension, Retirement Pension or Injury Benefit. Similarly, credits may be awarded for the weeks in which you received Jobseekers Assistance or Carer's Allowance, if you are eligible for credits. If you have never worked you would not get credits with Jobseekers Assistance.

A break in PRSI

If two consecutive tax years have elapsed without contributions having been paid or credited, no additional PRSI credits can be awarded until a further 26 PRSI contributions have been paid.

Voluntary contributions

A person who ceases to be insured under Pay-Related Social Insurance can, if under 66 years of age, opt to continue insurance on a voluntary basis for limited benefits, provided 260 PRSI contributions have been paid (156 before April 2002), and you apply within 12 months of the end of the tax year during which you had paid PRSI or had a PRSI credit.

There are three rates of voluntary contributions:

- The high rate of voluntary contributions apply if you were compulsorily insured at the higher rates of PRSI. Voluntary contributions at this rate normally provide pension benefits and a Bereavement Grant.

- The reduced rate of voluntary contributions applies to certain Public Servants insured at the lower rates. Voluntary contributions at this level normally provide for Contributory Widow(er)'s Pension and Orphan's Contributory Allowance and a Bereavement Grant.

- A flat rate voluntary contribution applies to self-employed people insured at Class S who cease self-employment or who are no longer obliged to pay Class S because their income falls below the insurable limit which is currently €3,174. This gives cover for Old Age Contributory Pension, Widow's/ Widower's Contributory Pension, Orphan's Contributory Allowance and Bereavement Grant.

PRSI classes and benefit entitlements

	A	B	C	D	E	H	J	M	P	S	See Page
Adoptive Benefit	*	-	-	-	*	*	-	-	-	*	164
Bereavement Grant	*	*	*	*	*	*	-	-	-	*	174
Carer's Benefit	*	*	*	*	*	*	-	-	-	-	170
Illness Benefit	*	-	-	-	*	*	-	-	*	-	171
Health & Safety Benefit	*	-	-	-	*	*	-	-	-	-	165
Invalidity Pension	*	-	-	-	*	*	-	*	*	-	159
Maternity Benefit	*	-	-	-	*	*	-	*	*	*	162
Occupational Injuries Benefit	*	*	-	*	-	-	*	*	-	-	172
Old Age Contributory Pension	*	-	-	-	*	*	-	-	-	*	151
Guardian's Contributory Allowance	*	*	*	*	*	*	-	-	-	*	158
Retirement Pension	*	-	-	-	*	*	-	-	-	-	148
Treatment Benefit - Dental, Optical, Hearing Aids & Contact Lenses	*	-	-	-	*	*	-	-	*	-	160
Jobseekers Benefit	*	*	-	-	-	*	-	-	*	-	166
Widow's/Widower's Contributory Pension	*	*	*	*	*	*	-	-	-	*	155
Working in the EU Jobseekers Benefit	*	-	-	-	-	*	-	-	-	-	176
Health Services											

Remember, Social Insurance contributions are not a tax but their effect is very similar as you pay contributions out of your gross income. However, it should also be pointed out that benefits are not means-tested and you are entitled to them as a right once you satisfy the necessary contribution conditions.

PRSI benefit entitlements

Summarised on page 147 are:

The main benefit entitlements applicable to the relevant PRSI Classes.

- The page reference to where you will find the necessary back-up information in this guide.

Social Welfare pensions

Social Welfare Pensions fall under two main categories;

- Contributory Pensions.
- Non-Contributory Pensions.

Contributory pension

Your entitlement to a contributory pension is based on the amount and contribution class of PRSI you have paid during your working life.

Any other income you have, will not affect your entitlement to a Contributory Pension.

Non-contributory pension

If you don't qualify for a contributory pension you may be entitled to a non-contributory pension. However, to qualify for this type of pension it is necessary to satisfy a means test. Any income or assets you have may affect your entitlement to a non-contributory pension.

Retirement Pension

A Retirement Pension is paid if you are insured for PRSI under classes A, E or H. To qualify for a Retirement Pension you must:

- Be aged 65 or over.

- Be retired from insurable employment.

- Satisfy the PRSI and retirement conditions.

Contributory conditions

The PRSI contribution conditions which must be met in order to qualify for a Retirement Pension are:

- You must have started paying contributions before you were 55 years of age.

  and

- You must have a certain amount of paid contributions

   - At least 156 if you reached age 65 before 6th April 2002

   - At least 260 if you reach age 65 from 6th April 2002

   - to 5th April 2012

   - At least 520 if you reach age 65 on or after 6th April 2012,of which at least 260 must be full-rate employment contributions.

  and

- A yearly average of at least 48 full rate contributions paid and/or credited from 1979 to the end of the tax year before you reach age 65 - this will entitle you to a maximum pension (this only applies if you reached age 65 on or after 6th April 1992).

  or

- For a minimum pension, you must have a yearly average of at least 24 weeks PRSI paid or credited from 1953 or the year you first become insured, whichever is later up to the end of the tax year before your 65th birthday. For a maximum pension, a yearly average of 48 weeks PRSI paid or credited in the relevant period is needed.

If you were insured in another member state of the EU, as well as in the Republic of Ireland, your full insurance record will be taken into account when deciding whether or not you are eligible for a Retirement Pension. Periods of insurance in countries with which Ireland has a bilateral social security agreement may also be used to help you qualify for a Retirement Pension.

Periods of insurable employment can be combined to ascertain if you would be entitled to a Retirement Pension from each country.

Retirement Condition

The retirement condition stipulates that at the age of 65 you must not enter into employment which is insurable under the Social Welfare Acts other than class gentlemen. This PRSI class applies to people employed under a contract of service whose reckonable earnings are less than €38 per week, or €3,174 per year if self-employed. At the age of 66 you are once more free to take up any employment you choose. Basically, you must actually retire from full-time work at the age of 65 in order to qualify for a Retirement Pension.

Retirement Pension Elements

A Retirement Pension is payable in three distinct elements:

- A personal amount.

- An increase for a qualified adult.

- An increase for each dependent child.

If you qualify for a weekly social welfare payment, you will normally get extra amounts for a qualified adult and child dependents. A qualified adult is usually a spouse but can be the person you are living with as husband and wife. Your spouse/partner is regarded as your dependent provided they are not getting a social welfare payment in their own right or have income of less than €88.88 per week and are not on a full-time FÁS non-craft training course. A spouse/partner can have income of up to €210.00 per week and still be regarded as partially dependent.

If you are entitled to an increase for a dependent spouse/partner and have dependent children you can claim the full rate for a dependent child. If you do not qualify for a payment for a qualified adult you are entitled to half rate for a dependent child.

The following are the maximum rates;

Retirement pension/old age contributory pension maximum weekly rates	Up to 31st Dec 2006 €	From 1st Jan. 2007 €
Maximum personal rate (under 80)	€193.30	€209.30
Maximum personal rate (over 80)	€203.30	€219.30
Increase for a qualified adult - under 66	€128.80	€139.50
Increase for a qualified adult - over 66	€149.30	€173.00
Increase per child - Full Rate	€19.30	€22.00
Increase per child - Half Rate	€9.70	€11.00
Living Alone Allowance for people age 66 or over	€7.70	€7.70
Allowance for people age 66 or over living on certain offshore islands	€12.70	€12.70

The increase for a qualified adult is paid at a reduced rate with certain reduced rates of Contributory Old Age Pension. The Living Alone Allowance is paid in full, irrespective of what rate of Retirement or Old Age Contributory Pension you qualify for personally. Recipients of Illness Allowance, Invalidity Pension, Jobseekers Supplement and Blind Pension who live alone, are also eligible for the Living Alone Allowance regardless of their age.

Contributory Old Age Pension

The Contributory Old Age Pension is payable to insured people from the age of 66. Unlike the Retirement Pension, it is paid to you even if you are still working. It is payable in respect of PRSI class A, E, H and S.

The three main conditions which must be met in order to qualify for the Contributory Old Age Pension are:

- You must have become insured before the age of 56

    and

- You must have a certain amount of paid contributions:

    - at least 156 if you reached age 66 before 6th April 2002

    - at least 260 if you reach age 66 from 6th April 2002 to 5th

April 2012

- at least 520 if you reach age 66 on or after 6th April 2012 (of which at least 260 must be full-rate employment contributions)

and

- For the minimum rate of pension, you must have at least 260 weeks PRSI paid and a yearly average of at least 10 paid and/or credited contributions from 1953 or the time you started insurable employment, if later to the end of the last complete tax year before you reached 66. For the maximum pension, an average of 48 is needed.

- To qualify for the maximum rate of pension, a yearly average of at least 48 weeks PRSI paid or credited for the period from 5th April 1979 to the end of the tax year before you reach pension age is needed. However, this only applies if you reached age 66 on or after 6th April 1992.

The maximum rates of Contributory Old Age Pension are the same as those listed for the Retirement Pension. A special 50% Contributory Old Age Pension is paid to self employed (Class S) contributors who were aged over 56 when social insurance for the self employed was introduced in April 1988 and who have at least five years paid contributions since then.

Pre-1953 Pension

This special half-rate Contributory Old Age Pension is for people who fail to get a pension under the normal rules. You must have at least 260 full-rate contributions paid of which at least one contribution must be before January 1953 for women or July 1953 for men.

Non-contributory old age pension

If you don't qualify for a Contributory Old Age Pension you may qualify for a non-contributory old age pension. To claim a non-contributory old age pension you must:

- Be aged 66 or over

- Be living in the State

- Satisfy a means test.

The following are the maximum rates.

Old age non-contributory pension/blind pension maximum weekly rates	Up to 31st Dec. 2006 €	From 1st Jan. 2007 €
Maximum Personal Rate Aged 66 - 79	€182.00	€200.00
Maximum Personal Rate Aged 80 or over	€192.00	€210.00
Increase for a qualified adult dependent	€120.30	€132.20
Increase per child dependent - Full Rate	€16.80	€22.00
Increase per child dependent - Half Rate	€8.40	€11.00
Living Alone Allowance	€7.70	€7.70
Blind Pension under 66	€165.80	€185.80
Increase for a qualified adult dependend	€110.00	€123.20
Allowance for People Aged 66 or over, living on certain offshore islands	€12.70	€12.70

Means test

When you make a claim for a non-contributory pension, a Social Welfare Inspector will normally investigate your entitlement to this pension in your own home and attempt to establish your weekly means.

In assessing your means, a Social Welfare Inspector will take account of;

- Cash income.

- The value of any property personally used by you, such as a farm or shop. Your home is excluded unless you are getting an income from it. Rental income received from a person living with the pensioner is not counted, provided the pensioner is living alone except for that person.

- The value of any investments or capital held.

- The means of your spouse or other person cohabiting with you as husband and wife.

You will get a **full** pension if you have savings or investments up to the amounts shown below and have no other means;

Pension	Savings
	€
Old age (non-contributory)*	
Single person	€20,315.80
Married/cohabiting couple	€40,631.60
Widow's/widower's (non-contributory)	€20,315.80

* If you have dependent children, you can have extra savings and still get a pension.

If you are applying for or getting a non-contributory pension, you will still be entitled to a minimum pension even if you have the savings shown in the following table and have no other means;

Pension	Savings
	€
Old age (non-contributory)*	
Single person	€68,565.84
Married/cohabiting couple	€137,131.70
Widow's/widower's (non-contributory)	€68,565.84

* If you have dependent children, you can have extra savings and still get a pension.

The 2007 Budget increased the means disregarded for Non Contributory pensions to €30 per week. From January 2007 the first €200 of employment income will be disregarded when assessing means for all non contributory pensions.

Mixed insurance pro-rata pension

People who have paid Class B, C and D (public service rate) and who have a certain number of full-rate (A,E,H & N) PRSI contributions paid since 1953 may qualify for a Mixed Insurance Pro-Rata Retirement or Contributory Old Age Pension. The rate of pension is paid in proportion to your full-rate contributions. The increase for a qualified adult is also paid on a pro-rata basis.

Contributory widow(er)'s pension

The Contributory Widow(er)'s Pension is payable on the death of a spouse provided the PRSI contribution conditions are satisfied that:

- you are widowed

- you are divorced from your late spouse and have not remarried

- you are not cohabiting, **and**

- you satisfy the PRSI contribution conditions, **or**

- your late spouse was getting a Retirement Pension or an Old Age Contributory Pension which included an increase for you or would have but for the fact that you were getting a Carer's Allowance, Non-Contributory Old Age Pension or Blind Person's Pension in your own right.

The PRSI conditions may be based on either your own or your late spouse's PRSI record. However, the two PRSI records cannot be combined. Whichever PRSI record is used must have;

- At least 156 weeks PRSI paid to the date pension age was reached or to the date your spouse died, if earlier, **and**

- Either an average of 39 weeks PRSI paid or credited over the three or five tax years whichever is more beneficial before reaching pension age (66 years) or before your spouse died, if earlier for a maximum pension, **or**

- For a minimum pension, a yearly average of at least 24 weeks PRSI paid or credited is needed since starting work up to the end of the tax year before reaching pension age (66 years) or the date your spouse dies, if earlier. For a maximum pension, a yearly average of 48 weeks PRSI paid or credited is needed.

With the exception of class J, K, M and P almost all PRSI contributions, including self-employed, civil servants and public sector workers, are included for the Contributory Widow(er)'s Pension and Contributory Orphan's Allowance. Your entitlement to the Contributory Widow(er)'s Pension is not affected by any other income you may have.

Extra benefits - household benefits package

If you are aged 66 or over and you qualify for a full or reduced pension or you satisfy a means test you may be entitled to Free Electricity/Natural Gas Allowance, Television Licence, Telephone Rental Allowance under the Household Benefits Package Scheme, subject to the qualifying conditions. All people aged 70 or over qualify regardless of income and who lives with them. Recipients of certain other payments e.g. Invalidity Pension, Carer's Allowance may qualify regardless of their age. You must be residing permanently, on an all year round basis at that address and no other person in the household can be in receipt of the allowances. The accounts must be in your name. The means tested Fuel Scheme is not part of the Household Benefits Package.

Since January 2003 the telephone allowance was extended to people aged over 70 who reside in Nursing Homes, where they have their own telephone accounts.

Free schemes were extended from January 2003 to pensioners under the age of 70 who are in receipt of a qualifying payment & whose spouse/partner is getting a Social Welfare payment in their own right and the total income of the spouse/partner is less than €210.00 per week.

Island Allowance

This is an additional allowance of €12.70 per week for social welfare pensioners aged 66 or over who are living on certain offshore islands. It is also payable to recipients of certain disability payments e.g. Invalidity/Blind Pension, Illness Allowance, Injury Benefit, Constant Attendance Allowance who are aged under 66.

The following are the maximum rates of contributory and non-contributory pensions:

Contributory widow(er)'s pension maximum weekly rates	From 1st Jan. 2006 €	From 1st Jan. 2007 €
Maximum personal rate - under 66	€171.30	€191.30
Maximum personal rate - aged 66 - 79	€193.30	€209.30
Maximum personal rate - aged 80 or over	€203.30	€219.30
Child dependent	€21.60	€22.00
Living alone allowance	€7.70	€7.70
Allowance for people aged 66 or over living on certain offshore islands	€12.70	€12.70

Non-contributory widow(er)'s pension

If you are a widow(er) and have no dependent children, you may be entitled to claim a Non-Contributory Widow(er)'s Pension on the death of your spouse, provided you are not already entitled to a Contributory Widow(er)'s Pension and can satisfy the means test. (See page 153).

Non-contributory widow(er)'s pension maximum weekly rates	From 1st Jan. 2006 €	From 1st Jan. 2007 €
Maximum personal rate - under 66	€165.80	€185.80
Living alone allowance	€7.70	€7.70
Allowance for people aged 66 or over living on certain offshore islands	€12.70	€12.70

One-Parent Family Payment

The One-Parent Family Payment is a payment for both men and women who, for a variety of reasons, are bringing up a child without the support of a partner.

A person who is unmarried, widowed, a prisoner's spouse, separated, divorced or whose marriage has been annulled and who is no longer living with their spouse, is eligible to apply for this payment.

If you are getting the One Parent Family Payment you can earn up to €146.50 p.w. and still qualify for full payment. If you earn between €146.50 p.w. and €400.00 p.w. you may qualify for a reduced payment.

Contributory Guardian's Allowance

Where both parents have died, or one parent has died and the other has abandoned the child, this allowance is payable, provided that the PRSI contribution conditions are met. These require that at least 26 weekly contributions have been paid at any time by the orphan's parent or stepparent, at the appropriate rate.

The PRSI contribution classes which cover the Contributory Guardian's Allowance are the same as those for the Contributory Widow(er)'s Pension. The allowance is payable up to the age of 18, or 22 if the orphan is in full-time education. From January 2007 the rate is €158 per week.

Non-Contributory Guardian's Pension

The Guardian's Non-Contributory Pension is paid for a child or children if:

- Both parents are dead.
- One parent has died and the other is unknown.
- One parent is dead and the surviving parent has abandoned or failed to support the child.
- The child satisfies a means test.
- The child is living in the State.

A claim cannot be made for a child living with stepparents. The allowance may be payable to the guardian of an orphan if the orphan does not already qualify for a Contributory Guardian's Allowance. The maximum rate of allowance payable from 1st January 2007 is €158 per week, where the estimated weekly means of the orphan do not exceed €7.60. If the estimated means of the orphan exceed €100.10 no benefit is payable. The allowance is payable up to the age of 18, or 22 if the orphan is in full-time education. However, the means test must be satisfied throughout the entire period.

Invalidity Pension

An Invalidity Pension is payable instead of a Illness Benefit if you have been incapable of work for at least 12 months and likely to be incapable of work for a further 12 months or you are permanently incapable of work or you are over age 60 and suffering from a serious illness or incapacity.

You must have paid PRSI at class A, E or H.

In order to claim Invalidity Pension you must have paid the appropriate PRSI contributions for at least 260 weeks and you must have had at least 48 weeks PRSI paid or credited in the last tax year before you apply. The following are the maximum rates.

Invalidity Pension maximum weekly rates	From 1st Jan. 2006 €	From 1st Jan. 2007 €
Maximum personal rate		
- Under 65	€171.30	€191.30
- Age 66 - 79	€193.30	€209.30
- Age 80 or over	€203.30	€219.30
Increase for a qualified adult dependent - under 66	€122.20	€136.50
Increase for a qualified adult dependent - 66 or over	€149.30	€173.00
Increases for child dependents - Full Rate	€19.30	€22.00
Increases for child dependents - Half Rate	€9.65	€11.00
Living Alone Allowance	€7.70	€7.70
Allowance for people living on certain offshore islands	€12.70	€11.00

Increases for dependent child payable with the pensions dealt with in this section are paid for children living with you and dependent on you up to the age of 18 or 22, if they are in full time education. The full rate for a dependent child is paid to you if you are entitled to an increase for an adult dependent. If you do not qualify for payment for a qualified adult, the increase for child dependents is paid at half rate.

If you are getting Jobseekers Benefit, Illness Benefit, Injury Benefit and Health and Safety Benefit and your spouse has income of €350 or less per week, you will be paid half-rate child dependant increase.

Qualified adult dependent payment

A qualified adult payment may be payable in addition to the basic benefit in respect of a claimant's spouse/partner, where the claimant's spouse/partner is wholly or mainly maintained by him/her. There are, however, certain exemptions, e.g. if the spouse has income of more than €220 (€240 from January 2006) per week or is receiving some other Social Welfare Benefit this supplement may not be paid.

Treatment benefits

Treatment Benefit covers Dental Benefit, Optical Benefit, Contact Lenses and Hearing Aids.

Dental benefit

Dental Benefit is available to persons who are paying PRSI at classes A, E, H and P and their dependent spouse.

Dental benefit covers a number of different items of dental treatment some of which are free, while for others you must pay part of the cost:

- Dental examination, diagnosis, scaling and polishing. For other treatment the Department of Social and Family Affairs will pay a set amount and you pay the balance.

- You can also have dentures fitted, repaired or replaced. The Department of Social and Family Affairs will give a fixed amount towards the cost and you must pay the balance.

Optical benefit

Optical Benefit is available to persons who are paying PRSI Classes, A, E, H and P and their dependent spouses. Optical Benefit covers a number of different items of optical treatment, sight test, advice from a doctor, optician or an ophthalmic surgeon are normally free.

Glasses with a certain kind of frame are also free. If you desire more expensive frames the Department will pay a fixed amount towards the cost and you pay the balance. Repairs to your glasses may also be free depending on the nature of the actual repairs. You can only claim Optical Benefit directly from a doctor, an optician or an ophthalmic surgeon, who is on the approved panel of The Department of Social and Family Affairs.

Contact lenses

If you get contact lenses instead of glasses, the Department of Social and Family Affairs will pay a fixed amount i.e. the same amount as is paid for glasses, and you must pay the balance. If, however, you need contact lenses for medical reasons the Department will pay up to half the cost subject to a maximum of €350, provided you have a doctor's recommendation.

Hearing aids

Hearing Aid Benefit is available to PRSI Classes, A, E, H and P and their dependent spouses. Before you make a claim for hearing aids, it is normally necessary to have a letter of recommendation from your doctor and to satisfy the contribution conditions.

You should then be entitled to a refund of 50% of the cost from Social Insurance up to a maximum of €700 for each hearing aid, provided you get your hearing aid from an approved supplier.

The Department of Social and Family Affairs will normally pay half the cost of repairs.

PRSI Conditions for Treatment Benefit (Dental and Optical Benefit, Hearing Aids and Contact Lenses)

Age	Contributions required
Under 21 years	39 weeks PRSI paid since starting work.
Between 21 and 24 years	39 weeks PRSI paid and 39 weeks PRSI paid or credited in the governing tax year, of which a minimum of 13 weeks must be paid contributions. The 13 weeks paid can be in any one of the last four tax years or in the current tax year - see below.

Age	Contributions required
Between 25 and 65 years	260 weeks PRSI paid and 39 weeks PRSI paid or credited in the governing tax year, of which a minimum of 13 weeks must be paid contributions - see below.
Over 66 years	260 weeks PRSI paid and 39 weeks PRSI paid or credited in either of the last two years before reaching age 66, of which a minimum of 13 weeks must be paid contributions.

The 13 weeks paid contributions can be in the relevant tax year on which the claim is based, in one of the two previous tax years or in any tax year after the relevant tax year.

If you satisfy the PRSI requirements at age 60 or 66 you retain entitlement for life.

Maternity Benefit

Maternity Benefit is payable to women in current employment or self employed women insured at PRSI Classes, A, E, H and S.

Maternity Benefit is not payable on your spouse's insurance. It is payable only where the mother is an insured person and satisfies the PRSI conditions on her own insurance record.

Who can qualify

You will qualify for Maternity Benefit if you are an employee and you;

- Are in employment which is covered by the Maternity Protection Act 1994 immediately before the first day of your maternity leave. The last day of insurable employment may be within 14 weeks of the expected date of birth of the baby;

- Are or have been self-employed;

and

- Satisfy the PRSI contribution conditions.

Contribution conditions

- You must have at least 39 weeks PRSI paid in the 12 months immediately before the first day of your maternity leave.

  or

- 39 weeks PRSI paid since you first started work and at least 39 weeks PRSI paid or credited in the relevant tax year.

  or

- 26 weeks PRSI paid in the relevant tax year and 26 weeks PRSI paid in the tax year prior to the relevant tax year.

For claims made in	The relevant tax year is
2006	2004
2007	2005

If you are self-employed you must have 52 qualifying PRSI contributions paid:

- In the relevant tax year

  or

- 52 qualifying PRSI contributions paid in the tax year prior to the relevant tax

  or

- 52 qualifying PRSI contributions paid in the tax year later than the relevant tax

PRSI paid at Class A, E, H, S are deemed as qualifying contributions.

The allowance is payable for a continuous period of 22 weeks (26 weeks from March 2007). To qualify for the maximum 18 weeks Maternity Benefit you must take a minimum of two weeks and a maximum of 14 weeks before the end of the week in which the baby is due. If your baby is born later than expected and you have less than four weeks maternity leave remaining, you may be entitled to extend your maternity leave to ensure that you have a full four weeks off following the birth.

Where Maternity Benefit has been in payment for a minimum period of 14 weeks, the balance of your payment may be postponed for up to six months if the child is hospitalised. The payment will resume within seven days following written notification of the discharge of the child from hospital.

The weekly rate of payment is 80% (January 2007), based on a weekly average of gross earnings in the relevant tax year, up to a limit of €265.20 per week maximum or a minimum of €207.80 per week.

Half rate payment is paid if your are receiving One Parent Family Payment, Contributory/Non-contributory Widow's Pension, Deserted Wife's Benefit, Prisoner's Wife's Allowance, Orphan's Allowance/ Pension.

Adoptive benefit

Adoptive Benefit is payable for 16 weeks to adoptive parents paying PRSI at class A,E, H and S who satisfy the contribution conditions. The rate of payment and the PRSI contribution conditions are the same as those applying to Maternity Benefit (see page 162).

Habitual Residence Test

A new habitual residence test came into effect from 1st May 2004. This means that in order to get certain payments, you will have to show that you have been habitually resident in Ireland or in the common travel areas of the UK, the Channel Islands or the Isle of Man for a substantial continuous period.

The following payments are now subject to a habitual residence condition:

- Jobseekers Assistance
- Old Age Non-Contributory Pension
- Blind Pension
- Widow(er)'s and Orphan's Non-Contributory Pensions
- One-Parent Family Payment

- Carer's Allowance

- Illness Allowance

- Supplementary Welfare Allowance (other than once-off exceptional and urgent needs payments)

- Child Benefit

Child Benefit

This is a benefit paid every month for each qualified child normally living with you and being supported by you. A qualified child is:

- A child under age 16

  and/or

- A child age 16, 17 or 18 who is in full time education or attending a FÁS Youthreach course or is physically or mentally disabled and dependent on you.

Child Benefit ceases when the child reaches age 19.

	Up to April 2006	From April 2007
First and second child	€150.00	€160.00
Third & subsequent children	€185.00	€195.00

Child Benefit Rate

For Multiple Births a grant and higher rates apply.

An early childcare supplement was introduced in 2006. This direct payment of €1,000 per year is payable to parents for each child up to the childs 6th birthday. This payment will be made on a quarterly basis and commenced in mid 2006.

Health and Safety Benefit

This is a weekly payments for women insured at Class A, E or H, who are pregnant or have recently had a baby or are breastfeeding (up to 26 weeks) and who have been awarded Health and Safety Leave under the Maternity

Protection Act, 1994.

Health and Safety Leave is granted to an employee by her employer when the employer cannot remove a risk to the employee's health or safety or her pregnancy or breastfeeding, or assign her alternative "risk free" duties.

Jobseekers benefit

- Jobseekers benefit is available to PRSI Classes A, H and P.
- Jobseekers benefit is paid weekly and to qualify you must:
- Be unemployed.
- Be capable of work.
- Be available for and genuinely looking for full-time work.
- Be under age 66.
- Have suffered a substantial loss of employment and earnings.
- Satisfy the PRSI conditions.

PRSI conditions

- You must have 52 weeks PRSI paid since starting work

  and

- 39 weeks PRSI paid or credited in the relevant tax year

  or

- 26 weeks PRSI paid in the relevant tax year and 26 in the tax year prior to the relevant tax year.

The relevant tax year is the second last complete tax year before the start of your claim. Jobseekers Benefit is normally paid from the fourth day after your claim. However, if you had lodged a claim for Illness or Jobseekers Benefit or Maternity Benefit in the previous 13 weeks, payment may be made from your first day of unemployment.

Age conditions

- If you are under age 18, Jobseekers Benefit can be paid for up to 156 days (6 months).

- If you are 18 or over and under age 65, Jobseekers Benefit can be paid for up to 390 days (15 months).

- If you are aged between 65 and 66 when your Jobseekers Benefit ends, you may continue to receive it up to age 66, provided you have at least 156 weeks PRSI paid.

The maximum duration of Jobseekers Benefit will be reduced to 312 days where a person has less than 260 PRSI contributions paid since first entering insurance.

People paying class "P" PRSI are entitled to Jobseekers Benefit for up to 13 weeks in each calendar year.

Redundancy Payments

If you receive a redundancy payment in excess of €19,046, you may be disqualified from receiving Jobseekers Benefit for up to nine weeks. This disqualification does not apply if you are aged 55 years or more.

How to claim

"Sign-on" for Jobseekers Benefit at your nearest Social Welfare office on the first day of your unemployment and bring your P45 (if you have it) with you, together with a household bill (e.g. ESB, Gas etc.) and two forms of identification. One of these should be your Birth Certificate or Passport.

Jobseekers Benefit can be paid by postal draft, cheque or directly into your bank account.

Short-time/night work

If you work on systematic short-time, you can get Jobseekers Benefit for the days you do not work. However, the total number of days at work and on benefit cannot be more than five in any week.

Re-qualifying for benefit

If you have exhausted your Jobseekers Benefit, you may re-qualify after working and paying PRSI for 13 weeks. Any weeks you work after you have drawn 6 months (156 days) benefit, count towards the 13 weeks needed to requalify. At age 65 you do not need the 13 weeks paid to requalify.

Jobseekers Benefit is made up of a personal rate plus extra amounts for your dependents.

Rates of Jobseekers Benefit

	2006 €	2007 €
Personal rate	€165.80	€185.80
Person with qualified adult dependend	€275.80	€309.10

Tax

Jobseekers Benefit is taxed at your relevant rate of tax. However, the first €13.00 per week of your Jobseekers Benefit together with additional payments for child dependents is exempt from tax. Systematic short-term working is exempt from income tax. This is short-term working for a limited time period is normally 6-8 weeks. Casual short-term working is liable to income tax. Casual short-term working differs from systematic short-term working in that casual working if for an unlimited period.

Reduced benefits

If you are getting a Widow's/Widower's Pension or One-Parent Family Payment from the Department of Social and Family Affairs, half the personal rate of benefit is payable. No increases are payable for child dependents.

Disqualifications

Jobseekers Benefit is not paid if you are:

- Out of work because of a trade dispute.

- Absent from the State (unless you are going to another EU country to look for work).

- Imprisoned.

- Convicted of an offence in relation to Jobseekers Benefit (you can be disqualified for three months).

You can be disqualified from payment for up to nine weeks if you:

- Lose your job through your own misconduct.

- Leave your job of your own will and without good reason.

- Refuse an offer of suitable work.

- Refuse to do a FÁS course without good reason.

- Do not avail of any reasonable opportunity of getting suitable work.

Back to work allowance

This scheme allows the unemployed aged 23 or over who have been unemployed for at least 5 years, or those receiving the One Parent Family Payment, Blind Person's Pension or Illness Allowance, Carer's Allowance (if no longer a carer), Farm Assist, Invalidity Pension, Unemployability Supplement, Pre-Retirement Allowance, Widow's /er's (non-contributory) pension, Deserted Wife's or Prisoner's Wife's Allowance for 15 months to take up employment and retain a percentage of their social welfare payment and secondary benefits (subject to certain conditions). For people over age 50 the minimum qualifying period is 12 months. Recipients of Illness Benefit for at least three years may also be eligible. You will be paid 75% of your existing Social Welfare payment the first year, 50% for the second year and 25% for the third year, along with your earnings.

Back to Work Enterprise Allowance

This scheme allows unemployed people and those in receipt of certain social welfare payments to set up a self-employment business and retain a percentage of their social welfare payment for up to four years (100% in the first year, 75% in the second, 50% in the third and 25% in the fourth). You must have been getting Jobseekers Benefit/Assistance (no age limit) for at least 3 years or one of the payments as listed above for the Back to Work Allowance Scheme for at least 12 months. Recipients of Illness Benefit for at least three years may also be eligible.

Other support is also available e.g. grants for training, market research and access to loans for the purchase of capital equipment. Assistance towards the cost of Public Liability Insurance is also available. The self-employment business must have been approved in writing in advance by a Partnership Company or a Job Facilitator in the Department of Social and Family Affairs.

Carer's Benefit

Carer's Benefit is payable to PRSI classes A,B,C,D,E and H. It is payable to people who leave work in order to care for a person(s) in need of full-time care and attention.

Who can qualify

You will qualify if you - the Carer;

- Are age 16 or over and under age 65/66.

- Live with the person(s) you are looking after or in close proximity.

- Satisfy the PRSI contribution conditions.

- Give up employment to care for a person(s) on a full-time basis. This employment must have been for a minimum of 17 hours per week or 34 hours per fortnight.

- Are not employed or self-employed outside the home. You may however work up to 15 hours per week from June 2006. The maximum weekly income which you can earn is €290 for a single person and €580 for a couple.

- Are living in the State.

- Are not living in a hospital, convalescent home or other similar institution

  and

- The person(s) you are caring for is/are;

  - So disabled as to need full-time care and attention (medical certification is required)

- Not normally living in a hospital, home or other similar institution

PRSI conditions

For a first claim you must have;

- 156 contributions paid since entry into insurable employment.

  and

- 39 contributions paid in the relevant tax year.

  or

- 39 contributions paid in the 12 month period before the commencement of the Carer's Benefit.

  or

- 26 contributions paid in the relevant tax year and 26 contributions paid in the relevant tax year prior to that.

Respite Care Grant

An annual Respite Care Grant is paid in June each year. From June 2005 this grant is extended to all carers providing full-time care to an older person or a person with disability, regardless of means, who are not in receipt of an unemployment payment or working outside the home for more than 10 hours per week. This grant is increased to €1,000 from June 2005 (€1,200 from June 2006) and is paid in respect of each person being cared for.

Illness Benefit

Illness Benefit is available to PRSI classes A, E, H and P.

It is payable if:

- You are under 66.

- Are unfit to work due to illness.

- Satisfy the PRSI conditions.

PRSI conditions:

- 52 weeks PRSI paid since starting work, **and**

- 39 weeks PRSI paid or credited in the relevant tax year, of which 13 must be paid contributions, **or**

- 26 weeks PRSI paid in the relevant tax year **and**

- 26 weeks PRSI paid in the tax year immediately before the relevant tax year.

If you do not have 13 paid contributions in the relevant tax year, the following years may be used to satisfy this condition:

- Either of the two most previous tax years.

- The most recent complete tax year; **or**

- The current tax year.

The relevant tax year is the second last complete tax year before the benefit year in which the Disability Benefit claim is made. The benefit year begins on the first Monday of January in each calendar year and ends on the Saturday immediately before the first Monday in the next calendar year.

Tax

Disability Benefit is taxed at your relevant rate of tax. However, additional payments for child dependents are exempt from income tax. The first six weeks (36 days) are also exempt from tax.

Occupational injuries benefit

Occupational injury benefit is available to PRSI Classes, A, D, J and M. People in employment insurable at PRSI contribution class B may qualify for limited benefit.

The Occupational Injuries Scheme provides social insurance cover for accidents at work, while travelling directly to or from work and for certain diseases contracted due to the work you do. It includes the following:

Injury benefit

This consists of a weekly payment during a period of incapacity for work as a result of an injury received or a disease contracted due to the work you do. It is payable for a maximum of 26 weeks. If you are still unable to work after 26 weeks you may be entitled to Disability Benefit (see page 167).

Disablement benefit

This is a payment in the form of a weekly or monthly pension or, in some instances, a lump sum. It is paid to persons who suffer the loss of physical or mental faculty as a result of an injury at work or a disease contracted at work.

Unemployability supplement

If you are receiving Disablement Benefit and you are not entitled to Illness Benefit, you may qualify for Unemployability Supplement. You must be permanently incapable of work in order to claim this payment.

Widow(er)'s benefits (death benefits)

These consist of Widow(er)'s Pension, Orphan's Pension, Dependent Parent's Pension and Funeral Grant.

Medical care

Any medical expenses incurred as a result of an injury at work or a disease developed due to the nature of your work may be claimed under the occupational injuries scheme provided:

- The expenses cannot be met under the Health Acts by your Regional Health Board, **and**

- They are reasonable and necessary.

Constant attendance allowance

This allowance is paid weekly as an increase in Disablement Pension if you are so severely disabled as to need someone to help you daily at home to attend your personal needs for at least six months.

Employees covered

With very few exceptions, all employees over 16 are covered under this scheme, regardless of the level of their earnings or their age. Permanent civil servants have limited cover only. Among those not covered by the scheme are members of the Defence Forces and the Garda Síochána, recruited prior to 6th April 1995.

If your accident does not immediately result in disablement or incapacity but you think that it might in the future, you should apply to the Department of Social and Family Affairs for a declaration that the accident was an occupational one, you should also notify your employer. In this way you will be safeguarding your right to benefit in the event of a future claim.

Early retirement due to ill health

This scheme applies if you are a Public Servant paying PRSI at Classes B,C and D and have to give up work because of ill health. It basically gives you PRSI credits to keep your insurance record up-to-date and protects your Contributory Widow's/Widower's Pension, Orphan's Contributory Allowance and Bereavement Grant.

To apply for these credited contributions, you should complete the application form CR35.

Bereavement grant

A Bereavement Grant of €850 is available to those paying PRSI at classes A, B, C, D, E, F, G, H, N and S. The grant, based on PRSI contributions, is payable on the death of:

- An insured person.

- The wife or husband of an insured person.

- The widow or widower of a deceased insured person.

- A contributory pensioner (or spouse of a contributory pensioner).

- A child under age 18, or under 22 if in full-time education (where either parent or the person that the child normally lives with satisfies the PRSI contribution conditions).

- The qualified adult of a contributory pensioner, including those who would be a qualified adult but are getting another Social Welfare payments, e.g. Carer's Allowance.

• A qualified child.

• An orphan or a person to whom an orphan's (contributory) allowance is payable.

When an adult dies, a death grant may be paid based on the PRSI record of the deceased or the spouse of the deceased.

When a child dies, a death grant may be paid based on the PRSI record of either parent or on the record of the person the child normally lives with.

PRSI conditions

The PRSI record used must have enough contributions to satisfy the following conditions:

• 156 contribution weeks paid since entry into insurable employment

or

• At least 26 PRSI contributions paid since entry into insurable employment

and

• 39 PRSI contributions paid or credited in the relevant tax year

or

• A yearly average of 39 PRSI contributions paid or credited over the 3 or 5 tax years before the death occurred or pension age was reached (age 66 at present)

or

• A yearly average of 26 weeks PRSI contributions paid or credited since 1979 (or since starting work if later) and the end of the tax year before the death occurred or pension age was reached (age 66 at present)

or

• A yearly average of 26 weeks PRSI contributions paid or credited since 1st October 1970 (or since starting work if later) and the end of the tax year before the death occurred or pension age was reached (age 66 at present)

The relevant tax year is the second last complete tax year before the year in which the death occurs or pension age was reached.

Claim forms are available from your local Department of Social and Family Affairs office.

Widowed Parent's Grant

A special grant of €4,000 is paid to widows or widowers with dependent children following the death of their spouse. It is payable to widows or widowers who qualify for the Widow/Widower's Contributory Pension or a One-Parent Family Payment or Bereavement Grant. This grant can be paid in addition to the €850 Bereavement Grant.

Funeral grant

If the death was due to an accident at work or occupational disease, a higher Funeral Grant under the Occupational Injuries Scheme may be payable instead of a Bereavement Grant.

Working in the EU

As Ireland is a member of the EU, you are legally entitled to look for work in any Member State without a work permit. Each Member State has a national placement service, similar to FÁS. If you wish to seek work in any of the EU countries, you can apply through a FÁS employment services office for a job in the country of your choice. Details of your application will be circulated abroad through the SEDOC system free of charge and if any suitable vacancies arise, you will be notified.

If you qualify for Jobseekers Benefit here and have been registered and in receipt of benefit for at least four weeks, you may have your Jobseekers Benefit transferred to another EU country for up to 78 days or for a shorter period if you have less than 78 days left on your claim, provided you look for and register for work in that country within seven days. You must register for work within seven days from the date you last claimed Jobseekers Benefit in Ireland for your unemployment payments to be continuous.

Form E301

This is required to claim Jobseekers Benefit. It gives details of your social insurance and employment record and is available from EU Records Section, Social Welfare Services Office, Floor 2, Oisin House, 212-213 Pearse Street, Dublin 2. Phone (01)7043000. You should also bring your birth certificate as it may be required in certain circumstances.

Health services

EU Regulations also apply to your Health Service entitlements. In the UK you are entitled to UK Health Services, as soon as you have an address in the UK and register with a doctor. If you are on a temporary stay in any other EU country you will be entitled to the same Health Services as the nationals of that country. The European Health Insurance Card which replaced Form E111 from 1st June 2004 is normally required to claim these Health Benefits in all EU countries, excluding the UK.

PRSI/EU documents

Form E104 is required if you are claiming Sickness or Maternity Benefit.

Form E301 is required if you are claiming Jobseekers Benefit.

The European Health Insurance Card (EHIC) is required to claim Health Service Benefits in EU countries excluding the UK.

Forms **E104** and **E301** are available from ;
> E.U. Records Section,
> Social Welfare Service Officer,
> Floor 2,
> Oisin House,
> 212-213 Pearse St.,
> Dublin 2.

while the **European Health Insurance Card** is available from your local Health Board.

Taxation of social welfare payments

Non-taxable

The following payments are not liable to Income Tax:-

- Jobseekers Assistance
- Maternity/Adoptive Benefit
- Family Income Supplement
- Back to Work Allowance
- Health & Safety Benefits
- Supplementary Welfare Allowance

Taxable

The following payments are taxable:-

- Retirement Pension
- Contributory Old Age Pension
- Disability Benefit
- Widow's/Widower's Contributory Pension
- Jobseekers Benefit
- Contributory Orphan's Allowances
- Occupational Injuries Benefit
- Invalidity Pension
- One Parent Family Payment
- Widow's/Widower's Non-Contributory Pension
- Carer's Allowance
- Deserted Wife's Benefit
- Carer's Benefit

Taxation of Jobseekers Benefit

The first €13.00 per week of Jobseekers Benefit, together with additional payments for child dependents paid with Jobseekers Benefit, is exempt from tax. Systematic short-term working is exempt from income tax. This is short-term working for a limited time period and is normally 6-8 weeks. Casual short-term working is liable to income tax. Casual short-term working differs from systematic short-term working in that casual working if for an unlimited period.

Taxation of Illness Benefit

The first six weeks payment (36 days) of Illness Benefit and payments for child dependents will be ignored for tax purposes. Any increases for child dependents are exempt from tax.

Non-Contributory Old Age Pension, Non-Contributory Widow's/ Widower's Pension, Non-Contributory Orphan's Pension, Carer's Allowance, Blind Person's Pension together with social assistance allowance for deserted wives, prisoner's wives and lone parents are also liable to tax. However, as these payments are subject to a means test it would be unlikely that a person in receipt of one of these payments would be liable to tax.

"With an Eagle Star pension,
I foresee great things for us..."

"Where's the goldfish?"

11

Pensions - savings for retirement

There is no denying that the proportion of older to younger people is growing, that we are generally all living longer, and that very few of us can be sure of having a secure and prosperous old age.

The State will provide a basic level of income for you in retirement through Social Welfare. At present this is payable from either age 65 or 66 depending on your employment status. But will it be enough? And could the retirement age be pushed forward to age 70 or 75?

Unless you plan to work until the day you die, you will need to make some kind of provision for an income in your retirement. And, of course, if you are not able to care for yourself you will need an even larger income to pay someone else to care for you.

Generally speaking, pension funding is like any saving or investment in that the longer the time period over which the fund has to accumulate, the greater the eventual amount in your fund. Alternatively, the earlier you start, say from the moment you start working, the smaller the amount you need to put aside each month or year compared to a person who waits a number of years before starting - every year can make a big difference.

Also, once you become involved in pension funding it is important to keep track of the eventual income that your scheme is likely to produce for you, compared to your current earnings and you may need to decide whether to increase your contributions to the scheme itself or start making additional voluntary contributions.

In addition to Social Welfare Pensions individuals can save for retirement through three recognised tax efficient methods.

1.   Personal Retirement Savings Accounts (PRSAs)

2.   Personal Pension Plans

3.   Occupational/Employee Pension Schemes (including SSAPS)

In this chapter we look at the attractions of savings for retirement through these methods, the investment strategies that may be pursued, and at the technical detail relating to the different methods. Of course, you could also consider making alternative arrangements, such as direct property investment. You would need to seriously consider the implications of such matters as tax charges and reliefs on your investments, however.

Seeking independent advice is to be recommended before making decisions about such matters.

Pension Funding - The Attractions

If you were to retire today and if you are one of the almost 50% not covered under a pension arrangement, provided you qualify for the full rate State Pension (Transitional or Contributory) this would be approximately 30% of the 'average industrial wage'. On a State Pension alone, many will not be able to enjoy anything near their current standard of living when they retire.

The State is keen to help you to save for your retirement by offering you four very valuable tax advantages.

Tax Relief on contributions paid

The first major attraction of saving for your retirement is the tax relief available on personal contributions made to retirement savings arrangements, subject to the age-related limits shown on page 184. If you pay income tax at 41% for every €1 you contribute you will get 41c back in the form of tax relief (within the limits outlined later).

You may also be entitled to claim relief from PRSI and Health levies on your contributions. In addition, certain contributions made by you before October 31st in any year may be backdated to the previous tax year for tax relief purposes, if you so wish. Also, in recent years the Revenue Commissioners have extended the deadline for making returns of income from October 31st to a date in the middle of November for those who "pay and file" on-line using the Revenue On-line Service (ROS), this includes payments for pension contributions.

A special, once-off Pensions Incentive has also been introduced for those people with maturing Special Savings Investment Accounts (SSIAs) to encourage them to invest part of the maturity value of those accounts into pension plans. (See page 227)

A non-taxable benefit

Most benefits provided as a "perk" by employers - such as company cars and preferential loans - will result in an increased tax liability for you. This does not apply to your employer's pension contributions.

Tax-free investment growth

Pension contributions are invested in funds, which are not subject to any tax on their investment profits. This is an important benefit which, when looked at in conjunction with the tax relief on your contributions, means your pension fund is very likely to grow much more quickly and higher in value than other types of savings/investments.

Tax-free cash on retirement

When you retire, you will have the option of taking a cash sum from your pension plan - which will be totally tax-free. The maximum amount will depend on the type of pension arrangement in which you participate. The different entitlements to tax-free cash will be covered in more detail later in this chapter.

In addition to the tax-efficiency of saving for retirement there is another even more important reason why you should fund for retirement - the provision of money for you and your dependents in your later years when you are no longer willing, or indeed able, to work as hard as you do now.

Pension Contribution Tax Relief Limits

When you retire, you will have the option of taking a cash sum from your pension plan - which will be totally tax-free. The maximum amount will depend on your pension arrangement. The different entitlements to tax-free cash will be covered in more detail later in this chapter, when we look at the technical details of the different types of pension plans.

In addition to the tax-efficiency of saving for retirement there is another even more important reason why you should fund for retirement - the provision of money for you and your dependants in your later years when you are no longer willing, or indeed, able to work as hard as you do now.

Pension Contribution Tax Relief Limits

Age	Percentage of Net Relevant Earnings/Remuneration
Up to 29 Years	15%
30 to 39 Years	20%
40 to 49 Years	25%
50 to 54 Years	30%
55 to 59 Years	35%
60 and over	40%

Notes:

• The above rates apply to the 2006 tax year and thereafter.

• Net relevant earnings/remuneration are limited to €254,000 per annum. This figure will be increased annually in line with an earnings index from 2007.

• **Relevant earnings** consist of income from non-pensionable employment or from self-employment. A husband and wife have separate relevant earnings, which cannot be aggregated for retirement saving purposes. Income from a claim under a Permanent Health Insurance (PHI) policy is considered to be relevant earnings for retirement saving purposes. Investment earnings are not treated as relevant earnings and cannot be taken into consideration in calculating your maximum allowable pension contributions. **Net relevant earnings** consist of relevant earning less capital allowances, trading losses and certain other charges e.g. covenants and mortgage interest, for which you can claim tax relief.

- **Remuneration** applies to the earnings of those who are members of occupational pension schemes. It can include basic pay, bonus payments, over-time payments and any other payments that are subject to Schedule E tax (PAYE) including the value of any benefit-in-kind.

- For some specific occupations the 30% limit applies irrespective of age (e.g. certain professional sports people)

- With the exception of AVC PRSA contributions, regardless of age and net relevant earnings an annual contribution of €1,525 to a PRSA will attract tax relief, even if this exceeds the figures shown above.

- For the self-employed and individuals in non-pensionable employment, the above limits relate to the total contributions made to Personal Pension plans or PRSA contracts.

- Where the employer is contributing to a PRSA on behalf of an employee the limits are inclusive of the total contributions (employer's and employee's) being paid.

- For employees who are members of occupational pension schemes the above limits apply to the total of personal contributions, Additional Voluntary Contributions (AVCs), and/or PRSA AVCs made. Employer contributions to Occupational pension schemes are not taken into account in calculating the maximum contributions for personal tax relief.

Retirement Benefits

Whether you are contributing to a PRSA or a Personal Pension, or you are a member of a company/employer scheme, you will be entitled to take a tax-free lump sum when you retire. You will also be able to use the balance of your accumulated fund to provide you with an income in retirement.

Prior to the Finance Act 1999 once the tax-free cash was taken, the only option available regarding the balance of capital was the purchase of a pension or retirement annuity. However, certain categories of individuals now have other options available to them – Approved Retirement Funds and/or Taxable Cash

With the exception of the tax-free cash available at retirement, income taken from a pension arrangement following retirement is liable to income tax under the PAYE system. However, the normal tax credits and tax exemption limits apply. (See Chapter 8)

Of course, you are not obliged to take the entire tax-free lump sum, or even a portion of it, and you could use the entire accumulated fund to provide an income. However, taking it and investing it separately makes a great deal of sense from a tax-efficiency viewpoint. If you do not take it at retirement you cannot opt to take it later, and any income you draw from the entire fund will be liable to income tax.

As a result of the Finance Act 2006 the maximum allowable pension fund an individual is allowed to have accumulated on retirement is €5 million, or if higher, the value of his pension fund on 7th Dec 2005. When a fund exceeds the relevant limit at retirement the excess is subject to a once-off income tax charge at 41%.

The maximum allowable tax-free lump sum payment is €1.25 million, provided the individual qualifies to take this amount under the rules/legislation relating to his pension arrangement. Any lump sum(s) taken in excess of this is taxed at the marginal rate as income.

The maximum allowable pension fund and the maximum allowable tax-free lump sum figures will be adjusted each year in line with an earnings index from Dec 31st 2007 onward.

Annuities

An annuity is a financial product sold by a life assurance company. It operates by you paying all or part of your retirement fund to the life assurance company and, in return, the life assurance company guaranteeing to pay you an income (annuity) for the rest of your lifetime and, depending on the type of annuity you purchase, the lifetime of your financial dependants after your death. The amount of your income will be expressed in terms of a percentage of the capital used to buy the pension - the annuity rate. For example, if your pension plan had a value of €500,000 and the annuity rate quoted was 5% then your pension income would be €25,000 p.a.

With annuities there is a combining of funds and some people benefit to a greater degree than others. Those who live well into old age benefit to a greater degree in that the total of all the years' income they receive back from the annuity before they die is likely to be much larger than their original investment.

The factors that usually decide the annuity rate are:

- Your age and your gender - the older you are at retirement, the higher the rate is likely to be, because the assurance company is likely to be paying out for a shorter term. Similarly, as women generally live longer than men do they can expect a lower annuity rate.

- Extra Benefits – pension escalation, dependant's pensions and guaranteed minimum payment periods can all be included in your pension from the outset; however, these extra benefits will result in a lower annuity rate and a lower pension payable to you initially.

- Interest rates – the higher the level of long term interest rates at your retirement the higher your annuity rate will be. The assurance company is guaranteed a rate of return on the investment of your money, through investing in fixed interest securities (bonds), the yield on which reflects interest rates at that time.

Annuities are made up of both the interest earned on the investment of your money and a return of part of the original capital invested.

The simplest form of annuity is a single life level annuity i.e. a pension payable to you solely for the rest of your life at a fixed annual rate.

Escalating Annuity

When you retire your retirement is likely to extend over 20 years or more. Over that time, rising prices can significantly reduce your standard of living if you are on a fixed income. Therefore, if you are buying an annuity you may be best advised to buy one that increases each year to help overcome the effects of inflation - "escalating annuity". Under conventional annuities escalation is provided by way of a fixed rate increase each year.

Joint Life Annuity

At retirement you can buy an annuity to provide for people who are financially dependent on you, should you predecease them. A spouse is the most common type of dependant but elderly family relatives and children (particularly handicapped children) may also qualify as dependants. You may choose to have a pension paid to them for the rest of their lives, starting after your death. Where the pension is for a husband and wife it is generally known as a Joint-life Annuity.

As you and your spouse together have a longer life expectancy than you do on your own the annuity rate under a joint-life annuity will be less than that under a single life annuity, resulting in a lower income payment. And, if your dependant is significantly younger than you, the reduction in the rate may be quite large.

Guaranteed payment period

The "guaranteed payment period" guarantees that your pension will be paid for a fixed term of years, even if you die within that term. Its purpose is to ensure your dependants get a minimum financial return from your pension plan. Of course, the annuity payments continue to be payable to you for as long as you live after the expiry date of the guaranteed payment period.

The Revenue Commissioners allow you to choose a guaranteed payment period from 0 up to 10 years. A guaranteed payment will also result in a reduction in the initial income paid to you or your dependants. The amount of the reduction will depend on your age and the guaranteed period chosen.

In recent years the levels of annuity rates available have fallen substantially mainly because of the substantial fall in interest rates. Low interest rates mean the assurance company can earn less on its fixed interest investments and less money is available to provide pension income for you in retirement.

At the same time as interest rates have been decreasing, pension providers have been noticing much improved mortality levels. Medical capabilities have improved substantially which means people are living longer. This means pensions will need to be paid over longer periods - this also reduces the initial level of pension payable at retirement.

In general, annuity terms quoted by insurance companies are offered to everyone regardless of the state of their health. People who are in poor health at retirement and unlikely to live for a long time are disadvantaged by this and deserve higher annuity rates. It may be possible to buy an "impaired life" annuity, which recognises this fact. The improved terms they offer will depend on individual circumstances.

Shopping around for the best annuity rate when you come to retirement makes excellent sense as rates can vary widely from provider to provider. As with most financial matters using an independent financial advisor to do the shopping for you can be very beneficial indeed.

Defined benefit pension scheme

If you are in this type of scheme (see Employee Pensions section page 214) you do not have to worry about interest rates and their effect on annuity rates at retirement as your pension will be directly related to your final salary - your employer carries the interest rate risk.

Retirement Options

If you are in one of the specified categories shown below, you have a choice of using your accumulated retirement capital to provide you with an income through any combination of the following:

1. **Buying an annuity**

2. **Investing in an Approved Retirement Fund (ARF) and gradually drawing down an income.**

3. **Taking your money in cash form, subject to immediate income tax**

These options are designed to give the individual involved more control over the use of their accumulated retirement fund; to address the problem of lower annuity rates; and to address the needs of those who wish to pass on the value of their pension funds to their dependants on death.

To avail of options 2 and 3 above there are requirements of which you are obliged to fulfil only one:

- Have reached age 75

- Have a guaranteed pension income of €12,700 per year, which is payable for your lifetime ("Specified Income")

- Have €63,500 invested in an Approved Minimum Retirement Fund (AMRF)

The pension income of €12,700 can include any ordinary pension annuity or Social Welfare Pensions (single rate) and foreign pensions. Timing your retirement under the new rules is important from the point of view of specified income e.g. if you retire a month before your Social Welfare pension becomes payable, it will not count as specified income. Once you invest in an AMRF your capital must stay in an AMRF until age 75. (see below)

Specified Categories

1. **PRSA plan-holders;**

2. **Personal Pension plan-holders;**

3. **Directors who own or control more than 5% of the shares in their companies (5% Directors) and who are members of employer sponsored pension arrangements;**

4. **Directors and employees who have made additional voluntary contributions (AVCs) to a company/employer pension arrangement and/or AVCs through a PRSA contract.**

For employees who make AVCs and/or PRSA AVCs, only that portion of their accumulated pension fund that relates to their AVCs and/or PRSA AVCs can avail of the retirement options. In addition, when it comes to the tax-free cash element of their pensions at retirement they are subject to the rules relating to occupational/employee pensions, and cannot take 25% of the AVC fund in addition to the maximum allowable benefit under those rules.

No other individual may avail of the options e.g. it is not possible for your personal representative to set up an ARF for your dependants after your death. Nor is it possible for you to pay funds directly into an ARF – they must come from an approved pension arrangement or another ARF.

For a 5% Director to qualify for the new retirement options he/she needs to have been a 5% Director within three years of reaching retirement or of leaving the employment where the pension fund was accumulated.

Approved Retirement Funds (ARFs) are defined in the 1999 Finance Act as funds "which are managed by a Qualifying Fund Manager and which comply with the conditions of Section 784B". ARFs taken out after April 6th 2000 are similar to pension funds in that investment growth within the fund is tax-free.

Approved Minimum Retirement Funds (AMRFs) are similar to ARFs with the exception that the draw down of money is limited to the investment growth only until you reach age 75. The purpose of AMRFs is to address the criticism that a spendthrift could dissipate their retirement benefits too quickly.

An ARF/AMRF enables you to control your pension fund assets at retirement and to direct future investment strategy through a Qualified Fund Manager. A Qualifying Fund Manager (QFM) can be one of the following:

- Bank

- Building Society

- Credit Union

- An Post

- Life Assurance Company

- Cash handling investment intermediary

- Stockbroker

- Equivalent institution authorised in another EU State.

A QFM must provide an annual statement, giving details of the investments held, the withdrawals made etc. to the beneficial owner of each ARF. This statement must be issued within three months of the end of the year of assessment (i.e. by 1st April each year).

Any withdrawal from an Approved Retirement Fund or Approved Minimum Retirement Fund taken out after April 6th 2000 is taxable under the PAYE system. Also, as a result of the Finance Act 2006, "deemed withdrawals" from ARFs will be liable to income tax. The tax will be payable on a percentage of the value of the ARF as at Dec 31st 2007 and as at Dec 31st each year thereafter. The applicable percentages will be 1% for 2007, 2% for 2008, 3% for 2009 and each year thereafter. Actual withdrawals made during the year can be deducted from the percentage value. Thus, if an individual withdraws in excess of the 1% of the value of the ARF as at Dec 31st 2007 during 2007 there will be no deemed withdrawals. While AMRFs are not subject to the deemed withdrawal taxation, withdrawals from AMRFs are treated as actual withdrawals.

On death your AMRF automatically becomes an ARF and the tax treatment of plan will depend on who benefits from the proceeds. The following chart shows the tax treatment on death of ARFs taken out after April 6th 2000.

ARF Funds Left To	Tax Due
ARF in surviving Spouse's name	No tax on transfer to a surviving Spouse's ARF. All subsequent withdrawals by spouse will be liable to Income Tax under PAYE. Exempt from Inheritance Tax.
Surviving Spouse - capital directly to a surviving spouse.	The full amount is treated as income of the deceased spouse in year of death and taxed accordingly under PAYE. Exempt from Inheritance Tax.
Children over 21 at date of parent's death.	Standard rate Income Tax (i.e. 20%) on amount inherited, deducted at source.Exempt from Inheritance Tax.
Children under 21 at date of parent's death.	No Income Tax liability. Amount is subject to Inheritance Tax - thresholds apply.
Others.	The full amount is treated as income of the deceased in year of death and taxed accordingly. Balance after payment of Income Tax is subject to Inheritance Tax - thresholds apply.

Taxes on Death

Note: If you intend leaving the money in your ARF to an ARF in your spouse's name on your death you are probably best advised to make provision for this in your will. This will have the effect of ensuring that the proceeds will not be treated as a transfer of capital directly to your spouse.

The main advantage of an Approved Retirement Fund is that it helps you retain flexibility and control over your pension fund investments after retirement. However, if you take a regular income from an Approved Retirement Fund, this income is not guaranteed for life, as it would be with a traditional annuity pension.

With a conventional annuity you are converting your pension fund into a guaranteed income for your own life and maybe that of your chosen financial dependants. It does not matter if the returns from investment markets are poor, or if you or your dependants live for a very long time because all the relevant pensions will be guaranteed to be paid by the assurance company.

The following table shows how drawing a regular income from an Approved Retirement Fund can affect the capital within the fund depending on different rates of investment return achieved. As can be seen, if you do not wish to deplete your fund it is important:

- not to have your withdrawals at too high a level.

  and

- to invest in a fund that is likely to give you an average rate of return higher than your chosen withdrawal rate over the years.

Of course, you do not have to make regular withdrawals from the fund such as those shown. You can decide what income you wish to withdraw and when you wish to withdraw it.

If you want to make regular withdrawals you can express these in monetary terms such as €2,000 per month, as against percentage terms as shown.

ARF Investment Fund: €500,000

Amount of Regular Withdrawals: 5% of remaining fund

Frequency of Withdrawals: Yearly in arrears

Projected Policy Values

End of Year	6% p.a. Investment Return		3% p.a. Investment Return	
	Projected Income Taken in year	Projected Policy Value	Projected Income Taken in Year	Projected Policy Value
	€	€	€	€
1	26,513	478,551	25,755	464,878
2	26,446	482,379	24,956	455,208
3	26,380	486,185	24,183	445,692
4	26,314	489,970	23,433	436,327
5	26,248	493,732	22,707	427,116
10	25,922	492,516	19,399	368,578
15	25,599	486,390	16,573	314,882
20	25,281	480,341	14,158	269,009

(Source: Eagle Star - 100% Balanced Fund. The rates of return shown are gross of charges and for illustration purposes only. They are not guaranteed. Actual investment growth will depend on the performance of the underlying investments and may be more or less than illustrated)

Your overall attitude to risk, and the risk/return concept will very much influence your choice of investment fund(s).

An ARF or an AMRF can purchase an annuity for you at any stage. However, once the annuity is purchased the process cannot be reversed.

A quick reference guide to the retirement options
Benefits being taken from a personal pension plan or PRSA

On retirement 25% of benefit can be taken as tax-free lump sum. The balance (note 1) can be taken as follows:

• Invested in an ARF (note 3),

- Taken as a taxable lump sum

or

- Taken in pension / annuity form

Benefits being taken from an occupational pension scheme

The two retirement options for a 5% proprietary director (note 2) are:

Option 1

- 25% of benefit can be taken as tax-free lump sum, regardless of service. The balance (note 1) can be taken as follows:

- Taken as a lump sum;

or

- Invested in an ARF (note 3), (ARF, not scheme trustees, can buy and annuity if so wished)

Option 2

- Tax free lump sum of up to 150% x final remuneration for 20 years or more service. (Lower percentage amounts for less than 20 years service or on early retirement.) The balance must be used by trustees to purchase an annuity for you and your dependents.

Benefits being taken from an AVC or PRSA AVC Fund (note 2)

Fund can be taken in conjunction with the main scheme benefits. Tax-free lump sum up to an overall maximum of 150% of final remuneration, for 20 years or more service. (Lower percentage amounts for less than 20 years service or on early retirement.) Depending on the main scheme rules it may be possible to take Revenue maximum tax-free lump sum from the main scheme, or to take it from the AVC or PRSA AVC fund, or a mix of both.

Balance of AVC fund (note 1) can be:

- Taken as taxable lump sum;

- Invested in an ARF (note 3)

or

- taken in pension/annuity form.

Note 1 Subject to €63,500 being invested in an AMRF or converted into a guaranteed pension income, if you do not have a pension income of €12,700 p.a. at that time, or have not reached age 75.

Note 2 See page 195. for more details regarding tax-free cash entitlements.

Note 3 You are not restricted to one ARF investment only, you can spread your ARF moneys amongst a number of Qualifying Fund Managers, but you can have only one AMRF.

Pensions Linked Borrowing

In recent years Pension Mortgages have become a very attractive and tax efficient method of funding property purchase. In addition, individual pension arrangements can now borrow to acquire assets for investment purposes, giving rise to what is termed Geared Property Pensions. Both pension mortgages and geared property pensions are particularly attractive where an individual may wish to use his/her pension to purchase a commercial property or a 'buy to let' residential property.

Pension mortgages

Pension mortgages are in effect "interest only" mortgages, where interest payments only are made to the lending institution. The individual borrower owns the property. But instead of making capital repayments to the lender, contributions are made to a pension arrangement. When the pension plan matures the tax-free cash and, if necessary a portion of the balance taken in taxable cash form, can be used to repay the capital borrowed. Tax relief is available on the pension contributions, subject to the normal limits. And, in the case of a commercial or a buy-to-let loan situation the interest payments can be offset against the rental income.

In many cases when the individual comes to retirement age or to the end of the loan term, the property is sold, the loan is repaid from the sale proceeds and the pension is used for its original purpose - to provide an income in retirement.

Geared property pension

Under a geared property pension arrangement the property is held within the pension trust. The trust does the borrowing, receives rental income and meets the costs of maintaining the property including meeting the capital and interest repayments. Holding geared property within a pension creates a tax umbrella under which all the income and outgoings of investing in a property can shelter. No tax will be paid on the rental income and contributions to the pension will receive tax relief, again within certain limits.

All moneys coming out of the pension arrangement, including the sale value of the property will be liable to tax, after any tax-free lump sum has been taken. The Revenue Commissioners require that the borrowing is done on a capital and interest basis, that the loan term is no longer than fifteen years and that the loan is repaid by retirement age. They also require that the property is held at arm's length, and as a result of this an individual will not be able to directly manage the property. Nor can the individual, or anyone connected with him/her, use the property.

Using a pension to purchase property either through a pension mortgage or through a geared property pension can be very attractive, particularly for higher rate taxpayers.

Deciding on whether one should use a pension mortgage arrangement or a geared property pension arrangement can be a complicated issue and using a pension to repay borrowings is not something that should be entered into without a full understanding of its working shortfalls. Seeking advice from an independent financial advisor is recommended.

Pension Funding - Important Points

The main aim of pension funding is to build up a large cash fund in a tax efficient manner for retirement. This cash fund will come from the contributions you, and/or your employer, make to the pension arrangement during your working life and the investment profits earned by these contribution within the fund over the years.

For Defined Benefit pension schemes, where the members are promised a certain level of benefits, the accumulated value of the scheme assets will be more important to the employer and the scheme trustees than to the individual members.

If you are a member of a Defined Contribution scheme or making Additional Voluntary Contributions (AVCs) on a defined contribution basis, in addition to the level of contributions made, the size of your accumulated fund at retirement will be determined by three main factors:

- **When you start.**

- **Investment strategy pursued.**

- **Growth rates.**

When You Start

The main aim of pension funding is to build up a large cash fund in a tax efficient manner for retirement. This cash fund will come from the contributions you, and/or your employer make to the pension arrangement during your working life and the investment profits earned by these contribution within the fund over the years.

For Defined Benefit pension schemes, where the members are promised a certain level of benefits, the accumulated value of the scheme assets will be more important to the employer and the scheme trustees than to the individual members.

John, Joanne, Mary and Pat are employees each of whom starts paying a contribution of €5,000 per year on a non-increasing basis to a Standard PRSA contract 10, 15, 20 and 25 years respectively before their 60th birthdays. Each qualifies for relief from Income Tax at 41% and for relief from the PRSI/Health Levy at 6% on the full contribution giving a net outlay of €2,650 p.a. each. Assuming each of their funds gives an investment return of 6% p.a. net they will have accumulated retirement capital, after the deduction of charges and expenses, as detailed in the following table:

Name & Term of Years to Retirement Age	Illustrative Retirement Capital at age 60	Total Gross Contributions made	Investment Growth
John – 10 years	€62,538	€50,000	€12,538
Joanne – 15 years	€107,121	€75,000	€32,121
Mary – 20 years	€163,872	€100,000	€63,872
Pat – 25 years	€236,113	€125,000	€111,113

(Source: Eagle Star. Based on a Standard PRSA contract with 5% contribution charge and 1% per annum fund management charge, the figures shown are for illustration purposes only. They are not guaranteed. Actual investment growth will depend on the performance of the underlying investments and may be more or less than illustrated)

Investment Strategy

Another very important factor that must be taken into consideration is the type of investment strategy that you choose. Choosing an incorrect strategy could have a very detrimental effect on the size of your accumulated fund at retirement age.

Historically, equity investing (i.e. company shares) has normally produced better returns over longer time periods than investing in property, fixed interest securities or cash. However, equities also likely to be much more volatile than the other types of investment assets.

Unit linked

Most pension funds operated by life assurance companies and other pension providers are operated on a unit-linked basis. That is, the moneys you contribute buy units within the fund, and the unit prices reflect the underlying value of the assets held by the fund. Thus as the value of these assets rises the unit prices rise and the value of your investments rise.

Unitised with-profit

Some life assurance companies also offer 'unitised with-profit' funds, where the investment profits earned are added to the fund on a systematic basis by way of bonuses or dividends, which increase the value of the units held within the fund. The life assurance company holds back some investment profits in good investment years to maintain bonus rates in poor investment years. The investments are normally held in Equities, Fixed Interest Securities and Property.

During and following periods of poor equity market performance, and in order to protect existing policyholders, companies can penalise those who are maturing their policies early by imposing 'market level adjustments' to their fund values.

Managed funds

The most popular funds for pension investment in modern times have been Managed (or Mixed) Funds, which invest in a mix of assets. Cautiously Managed Funds invest predominantly in fixed interest securities and cash. Managed Growth Funds have a mix of investments similar to with-profit funds, while Actively/Aggressively Managed Funds have more of an emphasis on equity investment – looking for the better long term investment returns.

Overall, possibly the best strategy to pursue is to have a greater exposure to equities the further from retirement age you are, reducing this exposure and investing in less volatile assets as retirement age approaches.

Self-directed and Self-administered

Recent times have seen the development of 'Self-Directed Pensions' that are aimed mainly at higher income individuals. Basically these are pension plans where life assurance companies allow individual policyholders to fully decide the assets that are to be used in the investment of the pension funds such as equities, fixed interest securities, property etc., giving the individuals more control over the investment of their pension funds. These assets are bought through stockbrokers and/or specialist pension providers.

'Self-Administered Pensions' are also available for employer-sponsored pension schemes. They are very similar to Self-Directed Pensions except a life assurance company is not involved. Instead a trust is put in place by 'Pensioner Trustees', who are responsible for the running of the scheme. (See page 228 for details.)

The importance of growth

Have a look at the chart on page... and you'll quickly see that the segment with the greatest potential for future value is the growth generated within the funds itself. See how much growth is generated within Pat's fund over 25 years as opposed to what John's contributions have achieved over 10 years. It is important therefore that you invest your contributions where they are most likely to give you good long-term investment returns.

While your tolerance for risk may be low it is important that you do not jeopardise your potential for building an adequate retirement fund over the long-term by being too conservative in your fund choice.

For example, if you contribute €5,000 per annum on a non-increasing basis to a Standard PRSA using an investment fund that produces an average investment return of 4% per annum your accumulated fund at retirement age is likely to be much less than if you had used a fund producing an average return of 6% per annum, as can be seen from the following table.

Term to retirement years	Illustrative Retirement Capital @ 4% pa Growth	Illustrative Retirement Capital @ 6% pa Growth	Percentage Difference
40	€365,842	€594,129	62.4%
35	€293,698	€445,125	51.6%
30	€231,359	€328,070	41.8%
25	€177,493	€236,113	33.0%
20	€130,948	€163,872	25.1%
15	€90,729	€107,121	18.1%
10	€55,977	€62,538	11.7%

((Source: Eagle Star. Based on a Standard PRSA contract with 5% contribution charge and 1% per annum fund management charge, the rates of return shown are gross of charges and are for illustration purposes only. They are not guaranteed. Actual investment growth will depend on the performance of the underlying investments and may be more or less than illustrated)

A good fund manager will make your money work hard for you. Yet, you – or your pension fund trustees - when completing the application forms and choosing a fund or combination of funds into which your contributions are to be invested set the parameters within which your investment manager must operate. If you do not feel comfortable in making the choice of investment fund(s) yourself many pension providers now offer predetermined investment strategies, often referred to as 'lifestyle strategies'. In fact, under the PRSA legislation PRSA providers are obliged to provide a predetermined strategy called a "Default Investment Strategy" as an investment option and this strategy must be designed to "fulfil the reasonable expectations of a typical investor".

Pensions and investments
that go further

Flexible and tax efficient client solutions

Dedicated service and support

Wide investment choice

Direct property
Shares
Standard Life funds
Multi-manager funds
Index trading funds
Bank deposits

Talk to your Standard Life Account Manager or call 1890 252 220

STANDARD LIFE

PRSAs (Personal Retirement Savings Accounts)

As a result of a political initiative to try to increase pension coverage Personal Retirement Savings Accounts (PRSAs) were introduced in 2003.

PRSAs - what are they?

PRSAs are intended to be low-cost, simple, accessible, portable retirement savings plans. They offer an attractive method of saving for retirement and should be seriously considered by anyone planning to fund for retirement.

The individual in whose name a PRSA contract is issued - the "Contributor" - is the sole owner of that contract. The individual's employer may contribute to the individual's PRSA plan, but once the employer's contributions have been made they become the property of the individual contributor through the PRSA contract.

PRSAs are available from Life Assurance companies, Credit Institutions (i.e. banks and building societies) and other Investment Management firms known as "PRSA Providers".

PRSAs are arranged on a "money purchase" basis. That is, the eventual level of benefits available will be based on four key factors:

- The number and level of contributions made over the years;

- The returns achieved by the investment fund(s) used;

- The term over which the retirement fund accumulates; **and**

- The charges deducted from the retirement fund by the PRSA Provider.

The greater the value of contributions made, the investment returns achieved and the longer the term over which the fund accumulates, the larger the eventual retirement fund. However, the higher the charges deducted, the lower the eventual level of retirement capital.

There are no limits to the maximum amount of money that can be accumulated within the fund, but tax relief is only available up to the levels shown on page 184.

Who can contribute?

If you are an employee, a self-employed individual, a homemaker, a carer, unemployed or any other category of person who wishes to save for your retirement you are eligible to take out a PRSA. However, you will only receive tax relief (see below) in respect of non-pensionable earnings and self-employed earnings from a trade or profession. If you are a member of an employer sponsored pension scheme (see Employee Pensions section later in this chapter) you may contribute to a PRSA by way of an Additional Voluntary PRSA Contributions (AVC PRSAs).

Transferring of tax reliefs between spouses is not possible, so if you are a stay-at-home spouse your partner cannot claim tax relief on your PRSA contributions. However, if you intend returning to the workforce at some time you will be able to carry the tax relief on you PRSA contributions forward to future years when you are again paying tax.

There may no great advantage in paying contributions unless you can claim tax relief, because 75% of your accumulated capital will be liable to tax when you draw it (see below), although the normal tax credits and tax exemption limits will apply. Other forms of saving, such as life assurance savings policies, where tax at 23% on the investment growth is currently payable on withdrawals from the accumulated fund, and where you do not have to wait until age 60 to collect your savings, may be a more attractive option for you if you are not likely to receive income tax relief on your contributions.

Portability

Once you take out a PRSA plan you can continue to contribute irrespective of your employment situation. For example, an employee who leaves employment to become self-employed can continue with his/her PRSA contributions. Likewise, if he/she returns to employed status he/she can also continue contributing, and so on. You can move from one PRSA provider to another without charge, and you can also hold PRSA plans with more than one provider.

In addition, if you wish to transfer your fund from a PRSA plan over to a company pension scheme on joining a new employment, for example, the legislation allows you to do so. If on leaving employment you wish to transfer your accumulated fund from a company pension scheme to a PRSA contract, subject to certain requirements, the legislation also allows you to do so, provided your membership of the scheme you are leaving does not exceed 15 years.

Types of PRSA and Charges

The legislation allows for two types of PRSA contracts:

- Standard

- Non-Standard

There are strict rules applying to the way in which charges can be made to PRSA products. Charges can only be levied on the basis of:

a   a percentage of the contribution entering the contract;

b   a percentage of the accumulated fund; and

c   a combination of (a) and (b).

For Standard PRSA's, charges are restricted to a maximum of 5% of contributions and 1% per annum of the accumulated fund. There are no maximum charge restrictions Non-Standard PRSAs.

In addition, Standard PRSAs must only use "pooled investment" funds, which include life assurance company unit-linked funds and unit trusts. Smoothed or guaranteed type funds such as unitised with profit funds are not considered to be pooled funds. As a result the investment choice under non-Standard PRSAs is wider from many PRSA providers, and very often includes the with-profit investment option mentioned earlier in this chapter.

Both types of PRSA must have a default investment strategy, which as mentioned earlier, must be designed to fulfil the reasonable expectations of a typical investor. The default investment strategies must be linked to pooled funds. If you do not wish to avail of the default investment strategy and you wish to make your own investment choice you must indicate this in writing on the application form.

The cost of risk benefits (i.e. life assurance cover, serious illness cover, PHI cover and contribution protection cover) cannot be deducted from PRSA contributions or funds. If you wish to arrange this cover in conjunction with your retirement savings you have do so separately.

Tax Relief

If you are an employee you can claim Income Tax relief at your marginal rate and PRSI/Health Levy relief on PRSA contributions, up to the limits shown on page 184. If you are self-employed you can claim Income Tax relief at your marginal rate subject to the same limits.

If you are self-employed or in non-pensionable employment the tax relief limits are inclusive of contributions that you may be making to any Personal Pension plans or any other PRSA contracts. If your employer is contributing to PRSA contract(s) on your behalf the limits are inclusive of the total contributions (employer's and employee's) being paid. For AVC PRSAs the limits are inclusive of any personal contributions you may be making to the main pension scheme or to any other AVC arrangement(s).

If the contribution limits are exceeded in any tax year relief may be carried forward to future years. In addition, you may elect to back date the tax relief on certain contributions paid between the start of the year and October 31st to the previous year (see below for further details).

Tax treatment of employer contributions

Employer contributions to your PRSA its contributions are treated as a benefit-in-kind under the terms of the legislation. However, as you are entitled to income tax relief on the total contributions up to the limits set out on page 184, a benefit-in-kind charge does not arise in practice, once the total contributions do not exceed these limits.

If you complete a return of income to the Revenue Commissioners you must give details of the PRSA contributions made on your behalf by your employer in the previous tax year. In addition, employers are obliged to make a return of details of PRSA contributions made on behalf of employees, where requested to do so by the Revenue.

Back dating tax relief

If you wish you may offset certain PRSA contributions made between January 1st and the following 31st October against your taxable income in the preceding tax year. If you are a self-employed individual any contributions made may be back-dated for tax relief purposes, but if you are an employee only once-off contributions may be back-dated.

Example

John is self-employed, under 30 and a 41% taxpayer. In September 2007 he pays an initial pension contribution of €19,500 to a PRSA. John's net relevant earnings are as follows:

2006	€60,000
2007	€70,000

John can claim relief up to 15% of his net relevant earnings in the current tax year (ending 31st December 2007). Under the backdating provisions he can claim up to 15% of his net relevant earnings in the preceding tax year (ending December 31st 2006) provided he paid the relevant contributions before 31st October 2007. However, he must elect to have the relevant part of this €19,500 contribution offset against his 2006 income, when making his self-assessment tax returns before October 31st 2007. His contribution will work out as follows:

Tax year	Net relevant earnings	Maximum contributions 15%	Tax Relief 42%/41%	Net Cost
2006	€60,000	€9,000	€3,780	€5,220
2007	€70,000	€10,500	€4,305	€6,195

Retirement Age

Normally PRSA plans can be matured whenever you wish once you have reached age 60. However, they must be drawn before age 75. It is not necessary to stop working to draw benefits.

Where an employee is retiring early from employment he/she can mature his/her PRSA plan(s), once he/she has reached age 50.

If you become seriously ill you will be able to mature your PRSA plan immediately, regardless of your age at that time.

Of course, the later you draw benefits from your plan the greater the accumulated fund is likely to be. This is due to the fact that you will have made more contributions and the fund will have had more time to benefit from investment growth.

Make your money work harder and smarter

Call for a free financial review today.

You've never had more savings and investment options. So how do you choose? How do you know if your money could do better? At EBS, we're offering free financial reviews to suit your personal needs.

Three great reasons to do a financial review:
- Review your existing investments
- Make sure your money is doing all it can for you
- Receive a FREE personalised report following your review

Let us show you what your money can do.

To set up your financial review,
just drop into your local EBS office or call 1890 923 205.

EBS
BUILDING SOCIETY

all together better

Retirement Benefits

It is normally possible to take up to 25% of the accumulated fund as a tax-free lump sum upon maturing the PRSA plan.

Note: For those who are members of employee pension arrangements and have been making AVC PRSA payments the maximum allowable tax free lump sum is subject to the legislation governing such arrangements, i.e. 150% of final remuneration if more than 20 years service with your employer.

Once the tax-free lump sum has been taken you are entitled to avail of the retirement options detailed on page 189. As an alternative to the ARF invest you are allowed to leave your money in the PRSA and, provided you leave at least €63,500 in the PRSA until age 75, the AMRF requirement is fulfilled.

Payment on Death

In the event of your death before you mature your PRSA the capital that has accumulated in your PRSA fund will be payable to your estate. The accumulated value of your PRSA fund is payable to your personal legal representatives and will be distributed according to the terms of your Will if you have made one, or according to the terms of the Succession Act if you have not.

Although the cost of life assurance cover and other risk benefits cannot be deducted from your PRSA it is important that you have adequate cover in place. You may be able to arrange life assurance cover through another pension contract type (e.g. Section 785 "stand alone" cover) thus entitling you to tax relief on the premiums.

Monitoring Your PRSA

Before you first take out a PRSA contract you will have be given a Preliminary Disclosure Certificate, giving you the technical details of the PRSA you are considering. Once you put the PRSA in place and every year thereafter, Statements of Reasonable Projection will have to be given to you by your PRSA provider. These are intended to illustrate the ultimate retirement benefits based on certain assumptions and related to future contributions and investment returns.

In addition, your PRSA provider will be obliged to provide you with a Statement of Account every six months detailing:

- contributions paid (both yours and your employer's, if applicable) from inception

- contributions paid since the previous statement

- the then current transfer value of the PRSA

A report on the performance of the investment funds(s) that you have chosen must also be issued on a six-monthly basis.

Additional Points to note

- Employers are entitled to relief against corporation tax if they are limited companies and against income tax if they are sole traders or partnerships on whatever contributions they decide to make to their employees' PRSAs. In addition, Employer's PRSI will not be payable on employee contributions deducted at source under the 'net pay' arrangement. However, they are not obliged to contribute to employees' PRSAs.

- If employers have "excluded employees" they are obliged to provide a payroll deduction facility through at least one PRSA provider in respect of at least one "Standard PRSA".

Excluded employees

Excluded employees are any individuals in employment where:

- There is no existing occupational pension scheme (i.e. an employer sponsored pension scheme for employees) in place;

- An occupational pension scheme exists but there is a waiting period of more than six months before employees can join it;

- An occupational pension scheme exists but it provides death-in-service benefits only; and

- An occupational pension scheme exists but there is no facility for employees to make AVCs to top up retirement benefits

If an employer is obliged to set up a Standard PRSA payroll deduction facility he must also

- notify "excluded employees" of their right to contribute to Standard PRSA's by payroll deduction

- allow PRSA providers and intermediaries work-site access to "excluded employees" to arrange Standard PRSA's

- allow "excluded employees" reasonable paid leave to enable them to make arrangements to put their Standard PRSA's in place

Once the PRSA scheme has been put in place the employer must

- remit the contributions deducted from the employees' salaries/wages in respect of all PRSAs to the PRSA provider(s) within 21 days of the end of the month in which the deduction is made

- notify employees each month of the all PRSA contributions deducted from their salaries/wages and of any contributions made on their behalf during the previous month (payroll slips are adequate for this purpose).

Personal Pension Plans

Personal Pension plans, or Retirement Annuity Contracts (RACs) as they are officially known, are of interest to the self-employed and to employees who are not in an employee/occupational pension scheme. Personal Pensions are similar to PRSAs in that the same limits for tax relief purposes, the same definition of Net Relevant Earnings, and the same rules regarding carry forward and back dating tax relief apply.

With the same exceptions as apply to PRSAs, the plan cannot normally be matured until after the age of 60 and must be matured by age 75. It is not necessary to stop working to mature your plan.

The same definition of disability applies if the plan is to be matured early – you must be "permanently incapable through infirmity of mind or body of carrying on your own occupation or any occupation of a similar nature for which you are trained or fitted".

25% of the total accumulated fund may be taken as a tax-free cash lump sum, on retirement.

- A pension may be provided, for a spouse or dependants, provided the total amount paid after your death does not exceed your own pension entitlements.

- You can retain ownership of the fund at retirement by transferring it to an ARF (Approved Retirement Fund) (See page 190).

Your employer may contribute to your Personal Pension plan and may deduct contributions directly from your earnings under the 'Net Pay' arrangement.

- You can transfer your Personal Pension plan over to another Personal Pension or PRSA in your own name.

- If you qualify, you are entitled to hold as many Personal Pension plans and/or PRSA contracts as you wish, but you are restricted in your overall contributions with regard to income tax relief.

Personal Pensions differ from PRSAs in that:

- While anyone can contribute to a PRSA only those who have relevant earnings can contribute to Personal Pensions. If you had relevant earnings in the past and made contributions to a Personal Pension plan at that time you can continue to make contributions to that Personal Pension but will not receive tax relief on your contributions if you no longer have relevant earnings.

- Additional life assurance cover can be arranged as part of a Personal Pension plan with the costs deducted from your fund – Section 785 "associated" cover. This cover has to be put place completely separately, on a Section 785 "stand alone" basis, if you are taking out a PRSA.

Provided the total of the pension contributions and the life assurance premiums within the Personal Pension plan remain within the limits detailed on page 179, tax relief can be claimed in respect of both. There is no limit with regard to the amount of cover that can be put in place.

If you decide to include this cover as part of your plan you will usually be offered the choice of having your life assurance paid in addition to your pension fund or of having the cover inclusive of the pension fund on your death. In order to minimise the amount being spent on life assurance cover and maximise the pension investment, having the cover inclusive of the fund makes most sense. Over the years the pension fund could grow in value to equal more than the life cover and no further premiums would then be required to pay for that cover.

Any death benefit lump sum is not assignable and cannot be used as collateral against a loan. The lump sum is payable to your personal legal representatives and will be distributed according to the terms of your Will or according to the terms of the Succession Act if you have no Will.

- Although covered by separate legislation Disability Insurance or Permanent Health Insurance (PHI) is another feature that can be arranged in conjunction with most Personal Pension plans, while it must be arranged completely separately to PRSA plans. For self-employed people this can be a very attractive cover.

In the event of your becoming disabled, or for any other reason you are too ill to work, disability insurance can provide a monthly income for the duration of your illness up to normal retirement age or your earlier return to work. The life assurance companies that provide this cover impose a limit on the total monthly benefit they will pay (normally 75% of your income prior to disablement less your Social Welfare entitlements). Payments normally commence after a deferment period has elapsed. This deferment period could be 13, 26, or 52 weeks, depending on the particular plan you choose. The calculation of deferment period starts on the date of your disability.

The full cost of Disability Insurance can be offset against your taxable income, provided it does not exceed 10% of your total income.

Another aspect of disability insurance that can be arranged as part of a Personal Pension package but cannot be added to a PRSA is 'Contribution Protection' cover, which means that your pension contributions are paid by the assurance company in the event of you being too ill to work. The same deferment periods as mentioned above normally apply here.

- If you are an employee wishing to retire early from employment you cannot mature your Personal Pension plan after age 50, which is allowed under PRSA legislation.

- Personal Pension providers are not obliged to provide you with the same degree of information regarding your contract as they are under PRSAs.

- While you can **transfer** a PRSA to an employer-sponsored pension scheme, a transfer from a Personal Pension to an employer-sponsored pension scheme is not allowed. Likewise, while a transfer from an employer-sponsored pension scheme to a PRSA is allowed under the legislation, a transfer to a Personal Pension is not allowed.

Employee / Occupational Pension Schemes

Although known officially as occupational pension schemes, these arrangements are also known under other names such as employee pensions, employer-sponsored, company-paid pensions, employee pensions etc.

An Employee Pension plan is one to which your employer, be he/she a sole trader, a partnership or a limited company makes contributions on the your behalf. You may also be obliged to contribute ("contributory schemes") or you may not ("non-contributory schemes").

Only those that pay Income Tax under the PAYE system (Schedule E) can become members of these schemes. Schemes may have as few as one member ("Executive Plans") or thousands of members ("Group Schemes"). Executive plans are normally put in place for proprietary directors of companies.

There is no legal obligation on an employer to put an employee pension scheme in place, although many do. If an employer does set up a pension scheme, it is not obliged to include all employees in the scheme but, with certain exceptions, it cannot discriminate on a number of grounds such as gender, age, sexual orientation etc.

Under Revenue rules the plan must be 'exempt approved' and one of the criteria for this is that the employer is obliged to contribute a 'meaningful contribution' to the total cost of the benefits provided. In effect, this meaningful contribution usually means 1/10th of the overall cost of scheme benefits. For larger schemes the employer paying the cost of any life assurance benefits provided and the cost of administering the scheme is also taken to be a 'meaningful contribution'.

When the scheme is being established, a trust arrangement must be put in place to keep the scheme assets separate to the business assets, and a set of rules must be put in place to govern the administration of the scheme. These rules must comply with Revenue practice. A Normal Retirement Age (NRA) between ages 60 and 70, upon which members are normally expected to retire from the employment, must be mentioned in the scheme rules.

Very often the employer will appoint a life assurance company to administer the scheme on its behalf. This administration service includes record keeping, investment of scheme assets, claims payments etc. Such schemes are generally referred to as insured schemes.

Under self-administered schemes the employer may take on the administration of the scheme itself, particularly with regard to the investment of the scheme assets. Often specialist pensions providers will provide the administration services and the fund management can be handed over to one or more specialist investment companies, which could include a life assurance company. The employer may also invest the assets, subject to certain Revenue requirements. (See Small Self Administered Schemes section later in this chapter)

The players

- The Employer: Sets up the pension scheme and is usually responsible for the major share of the operating costs.

- The Members: Employees (including Proprietary Directors) covered by the scheme. They must be given written particulars of all the essential features of the scheme.

- The Trustees: Individuals responsible for controlling the assets of the scheme, collecting and investing the contributions and for paying out the pension benefits in accordance with the scheme rules. Very often the employer will act as trustee. Named individuals, resident within the State may also act as trustees, or the employer may appoint an independent firm that offers trusteeship services.

- The Administrator: The manager of the scheme.

- The Revenue Commissioners: Vet and approve each scheme.

- The Pensions Board: The statutory Government agency that supervises the registration, funding and operation of employer pension schemes under the provisions of the Pensions Act 1990.

- Pensions Ombudsman: Where a scheme member has a complaint of maladministration against the pension scheme trustees causing financial loss, or if there is a dispute on a matter of fact or a point of law relating to the scheme, the Pensions Ombudsman is the forum for the resolution of such disputes. The aggrieved member must outline his/her complaint in writing to the Pensions Ombudsman's office, which will investigate the matter and come to a decision. This decision is binding upon the parties, although they may appeal to the High Court within 21 days of the Pensions Ombudsman's determination.

Defined Benefit Schemes

Defined Benefit schemes, also known as "final salary" schemes, are where the employer promises to pay a pension that in most cases reflects your years of service and your income as you approach retirement. In many schemes if you have 40 years service, you will receive 2/3rds of final "pensionable salary" (i.e. 1/60th for each year of service).

Members are usually required to contribute about 5% of their income - a small proportion of the overall cost of funding a pension. If your promised benefits are likely to be less than the maximum benefits allowed by the Revenue you will usually be entitled to make Additional Voluntary Contributions (AVCs). These can be made either to the scheme itself on a group basis; or to a separate group AVC arrangement set up under trust; or to a PRSA AVC plan.

Unlike Personal Pensions and Defined Contribution schemes where each individual has his/her own investment account, under Defined Benefit schemes all the contributions are pooled together in a fund and the benefits are paid out of the fund. There is usually no need for the purchase of an annuity at retirement, therefore, unless the scheme is quite a small one.

In the past Defined Benefit schemes were generally considered to be the best type of pension plan for employees, particularly for those who remained with the same employer until retirement. They offer certainty with regard to the amount of pension income that you will receive on retirement. However, they are proving less popular with employers than in the past because of the extra costs involved in administering them and because of the lack of control the employer has over these costs. The employer is taking the investment risk in that if the investments do not achieve the desired levels of return the employer will have to increase its contributions.

Many Defined Benefit schemes have been changed to a Defined Contribution basis or closed to new employees in recent years. In many instances new employees have had to settle for Defined Contribution schemes instead.

There is likely to be an element of death benefit to provide protection for your family should you die before you reach retirement and many schemes, particularly the larger ones, also offer Disability or PHI cover. The disability payment will be made by the insurance company to the employer who will then pay it to the employee as income for as long as he/she is out of work or up to retirement age, when the pension will become payable.

Public sector pensions

Pension schemes in the Public Sector are normally arranged on a Defined Benefit basis and typically offer the following benefits at normal retirement age:

- A pension of 1/80th of final remuneration for each year of service, with a maximum pension of 40/80ths (50%), plus

- A separate lump sum benefit of 3/80ths of final remuneration for each year of service, with a maximum of 120/80ths.

For those who joined employee in the public sector since 1995, and who now pay the full employee PRSI rate, there is a reduction in their pensionable earnings to take account of their entitlement to the Contributory Social Welfare Pension at retirement.

Defined Contribution Schemes

Defined Contribution schemes are ones which the employer normally pays a specific percentage of the scheme member's salary into a pension fund, and the employee is usually obliged to contribute a similar or smaller amount. However, the employer makes no promises about the size of the actual pension that will be paid upon retirement. Each individual member has their own investment 'account' and the eventual retirement income will depend entirely upon:

- The number and level of contributions made over the years;

- The returns achieved by the investment fund(s) used;

- The term over which the retirement fund accumulates;

- The charges deducted from the retirement fund;

- The annuity rates prevailing at the date of retirement.

If you belong to a Defined Contribution scheme and you wish to ensure that you have an adequate pension income when you retire, you will need to take a more active role in monitoring the performance of your pension fund. Members will generally have the right to make AVCs or PRSA AVCs to help boost the eventual benefits.

There is also likely to be an element of **death benefit** (i.e. life assurance cover) to provide protection for your family should you die before you reach retirement. This cover may be on a defined benefit basis (e.g. 3 times basic salary).

Defined Contribution schemes may also include **Disability (or PHI)** cover as an integral part of the pension plan in order to offer a level of security for employees that will become ill before their pension 'accounts' have grown to worthwhile values. The PHI contract will guarantee a specific level of income in the event of a prolonged illness or injury and can also ensure that pension contributions will continue to be paid for the duration of the illness or injury, or up to normal retirement age.

Serious Illness cover is sometimes provided, particularly where PHI cover is not available, or too expensive. In the event of a claim the serious illness benefit has to be added to the individual member's pension fund and, if the individual qualifies for ill-health early retirement, the enhanced fund can be used to provide their retirement benefits. This applies to both ordinary employees and directors.

Contributory Schemes

If you are obliged to contribute to your company's pension scheme this scheme is a "Contributory Scheme" and your contributions are known as "Personal Contributions".

Personal Contributions are normally deducted from your salary/wages under the Revenue approved 'net pay' arrangement. This means that your contributions are deducted before the calculation of Income Tax and PRSI/Health Contribution and you receive immediate tax relief.

The normal limits apply in respect of your personal contributions for tax relief purposes (see page 184), although it is very unlikely that a scheme would oblige you to contribute these amounts. Under a normal contributory scheme the employees would be obliged to contribute approximately 5% of basic salary.

There are no limits on the contributions that your employer may make provided that the expected retirement benefits do not exceed the maximum approvable benefits allowed by the Revenue Commissioners.

Maximum Approvable Benefits

Under a Defined Benefit scheme the benefits that would be available upon retirement or earlier death are contained in the rules of the scheme and these will vary from scheme to scheme. Under a Defined Contribution scheme the benefits will be dependent upon the fund accumulated in the individual member's name. In either case the benefits payable at retirement or on earlier death may not exceed the maximum approvable benefit limits set down by the Revenue Commissioners, see page 230.

Where a 5% director chooses the Approved (Minimum) Retirement Fund or taxable cash option they must first ensure that the total fund accumulated would not result in a situation where the maximum benefits would be excluded had they gone down the traditional annuity purchase route.

Benefits on Leaving Service

If you leave employment any time before normal retirement age with two or more years 'qualifying service' you are entitled to a 'preserved benefit' under the terms of the pensions legislation. 'Qualifying service' means service as a member of your employer's pension scheme for retirement benefits - as against death benefits - or service applying to any benefits you may have transferred into your employer's pension scheme.

In the case of a Defined Contribution scheme, the preserved benefits are the benefits secured by all contributions, paid by your employer and yourself.

In the case of a Defined Benefit scheme, the preserved benefit is calculated in accordance with the following formula:

T/N x Pension expectation, based on scheme rules, where

T = scheme service for retirement benefits (i.e. qualifying service), and

N = total potential scheme service

Example

Mary commenced employment at age 18. She joined the pension scheme at age 25. She leaves service at age 45 and her remuneration is €30,000 p.a. Her pension expectation under the scheme is 2/3rds x final remuneration at age 65.

Calculation of "Preserved Benefit"

Final pension expectation: €20,000 (i.e. 2/3rds x €30,000).

T (Qualifying Service):		20 years
N (Total Potential Scheme Service):		40 years
Preserved Pension Benefits	=	20/40 x €20,000p.a.
	=	€10,000 p.a. at age 65.

The preserved benefit under a defined benefit scheme must be 'revalued' at the end of each calendar year from 1st January 1996 onwards, by the lesser of 4% or the increase in the CPI.

As an alternative to maintaining the preserved benefit in your old employer's scheme, you may elect, within two years of leaving service, to have the value of the preserved benefit transferred to:

- The pension scheme of a new employer;

- To a 'Buy out Bond' (Personal Retirement Bond);

- To a PRSA (certain restrictions apply)

The trustees of the scheme you have left also have the right to transfer the value of your preserved benefits to a "Buy out Bond", with or without your consent, after the end of the same two-year period, if the transfer value is less than the specific amount - currently this is €3,800.

Refund of personal contributions

Many contributory pension schemes will allow you take a refund of your personal pension contributions, with or without interest, when you leave employment. The Pensions (Amendment) Act 2002 curtailed the right to take a refund of contributions and early leavers with more than two years' Qualifying Service are no longer allowed to receive a refund of their personal contributions on leaving service. Instead they are automatically entitled to a preserved benefit as detailed earlier.

Where allowed refunds will normally be subject to tax at 20%, unless the refund is being transferred directly to a PRSA, when no tax is payable.

If you take a refund of your own contributions when you leave, your employer will also get back its contributions over this same period and you cannot retain any rights to pension benefits in respect of that employment.

Integration with Social Welfare Benefits

Very few Defined Benefit Schemes will reflect the maximum Revenue approvable pension benefits. Indeed, in order to help keep down the costs of the scheme many integrate their employees' Contributory Old Age Pension benefit entitlements with the pension scheme.

Typically, the objective is that the benefits from your employer's pension scheme and your Social Welfare pension at normal retirement age will amount to 2/3rds of your final remuneration, if you have 40 years service with the employer.

This objective is met by defining your 'pensionable salary' as actual salary less a deduction to allow for Social Welfare benefits. Typically, this deduction would be 1.5 times the Contributory Old Age Pension benefit for a single person in the case of a scheme that provides 1/60ths of final salary for each year of service (i.e. N/60ths scheme).

Example

Retirement Pension (January 2007) for a single person	€209.30 per week	€10,883.60
SW deduction for pensionable salary	€10,883.60 x 1.5	€16,325.40
John's Final Salary	€40,000	
John's Pensionable Salary	€40,000 - €16,325.40	€23,674.60
Expected Retirement Benefit	2/3rds x €23,674.60 p.a.	€15,783.07
Expected SW Retirement Pension		€10,883.60
Total Expected Pension (Scheme plus Social Welfare)	(i.e. €40,000 x 2/3rds)	**€26,666.67**

Some schemes will calculate the pension amount first and then reduce it by the amount of the Social Welfare pension. This will work out the same as the above example where you have 40 years service, but not as well where the service is less than 40 years.

Hanock Annuity

Occasionally, an employer may wish to provide a pension for a retiring employee/ director where no pension provision already exists, or to enhance an existing pension entitlement. In this situation, a Hanock Annuity, which can provide a retirement package similar to a conventional pension plan, can be bought by making a large contribution on behalf of the employee. The cost of purchasing the Hanock Annuity is treated as a business expense for the employer in the relevant year, and it is not treated as a benefit-in-kind from an employee's point of view.

Proprietary Directors

Proprietary Directors - defined as those who own or control **more than 20% of the voting rights** in their companies - are allowed to become members of occupational pension schemes but certain restrictions apply:

- As mentioned later in the section covering Revenue Maximum benefits, their definition of final remuneration is restricted.

- They must dispose of their shares in the company in the event of voluntary early retirement (i.e. retiring for reasons other than ill health before their Normal Retirement Age)

- On leaving the service of the company, they are not entitled to a refund of their contributions to the scheme under any circumstances.

Proprietary directors of investment companies cannot become members of any pension arrangements even if they are taxed under the PAYE system.

Directors who own or control more than 5% of the voting rights in their companies are entitled to avail of the retirement options – A(M)RF Investment and/or Taxable Cash (see page 189)

Thus, if you are a 5% Director in an Occupational Pension Plan you have a choice of two different options:

- You have a right to take the normal lump sum in accordance with your Occupational Pension Scheme Rules. This typically amounts to a maximum of 150% of final remuneration with 20 years service. However, if you choose this option your cannot avail of the ARF and Taxable Cash options. The scheme trustees must buy an annuity for you with the balance of your retirement capital..

- You can decide to opt for a tax-free lump sum of up to 25% of your accumulated fund and avail of the Approved Retirement Fund or Taxable Cash options (subject to the restrictions detailed earlier).

Additional Voluntary Contributions (AVCs) and PRSA AVCs

Very few employee pension schemes provide the maximum pension benefits allowed by the Revenue Commissioners. Therefore you need to check the position with regard to the benefits you are likely to receive from your own employer's scheme. If you don't have a member's handbook, get one and read it carefully. You may, depending on the rules of your scheme, be able to top up your pension benefits at your own expense by paying what are known as an Additional Voluntary Contributions (AVCs).

Reasons for commencing an AVC

If you are a member of a Defined Benefit scheme you may wish to top-up your scheme's benefits for a number of different reasons, such as:

- If your scheme provides 1/60th of your final remuneration per year of service and your service with your employer at retirement age will be less than 40 years your pension will fall short of the allowable maximum of 40/60ths.

- Your scheme may not provide you with the maximum allowable tax-free lump sum at normal retirement age – it may be based on basic salary rather than total earnings.

- Your pensionable salary may be adjusted to make allowance for your Social Welfare entitlements

- Your scheme may not take into account non-salary benefits like a company car, annual bonus, overtime etc.

- Your scheme may not make provision for a spouse's pension if you die in retirement, or that provision may be less the maximum allowable.

- Your retirement pension may not be indexed, to take account of cost of living rises..

- Your scheme may not provide for any death-in-service benefits or, at best, these are likely to fall short of the maximum allowable.

If you are a member of a Defined Contribution scheme chances are that the scheme is unlikely to provide you with the maximum allowable benefits due to the contributions over the years not being adequate to do so. In fact, the actual benefits may fall well short of your own expectations if you do not monitor them closely and make AVCs when necessary.

If you wish to retire early as a member of a Defined Benefit scheme your scheme rules are likely to give a much reduced pension, while in a Defined Contribution situation the capital accrued is unlikely to provide you with adequate benefits. While the Revenue rules do not actually allow you to fund for early retirement making AVCs for any of the reasons detailed above is allowed, and any moneys accumulated for these reasons can be used to help fund early retirement.

Tax relief

You can claim full tax relief at your marginal rate on your AVC and/or PRSA AVC payments subject to the normal limits (see page 184). The contribution limits include any other personal contributions you may be making to the main scheme and your resultant topped-up benefits may not exceed the maximum benefits permitted by the Revenue.

If your AVC and/or PRSA AVC contributions are deducted at source under the 'net pay' arrangement, full relief in respect of both PAYE and PRSI/Health Levy will be granted automatically. If you pay by direct debit you claim the income tax relief direct from your Inspector of Taxes by way of a credit, and at the end of the year you may also claim a refund of the PRSI relief due to on your contributions.

Where you pay a lump sum contribution, which brings your total personal contributions over the percentage limits allowed, the excess may be carried forward for relief into future years. You can also elect to backdate the tax relief on lump sum contributions made before October 31st in any year to the previous year, subject to the usual limits.

Retirement options

Those who contribute to AVCs and PRSA AVCs are entitled to exercise the ARF/AMRF Investment and/or Taxable Cash options in respect of the moneys accumulated in their AVC fund. They are not entitled to the 25% of the accumulated fund tax free cash option which applies to Personal Pension holders and 5% Directors. However, they are entitled to take up to 150% of final remuneration as per the Revenue Rules from the main scheme, or the AVC fund, or a mix of both, subject to the main scheme rules.

Making AVCs

An employee can make AVCs, with the agreement of the employer and/or the scheme trustee, on one or more of the following bases:

- As part of the main scheme;

- As part of a separate Group AVC scheme;

  or

- As an individual PRSA AVC plan taken out with an approved PRSA Provider, where the main scheme have been amended to allow them, or where the trustees of the main scheme indicate that they intend to change the rules.

Under these arrangements the contributions are normally made by salary deduction.

Stand alone PRSA AVC's

A very important development in recent times has been the introduction of 'stand-alone PRSA AVCs' to the market. The agreement of the trustees and employer is not required for these contracts to be put in place provided the PRSA provider does a check when the plan is being put in place and also at retirement that the maximum allowable retirement benefits are not being exceeded. The PRSA provider must also inform the trustees of the main scheme of each stand-alone PRSA AVC that has been put in place.

Buying back years

If your main pension scheme is arranged on a Defined Benefit basis then your group AVC arrangement may also be on this basis. This will give you the option of "buying back years". In other words, if you will be short of the full 40 years service at normal retirement age you will be able to make up the shortfall by contributing a predetermined percentage of your earnings by way of AVCs. The percentage will depend on the number of years you wish to make up, your age when you start contributing and the term to run to retirement age.

Both Defined Benefit schemes and Defined Contribution schemes often allow AVCs to be made on a Defined Contribution basis. You will not know the exact worth of your AVCs benefits until you get to retirement age, but you will be able to make on going estimates, based on certain assumptions.

If your scheme already makes provision for AVCs, you could simply contact your employer and ask about joining. Alternatively, if you would like to diversify your pension investment you could contact an independent life assurance and pensions broker and talk to him about PRSA AVCs.

If your scheme doesn't allow AVCs your employer must provide you with the facility to contribute to a Standard PRSA (i.e. a PRSA AVC) by salary deduction. Your employer should have informed you of the existence of this facility and should have given you details regarding the selected PRSA provider(s).

SSIA Pensions Incentive

As mentioned earlier in this chapter, the Finance Act 2006 introduced an incentive for those with maturing Special Savings Investment Accounts (SSIAs) to invest part or all of the maturity value of these accounts into pension plans.

The plan is limited to those whose individual gross income in the year preceding the year in which the SSIA matures was less than €50,000. For those with SSIAs maturing in 2007 the limit is based on 2006 income. However if gross income for 2006 has not been determined, the gross income for the previous year, plus 5%, can be used to determine if the €50,000 limit is satisfied.

The Exchequer will add €1 for every €3 invested by the qualifying individual to the investment, subject to a maximum contribution from the Exchequer of €2,500. In addition, the Exchequer will add that part of the exit tax charged on the SSIA maturity corresponding to the amount of the individual's pension contribution.

The pension contribution must be made within three months of the SSIA maturity date. The pension does not have to be put in place with the same institution as the SSIA was with. The SSIA provider will furnish a maturity statement, which the individual must give to the pension provider. The individual must also sign a declaration stating that his/her income does exceed the income rule; he/she will not claim tax relief under normal tax rules for amounts up to and including €7,500 invested under the incentive; and he/she will not use the incentive to replace any amounts he/she is already committed to contributing to a pension product.

For sums in excess of €7,500 the applicable exit tax credit is added by the Exchequer and the individual may able to claim tax relief, under normal income tax rules, for the excess of the investment over €7,500. In addition, the first €7,500 of the investment is not taken into account for the purpose of the limits set out on page 184.

The qualifying pension contributions can be made to

- PRSAs

- Personal Pensions

- AVCs / PRSA AVCs

For those whose earnings are less than €50,000 but who pay tax at the 41% rate normal pension tax relief will provide better value, than the incentive. However, if they are already using up the age-related limits shown on page 184. they could use this incentive to avail of the €2,500 contribution, plus exit tax refund, from the Exchequer.

Small Self-Administered Pension Schemes (SSAPS)

An SSAP is a type of occupational pension scheme, established by an employer where the company director(s) wish to have more choice and control over the investments made by the scheme. They are normally established for the benefit of the proprietary directors of the employing company and they can include one or more members. As with all occupational pension schemes, SSAPS provide a tax-efficient environment in which a company's profits can be invested - free from creditors should the company go into liquidation.

An SSAP can be established with one or more of the members acting as trustee. The trustees are responsible for and control all aspects of the SSAP's investment strategy and payment of retirement benefits.

In addition the trustees must include a professional trustee, known as "Pensioneer Trustee". This is a company or individual who is expert in pensions matters and is approved by the Revenue Commissioners. Pensioneer Trustees provide the legal documentation required to set up the SSAP, seek initial Revenue approval from the Revenue, and provide ongoing services to the arrangement. SSAPS can be either Defined Benefit or Defined Contribution schemes, although most are now arranged on a Defined Contribution basis.

The range of investment options is extensive and includes property, structured deposits, direct investment in stocks and shares etc. However, as a result of the Finance Act 2006, where a pension scheme makes any of a comprehensive list of investments or transactions the value of the amount invested is treated as a taxable pension payment to the relevant pension scheme member from the scheme, and that amount is then no longer part of the scheme. In addition, there are Revenue rules regarding the types of investment that a Small Self-administered Scheme can make and the pensioner trustee must ensure that these are adhered to.

There is a prohibition on pension schemes borrowing to invest, except for short-term liquidity purposes. However, the prohibition does not apply to a scheme which is a "one member arrangement." To qualify as a one member arrangement the scheme must be established for one person only and that person must have discretion over how the scheme funds are invested.

Maximum Allowable Benefits

As mentioned earlier the benefits payable by an occupational pension scheme at retirement or on earlier death may not exceed the maximum limits set down by the Revenue Commissioners. The calculation of some of the maximum benefits can be very complicated indeed for the ordinary individual to understand, particularly with regard to early retirement. Normally your pension provider or financial advisor will be able to explain the calculations of benefits to you, if the need arises.

Maximum Pension at Normal Retirement Age

In general, a maximum pension of at least 1/60th of final remuneration for each year of service with the employer up to a maximum of 40 years may be provided for an employee at normal retirement age. This is referred to as the n/60ths scale where "n" is the number of years service the employee will have had with the employer at retirement. However, if you have more than five years service with your employer an "uplifted 60ths" scale may be used, as follows:

Years of Service at Normal Retirement Age	Maximum pension as a fraction of your final remuneration
1	4/60ths
2	8/60ths
3	12/60ths
4	16/60ths
5	20/60ths
6	24/60ths
7	28/60ths
8	32/60ths
9	36/60ths
10 or more years	40/60ths (i.e. 2/3rds)

The **overall maximum pension** that can be provided for an individual retiring at Normal Retirement Age from his employer's pension scheme is the **lower** of:

- A pension based on the up-lifted scale shown above,

   and

- 2/3rds of final remuneration less any retained pension benefits,

if the resultant amount is greater than that calculated under the n/60ths scale.

Retained pension benefits are pension benefits arising from a previous occupational pension scheme or from any paid-up benefits under a personal pension plan or PRSA. Benefits accumulated through AVCs and PRSA AVCs in respect of the same employment are treated as benefits arising from the main scheme and not as retained benefits.

As a result of the Finance Act 2006 the overall maximum fund that an individual can have accumulated is €5 million, or whatever amount he/she had accumulated as at Dec 7th 2005 if larger.

Final remuneration

Final remuneration may be defined as any one of the following:

A 1. Remuneration for any one of the five years before the retirement date. "Remuneration" means basic pay for the year in question plus the average of any fluctuating emoluments (e.g. bonuses, over-time payments etc.) over a suitable period, usually three years or more

or

B The average of the total emoluments of any three or more consecutive years ending not earlier than 10 years before your normal retirement age

or

C The rate of basic pay at the date of retirement, or on any date within the year ending on that date, plus the average of fluctuating emoluments over three or more consecutive years ending with the date of retirement.

Notes:

- **"Remuneration"** includes all income and benefits that are assessable to income tax under PAYE in the relevant employment e.g. BIK on a company car can be included as part of your final remuneration.

- In the case of the first two definitions each year's remuneration may be increased in line with the Consumer Price Index from the end of the relevant year up to your retirement date. This is referred to as 'dynamising' final remuneration.

- If you own or control more than 20% of the voting rights in your company (i.e. "a proprietary director") you can only use definition 2 above when calculating your final remuneration. This is to stop controlling directors substantially inflating their earnings in the last years before retirement in order to increase the tax-free lump sum they can take from their pension.

Calculate your Pension

It's your responsibility!

Visit the online pensions calculator at
www.pensionsboard.ie

The Pensions Calculator allows you to estimate the amount of money you would need to contribute to your pension, in relation to your age and current yearly salary, to end up with the level of pension you would like to receive in retirement.

The time for action is now, so talk to your employer, trade union, bank, insurance company, building society or financial advisor about starting your pension today.

An Bord Pinsean -
The Pensions Board
Authority for Pensions

Locall Number 1890 65 65 65

Maximum Tax Free Cash Lump Sum at Normal Retirement Age

When you retire from an occupational pension scheme you can normally convert part of your pension benefits into a tax-free lump sum. In general, a maximum lump sum amount of at least 3/80ths of final remuneration for each year of service up to a maximum 40 years, or 1.5 times your final remuneration, can always be provided at normal retirement age. However, if you have more than eight years service with your employer, an "uplifted 80ths" scale may be used as follows:

Years of Service at Normal Retirement Age	Maximum Tax Free Lump Sum as a Fraction of Final Remuneration
1 - 8	3/80ths for each year
9	0/80ths
10	36/80ths
11	42/80ths
12	48/80ths
13	54/80ths
14	63/80ths
15	72/80ths
16	81/80ths
17	90/80ths
18	99/80ths
19	108/80ths
20 or more years	120/80ths

The **overall maximum tax-free lump sum** that can be provided for an individual with more than 8 years service in the employment from which he/she is retiring is the lower of:

- ·a lump sum based on the up-lifted scale shown above,

   and

- 1.5 times final remuneration less any retained lump sum benefits,

if the resultant amount is greater than that calculated under the 3n/80ths scale.

Retained lump sum benefits are benefits arising from a previous occupational pension scheme or from any paid-up benefits under a Personal Pension plan or PRSA. Benefits accumulated through AVCs and PRSA AVCs in respect of the same employment are treated as benefits arising from the main scheme and not as retained benefits.

Normally the tax-free cash cannot be taken without also taking the pension benefits.

Maximum tax-free cash figure of €1.25 million also applies.

Maximum Ill Health Early Retirement

Whereas there is no specific definition of ill health in the Revenue pension guidelines, incapacity is defined as follows:

"Physical or mental deterioration which is bad enough to prevent the individual from following his normal employment, or which very seriously impairs his earning capacity. It does not mean simply a decline in energy or ability."

If you retire early due to ill health, the maximum pension you can receive is the equivalent of the one you could have expected to receive had you worked until your normal retirement age.

Example

John commenced employment with his current employer at age 35. The normal retirement age under the scheme rules is 65 years.

Now, five years later, John aged 40 retires on grounds of ill health, after suffering a serious illness. He has no retained pension benefits. His final remuneration prior to ill health was €50,000 per annum.

John would have had 30 years of service to normal retirement age, entitling him to a maximum pension on the "up-lifted 60ths" scale of 40/60ths of final remuneration. His maximum ill health retirement pension is:

40/60ths x €50,000   =   €33,333 per annum

In the case of early retirement due to ill health, "final remuneration" is calculated by a reference to the period preceding actual retirement.

If John were a member of a Defined Contribution scheme he is very unlikely to have accumulated enough capital to be able to provide that level of benefit. This is where his PHI cover is likely to be called on to provide him with an income until normal retirement age, when the pension benefits would become payable. It would be important to have Contribution Protection cover in place to ensure the continuation of John's pension contributions up to retirement age.

In the case of a Defined Benefit scheme only the very large schemes would be able to afford to pay him this level of benefit at such an early age and PHI cover would probably be required also.

If you are retiring in 'exceptional circumstances of serious ill health' (i.e. your expectation of life is less than 12 months) the Revenue will allow you to take your pension entitlement in cash form. The non tax-free part of the full lump sum taken in these circumstances is liable to income tax at 10%.

Maximum Pension on Voluntary Early Retirement

Where early retirement is taking place after age 50 other than due to ill health, then the maximum immediate pension allowed is the greater of:

- 1/60th of final salary remuneration for each year of actual service completed, **or**

- The pension worked out by the following formula -N / NS x P

N = The actual number of years service to early retirement,

NS = The number of years of potential service to normal retirement age.

P = The maximum pension allowable if the scheme member had remained in service to your normal retirement age.

Example

John joined his employer at age 35. The normal retirement age under the scheme rules is 65. John is now aged 50 with a salary of €40,000 p.a. and he elects to take voluntary early retirement with his employer's consent.

N is 15, actual years service completed to age 50.

NS is 30, Potential Service to Normal Retirement Age.

P is 2/3rds of final remuneration – Revenue maximum pension.

So John's maximum early retirement pension is to be the greater of:

> 15/60ths x €40,000 = €10,000 per annum.

> **and**

> 15/30 x 2/3rds x €40,000 = €13,333 per annum.

If the individual has less than 10 years service completed by the date of early retirement the maximum immediate pension is the lowest of:

- N/NS x P, as calculated above,

- The maximum pension as calculated on the uplifted scale shown earlier, taking account of actual service to date, and

- 2/3rds of final remuneration less retained pension benefits.

While the above outlines the maximum pension benefits that may be allowed by Revenue on early retirement, it would be rare for most employers to provide this level of benefits on early retirement. Typically, the rules of a Defined Benefit scheme would provide for the calculation of benefits based on the n/60ths scale, related to service to the date of retirement, with penalties for early retirement. For example, these penalties could mean a reduction of 0.3% per month for each month between of the period between the date of early retirement and the normal retirement age (i.e. a 36% reduction if you are retiring 10 years early).

For Defined Contribution schemes the early retirement benefits would be dependent on the fund accumulated at that stage and, in reality it is very unlikely that this would be sufficiently large to exceed the Revenue maximum allowable figures.

Maximum Tax Free Lump Sum on Early Retirement

In the case of ill health early retirement, the maximum tax-free lump sum is similar to that available had you remained in your employer's service up to normal retirement age. This would give up to a maximum of 1.5 times final remuneration at the date of retirement, if you were to have had 20 years service at normal retirement age.

In the case of voluntary early retirement the maximum tax-free lump sum is normally calculated by taking the **greater** of:

- 3/80ths of remuneration for each year of actual service, **or**

- the sum calculated in accordance with the following formula - N/NS x LS

  N   =   number of years service completed up to early retirement

  NS   =   the potential number of years that could have been completed by normal retirement.

  P   =   the maximum allowable tax-free lump sum which could have be provided at normal retirement age, after the restriction for any retained lump sum benefits where relevant.

In the example earlier John could get the greater of:

      15 x 3/80 x €40,000 = €22,500 **and**

      15/30 x 1.5 x €40,000 = €30,000

      N = 15   John's actual Service

      NS = 30   Potential Service

      LS = 150% of final remuneration   Revenue maximum

In this example **€30,000** could be taken.

If the individual has **less than 20 years** service completed by the date of early retirement the maximum immediate lump sum benefit is the **lowest** of:

- N/NS x LS, as calculated above

- The maximum lump sum on the uplifted scale as shown earlier, taking account of actual service completed to the date of early retirement, **and**

- 150% of final remuneration less retained lump sum benefits.

Of course if a tax-free lump sum is taken on voluntary early retirement the early retirement pension benefit has to be reduced by the pension equivalent of the tax-free lump sum.

In the case of Defined Benefit schemes, the lump sum on voluntary early retirement may be restricted by the scheme rules; in the case of Defined Contribution schemes taking the tax-free cash may actually deplete the retirement fund completely, leaving no capital to provide an income.

Maximum Death-in-Service Benefits

A pension scheme may provide two benefits if you die in service before normal retirement age.

The maximum allowable **lump sum benefit** is four times your remuneration at the date of death, together with a refund of any personal contributions to the scheme with "reasonable interest". This benefit would be payable to the trustees who, under the rules of the scheme, would have some discretion as to which of your dependants should receive the proceeds.

The maximum allowable **death-in-service pension,** which could be paid to your spouse, or to any one or all of your dependants is 100% of the maximum pension that you could have received if you had retired on grounds of ill health at the date of your death.

Maximum Death-in-Retirement Benefit

Many pension schemes provide a guaranteed period of pension payments after your retirement in the event that you die early. This guaranteed period may be up to 10 years. If the guaranteed period is five years or less the remaining instalments may be paid at the Trustees' discretion in a lump sum to your dependants. If the guarantee is more than five years, the outstanding instalments will be paid in pension form to your beneficiaries.

Spouses' and dependants' pensions may be provided in addition to this guarantee. The maximum pension that may be provided for your spouse, or for any one or all of your dependants is 100% of the maximum pension that could have been provided for you at retirement.

The term "maximum pension" is defined as the maximum pension at normal retirement age, increased in line with the Consumer Price Index from the date of retirement up to the date of death.

Maximum Pension increases

Generally speaking, a pension may be increased in line with the rise in the Consumer Price Index each year. Alternatively, increases at a rate of 3% per annum compound may be promised and paid, regardless of the Consumer Price Index. However, if your pension at retirement was less than the maximum Revenue allowable pension at retirement age, this pension may be increased at a faster rate than the increase in the Consumer Price Index until it reaches the level of the maximum allowable pension.

Retirement Funding Options

The following pages give a short synopsis of the retirement funding choices available to different types of individuals based on their employment status. We cannot give advice as to the best options for any individual to take. All we can say is that if you feel you do not have the necessary expertise yourself seek professional advice from a qualified, independent financial adviser.

Whereas Standard PRSAs were introduced to provide low cost pension funding, the long- term value of other contract types may actually be better depending on the charging structure etc., involved. Just make sure that all charging structures and the other options such as Life Cover, Disability Cover and Contribution Protection are fully explained.

Your advisor should complete a thorough a personal financial planning review (i.e a 'fact-find') with you to ascertain information regarding your financial planning needs, your investment risk tolerance levels etc.

Self Employed

- If you are self-employed and not operating your business through a company you will be entitled to contribute to PRSA contracts and/or to Personal Pension plans. You will be entitled to contribute to both PRSAs and Personal Pension Plans simultaneously, subject to the overall age-related limits for tax relief purposes.

- If you wish to have life assurance cover as part of your plan you can put this in place under a Personal Pension plan either on an "inclusive" or "exclusive" of fund basis under a Section 785 'associated' contract. Separate Section 785 cover can also be arranged on a "stand alone" basis and tax relief obtained.

- Separate Section 785 'stand alone' cover can be arranged where life cover is to be arranged with a PRSA. Life cover costs cannot be taken from of PRSA contributions or funds.

- 'Contribution Protection' cover cannot be put in place under a PRSA plan as it can under a Personal Pension plan.

Proprietary Directors

- If you are operating your business through a company, you and your company, on your behalf, are entitled to contribute to Occupational/Executive Pension arrangements or to PRSA plans. Unlike an Occupational/Executive Pension arrangement, a PRSA contract is individually owned by you and is not arranged under trust. If you are already contributing to a Personal Pension plan you may continue to make contributions but you will not receive tax relief on your contributions while your company is contributing to an occupational/executive plan on your behalf.

- The total contributions (i.e. your own and your company's) that can be made to occupational/executive pension arrangements are much higher than those allowed under PRSAs and Personal Pensions. Having your company contribute to a pension arrangement on your behalf is an excellent way of extracting money from your company on a tax-efficient basis.

- If you are already a member of an Occupational/Executive pension arrangement you can make personal contributions to that arrangement and/or to a group Additional Voluntary Contribution (AVC) scheme and/or to an AVC PRSA.

- If you wish to have life assurance cover as part of your plan you cannot put this in place under PRSA legislation.

- 'Contribution Protection' cover cannot be put in place under a PRSA plan

Employees

It is important here to make a distinction between those who are and are not "excluded employees".

If you are an "Excluded Employee"

- You may take out PRSAs and, if you are not a member of an occupational pension scheme, you can take out a Personal Pension. If you are a member of an occupational pension scheme you can only take out a PRSA if it is an AVC PRSA.

- If you are not a member of an occupational pension scheme your employer is obliged to provide you with access to at least one Standard PRSA contract through salary/wages deduction..

- If you are not a member of an occupational pension scheme your employer may contribute to your PRSA contract, but is not obliged to do so.

- If you wish to have life assurance cover as part of your plan life cover costs cannot be taken from of PRSA contributions or funds.

If you are not an "Excluded Employee"

- The occupational pension scheme of which you are a member may allow you to make AVCs and/or PRSA AVCs, or you may put a 'standalone PRSA AVC' in place.

Pensions and Marriage Break-Up

The break-up of a marriage can impact on an individual's retirement benefits or on any associated benefits that may be payable on death before retirement.

The Family Law Act 1995 and the Family Law (Divorce) Act 1996, provide for a range of ancillary orders that can be made on or after

- A decree of judicial separation, **or**

- A decree of divorce.

With regard to pensions and associated death benefits the applicable ancillary order is a Pension Adjustment Order. Either of the spouses involved, or a person acting on behalf of a dependant child, can apply to the courts for the order to be made. The order can also be sought where either dissolution of marriage or a legal separation were granted after August 1st 1986 under the laws of a foreign country or jurisdiction, which is recognised as valid in the State.

Two important points to note are:

- The courts will not make the order automatically – the individual has to apply

- While the courts are not obliged to make the order once the individual has applied, they must endeavour to ensure that proper provision is made for each spouse, rather than just the applicant spouse, having regard to the circumstances involved.

If granted by the courts a Pension Adjustment Order can compel the trustees (or the administrator if no trust applies) of the pension arrangement to:

- Pay a designated part of the individual's retirement benefit to either

  - His/her spouse, or the personal representative of the spouse in the case of the spouse's death, **or**

  - A person specified in the order, for the benefit of a dependant child, for as long as that child remains a dependant child.

Pay a specified percentage of whatever death-in-service benefits there are, when they become payable to

  - The spouse, **or**

  - A person specified under the order for the benefit of a dependant child, **or**

  - To both the above, in such proportions as decided by the courts.

The Family Law Acts provide guidance as to the factors that the courts should take into account when making the order and they lay down formulae for the calculation of the designated parts of the benefits payable.

12

Employee benefits & shares

Major changes came into effect on 1st January 2004, in respect of the taxation of benefits from employment.

A summary of these changes are as follows:

- PAYE is now charged through the payroll system on taxable benefits provided by the employer. Prior to the 1st January 2004 the amount of the taxable benefit was "coded in" under the PAYE system i.e. the employees tax credits were reduced, increasing the tax payable on the employees salary to such an extent that it covered the tax payable on the benefits provided.

- Both employee and employer PRSI now applies to Benefits in Kind

- Specific rules for arriving at the taxable value of benefits were introduced in order to establish an amount of "notional pay", which enables the benefit to be taxed through the payroll.

- The compliance risk, in respect of both the reporting requirements and tax exposure, has moved from the employee to the employer. Prior to the 1st January 2004 the responsibility for declaring and paying the tax on benefits provided from your employment rested with the employee. From the 1st January 2004 it is now the employers responsibility to deduct income tax and PRSI on any taxable benefits provided and pay this over to the Revenue Commissioners.

Where the amount of salary paid to an employee is insufficient to collect the full amount of PAYE/PRSI due on the "notional pay", the employer must pay any shortfall to the Collector General.

Any shortfall in PAYE (but not PRSI), paid by an employer must be recovered from the employee. Any amount not recovered by the 31st March following the end of the tax year in which the benefit is received, is treated as a taxable benefit in the following year and liable to PAYE and PRSI. Resulting in a double charge to tax.

Small Benefits

These new rules do not apply to every single benefit paid to staff. Where an employer provides a benefit of less than €250 per annum to employees no PAYE/PRSI will apply. If the value of the benefit exceeds €250, PAYE/PRSI will apply to the full benefit.

Best Estimates

In order for the employer to calculate the PAYE/PRSI on benefits provided, they must make a "best estimate" of notional pay in respect of certain benefits. For instance if a company values the use of a company car at €10,000 per annum, then this is the "notional pay" amount.

However, in many cases e.g. on the provision of vouchers, the employer will be aware of the exact value of the benefits provided. This again will be called the "notional pay" amount.

The PAYE/PRSI due on the benefits should normally be deducted in the month the benefit is provided. However, in certain cases e.g. the provision of a company car the liability to PAYE/PRSI may be spread out over the full tax year.

Valuation Rules

Except where there are specific rules e.g. company car (see page 245), the amount of the taxable benefit (i.e. the notional pay), which will be liable to PAYE/PRSI will be the higher of:

- The expense incurred by the employer in connection with the provision of the benefit to the employee

  or

- The value realisable by the employee for the benefit in money or money's worth.

Less any amount made good to the employer by the employee.

Payments made on behalf of the employee

In the case of the payment made on behalf of an employee e.g. club subscription, it is the expenses incurred by the employer (less any reimbursement by the employee direct to the employer) that is to be taken into account for PAYE and PRSI purposes.

Payment of Medical Insurance

In the case of medical insurance premiums, the cost to the employer is based on the gross premium, before tax relief, at source. The employee then receives tax relief at the standard rate on the gross premium amount.

To claim the relief due you should notify your local tax office of the relevant details or complete an annual tax return form and send it to your local tax office.

Company Cars

Where a company car is available for the private use of an employee, the employee is liable to PAYE and PRSI in respect of the car.

The "notional pay" to which PAYE and PRSI applies, is on the cash equivalent of the car. This cash equivalent is normally calculated at 30% of the "original market value" (OMV) of the car supplied. This calculation is applied regardless of whether the car is acquired new or second hand. However, this 30% can be reduced for high business mileage as follows;

Annual Business Mileage	2006	2007
15,000 or less	30%	30%
15,001 – 20,000	24%	24%
20,001 – 25,000	18%	18%
25,001 – 30,000	12%	12%
30,001 or over	6%	6%

Travel to and from work is considered private use.

Calculation of notional pay

Step 1:   Find out the original market value of the car.

The 'OMV' of the car is usually as the list price of the car including duties, VRT and VAT, when it was first registered less a 10% discount.

Step 2:   Ascertain the business mileage for the year, and calculate the cash equivalent using the appropriate percentage (see page 245)

Example

> You are provided with a company car on the 1st January 2007. The OMV of the car is €35,000, and your business mileage is less than 15,000 a year. You make no payments towards the running costs of the car.
>
> Your "notional pay" in respect of the company car would be calculated as follows;
>
> $$€35,000 \times 30\% = €10,500$$
>
> If you are paid weekly, €201.92 "notional pay" (€10,500 / 52) will be added to your normal salary and income tax and PRSI will be applied to this amount.

Step 3:   Deduct amounts paid by the employee to the employer in respect of the car. Taking the above example, but assuming you make a payment directly to your employer of €1,000 in respect of the running cost of the car, you also pay all your own private fuel. Your BIK would work out as follows:

	Notional pay as per previous example	€10,500
Less:	The running expenses paid directly to employer	€ 1,000
	Notional pay amount	€ 9,500

There is no deduction for the private fuel, as you did not make this payment directly to your employer.

In some cases an employee will pay a lump sum contribution towards the purchase of a company car. In this case, the lump sum is deducted from the "notional pay" in the first year the car is provided. This deduction is only allowed in the first year.

20% reduction in BIK

Your BIK charge can be reduced by 20%, provided all of the following conditions are met:

- You spend 70% or more of your time away from your place of work.

- Your annual business mileage exceeds 5,000 miles p.a. but does not exceed 15,000 miles p.a.

- You work an average of at least 20 hours per week.

- You keep a log book, detailing the mileage, nature and location of business and amount of time spent away from your employer's business premises. This log must be available for inspection by your Inspector of Taxes, if requested and must be certified by your employer as being correct.

End of year adjustment

The exact business mileage for an employee cannot be determined until the end of a tax year. So during the year employers should make a best estimate of the business mileage for the year, based on available information and records. However, prior to the end of the tax year this best estimate should be reviewed to ensure that it is correct. Any necessary adjustment should then be made before the end of the tax year.

Meaning of "car"

A car is defined as all cars and includes crew cars and jeeps.

Car available for less than a full year

If a car is only available for part of the tax year, e.g. when you first get the car or the year you leave employment with the company, the business mileage threshold and percentage cash equivalent used are calculated by reference to the following percentage;

Number of days in the tax year the car is available for private use   x 100
365

Example

You receive a company car on 1st October 2006. The original market value (OMV) of the car is €25,000 and the company pays all the running expenses. Your business mileage for the period from 1st October 2006 to 31st December 2006 is 7,500 miles.

The percentage is calculated as follows:

Number of days you have the company car is 92 days
$\frac{92 \times 100}{365}$ = 25.20%

The adjusted business mileage and percentage BIK change apply the 25.20% to the normal rates as follows:

Annual Business Mileage	Reduced % charge
3,780 or less	7.56%
3,781 - 5,040	6.05%
5,041 - 6,300	4.54%
6,301 - 7,560	3.02%
7,561 and over	1.51%

The "notional pay" will be calculated as follows:

€25,000 x 3.02% = €755

Company Car or Mileage Allowance?

Many people now look at the option of using their own car and motor bikes for business and taking a mileage allowance for business travel instead of a company car.

To see which option is best for you, first work out how much your car costs;

Motoring costs

Each year the AA publishes a leaflet entitled "Motoring Costs" in which they divide motoring costs into two distinct categories:

- Standing Charges
- Operating Costs

A Standing Charge is any fixed annual cost which remains the same no matter how many miles you drive. An Operating Cost, on the other hand, is a cost which is directly related to the number of miles you travel, say for example, petrol.

Of course, your overall motoring costs depend to a large extent on the type of car you drive, your age, driving experience etc., but to make everything as straightforward as possible, we have outlined below what the AA estimated were the average Standing Charges for a 1001 - 1250cc and for a 1751 - 2000cc car.

Now that you can identify the Standing Charges, we next outline what the AA estimated were your Operating Costs in June 2006 expressed in cents per kilometre.

By referring to these two tables, you can see quickly that if you own a 1001-1250cc car, drive 15,000 kilometres per annum between Standing Charges and Operating Costs. The AA estimates it will cost you an average of €9,995 p.a. or €192 p.w. The corresponding figure for a 1751-2000cc car is €12,480 p.a. or €240 p.w.

Standing charges

Item	1001 - 1250cc	1751 - 2000cc
	€	€
Car Tax	€251	€511
Insurance	€940	€1,301
Driving Licence	€3	€3
Depreciation	€1,858	€2,525
Interest Costs	€409	€560
Garage/Parking	€3,761	€3,761
NCT Test	€18	€18
AA Subscription	€120	€120
Total Standing Charges	**€7,360**	**€8,799**

Operating costs (in cents)

Item	1001 - 1250cc	1751 - 2000cc
	€	€
Petrol *	8.761c	12.332c
*Based on 117.2c per litre. For each cent more or less add or subtract	+/- 0.74c	+/- 0.108c
Oil	0.111c	0.172c
Tyres	1.474c	2.195c
Servicing	1.761c	2.321c
Repairs & Replacement	5.457c	7.523c
Total Operating Cost per kilometre	**17.564c**	**24.543c**

Civil service mileage rates

The Civil Service Mileage rates for cars and motor bikes effective from 1st July 2006 were as follows:

Cars

	Rates per kilometre		
	€ **Under 1200 cc**	€ **1201 to 1500cc**	€ **1501cc and over**
Up to 6,437 km	52.16c	61.66c	78.32c
6,437 km & over	26.97c	30.96c	36.65c

Motor bikes

Rates per kilometre		
€ **Under 150 cc**	€ **151 to 250cc**	€ **251cc and over**
15.35c	21.46c	28.33c

Provided your employer agrees and provided you do not charge mileage in excess of the Civil Service Mileage Rates, these charges will be tax free into your hand.

Evaluating which is best for you in your particular circumstances can be a complex exercise and we suggest that you go about it as follows:
- First estimate your annual Standing Charges (A).
- Estimate your Operating Costs per mile (B).
- Estimate your total annual mileage (C).
- Calculate how much of your total annual mileage is business mileage.

From A, B and C above you can calculate your total annual cost. By simply applying the Civil Service mileage rate to your annual business mileage you can calculate the value of reimbursements your employer may pay you tax-free.

Taking a salary increase instead of a company car

Another consideration is salary in lieu of a company car. For example, if you do relatively low business mileage and are considering the option of giving up the company car in favour of a salary increase coupled with the ability to claim a small mileage allowance. The question you must ask yourself is "Will I lose money"? The example on page 252 will help you to answer this important question.

Car Pools

Cars included in car pools are treated as not being available for an employee's private use and no tax liability arises on the provision of a car from a car pool provided all of the following conditions are met:

- The car is made available to, and actually used by, more than one employee and in the case of each of them it is made available to them by reason of their employment, but is not ordinarily used by any one of the employees to the exclusion of the others.

- Private use by each employee is incidental to other use.

- The car is not normally kept overnight at, or in the vicinity of, any of the employee's homes.

Company Van

If an employee has the use of a company van for private use the Benefit in Kind is calculated at 5% of the OMV of the van.

No BIK will be charged on company vans were the following conditions are met:

- The van is supplied to the employee for the purposes of the employee's work.

- The employee is required by the employer to bring the van home after work.

- Apart from travelling from work to home and back to work, other private use of the van by the employee is forbidden by the employer and there is no other private use.

Example

You have a company car with an original market value of €25,000. You do 8,000 business kilometres a year, assuming you pay tax at 42% (41% in 2007), your BIK will work out as follows with a company car.

	€
Original Market Value of Car	€25,000
BIK @ 30%	€7,500
Your increased tax bill (€7,500@ 44%) (Income tax @ 42% + Health Levies @ 2%)	€3,300

*Assuming your salary income exceeds the threshold for PRSI (see page 144).

The estimated cost of running your car is €9,200 per annum.

You have the option of giving up your company car, taking a salary increase of €3,500 and a mileage allowance of €5,500. (8,000 kilometres @ 68.75c per kilometre). Should you take it?

	€
Running Cost of Car	€9,200
Salary Increase of €3,500 (Net of Tax @ 42% + Levies @ 2%)	(€1,960)
Mileage Allowance	(€5,500)
Net Annual Cost of Car	**€1,740**

Your position

The cost to you of the company car is €3,300 per annum i.e. your additional tax bill. If you provided your own car and you got an increase in salary of €3,500 and mileage allowance of €5,500, the net cost of running your car will work out at €1,740. A saving of €1,560 per annum.

253

- In the course of their work, the employee must spend at least 80% of their time away from the premises of the employer to which they are attached.

Business Kilometres involving travel direct from/to home

Where an employee proceeds on a business journey directly from home to a temporary place of work (rather than commencing that business journey from his/her normal place of work) or returns home directly, the business kilometres should be calculated by reference to the lesser of :

- The distance between home and the temporary place of work or

- The distance between the normal place of work and the temporary place of work.

Preferential loans

A preferential loan is a loan made to an employee by their employer (directly or indirectly) on which they pay no interest or interest at a rate lower than the specified rate.

The Benefit in Kind for tax purposes is the difference between the interest paid (if any) and interest calculated at the specified rate. However, the amount of interest assessed to tax will qualify for mortgage interest relief as "deemed interest" subject to the normal limits.

For the tax year 2006 the specified rate for a loan used to purchase, repair or improve your main residence is 3.5%. For other loans the specified rate is 11%. (see example on page 255)

Budget 2007:   The specified rate has changed to 4.5% on a residential loan and to 12% on other loans to take effect from 1st January 2007.

Example

You are married and joined the bank in January 1998. In April 1998, you were granted a preferential house purchase loan of €60,000 @ 3% p.a. You pay tax at 42%, your position is as follows for 2006:

		2006 €
	Preferential House Purchase Loan	€60,000
	Interest Paid €60,000 @ 3%	€1,800
	Benefit-In-Kind (BIK) €60,000 @ 3.5%	€2,100
Less:	Interest Paid	€1,800
	Taxable Benefit in Kind	€300
	Interest Relief for Tax Purposes	
	Interest Paid	€1,800
	Deemed Interest Paid	€300
		€2,100

Accommodation

If your employer provides you with accommodation rent free or at a reduced rate and this accommodation is not necessitated by your job, then a taxable benefit arises. This benefit is normally the market rate of the annual rent which could be obtained on a yearly letting of the accommodation.

Any amounts paid by the employee to the employer by way of rent are deductible from the taxable benefit.

Relocation costs - relating to employment.

Strictly, the cost of relocating your home is a personal expense. However, if it is a requirement of your job to move home and certain procedures are followed, your employer may compensate you for these costs in a tax free manner.

The types of expenses covered are:

- Auctioneer's fees, solicitor's fees and stamp duty arising from moving home.

- Furniture removal costs.

- Storage charges.

- Insurance of furniture and items in transit.

- Cleaning stored furniture.

- Travelling expenses on removal.

- Temporary subsistence allowance while looking for new accommodation.

Formal Requirements

- The cost must be borne directly by the employer in respect of actual expenses incurred by you.

- The expenses must be reasonable.

- The payments must be properly controlled.

Receipts must be provided (apart from temporary subsistence), and your Inspector of Taxes must be satisfied that moving home is necessary for your job.

Share schemes

More and more employers are looking at Share Schemes as a way of rewarding their employees. Some, of these schemes attract favourable tax treatment provided certain conditions are met.

Approved Profit Share Scheme

An Approved Profit Sharing Scheme allows a full or part time employee or a full time director to receive shares tax free from their employer up to an annual limit of €12,700 provided certain conditions are met.

A trust is set up by the company, this trust must purchase shares in the company on behalf of the employees with funds received from the company. The trust must hold the shares for two years before transferring them to the employee, who must then hold the shares for three years after receiving them. If the shares are disposed of by the employee before the end of the three year period income tax is charged on the lower of:

* The market value of the shares at the date they were initially apportioned to the employee

  or

* The sale proceeds from the sale of the shares

However, if the employee/director ceases employment or reaches retirement age within the three year period, income tax will be payable at 50% of the lower of the above.

Approved Profit Sharing schemes are tax efficient for both the employee and employer as the employee can receive shares tax free up to an annual limit of €12,700 and the employer can offset the cost of the shares against the company's profits.

Employee Share Ownership Trusts

Employee Share Ownership Trusts (ESOT's) were first introduced in the Finance Act 1997.

A company can place shares for a maximum of 20 years in an ESOT. They are designed to work in conjunction with profit sharing scheme as shares can be released from the ESOT each year into the company's profit sharing scheme.

The €12,700 tax free limit which applies to Profit Sharing Scheme can be increased to a once-off €38,100 after 10 years in respect of shares previously held in an ESOT provided;

- The shares have been transferred to the Trustees of an approved profit sharing scheme by the Trustees of an ESOT;

and

- In the first five years of the establishment of the ESOT, 50% of the shares retained by the Trustees were pledged as security on borrowings.

- No shares which were pledged as security for borrowings by Trustees of the ESOT were previously transferred to the Trustees of a profit sharing scheme.

Stock Options

A Stock Option arises where a company grants to its employees or directors an option to subscribe for shares in the company at a preferential price. A taxable benefit arises when the predetermined share price is less than the market value.

The amount liable to tax is the difference between the market value of the shares at the exercise date and the price you actually pay. This liability arises at the date you exercise the option.

If the options are capable of being exercised more than seven years after they were granted, income tax may also arise on the date the option is granted. The amount liable to income tax is the difference between the market value of the shares at the date the option was granted and the option price. Any tax paid at this early stage can be offset against the total tax liability when the option is eventually exercised.

Capital Gains Tax may also be payable on the shares if they increase in value from the date you exercise the option. Any amounts assessable to income tax are deemed to be part of the cost for Capital Gains Tax purposes.

Example

> You are granted an option in August 2002 to purchase 2,000 shares in your employer's company at a future date for €7 per share. When you exercise your options in August 2006 the share price was €9 per share.
>
> | The amount liable to income tax in 2006 | | € |
> |---|---|---|
> | | Market value of shares in August 2006 | €9 x 2,000 = €18,000 |
> | **Less:** | Option price | €7 x 2,000 = €14,000 |
> | | Benefit liable to income tax | €4,000 |
>
> This tax would be payable 30 days after the date of exercise of the stock options.

Stock options and non resident

Prior to the 2005 Finance Act, if you were granted a stock option you are liable to income tax when you exercise the option regardless of your resident position at the date of exercise.

If you were granted an option before you came to Ireland, but exercised it after your arrival here no income tax liability would arise in Ireland provided there was no connection between the Irish employment and the granting of the option and no tax planning or avoidance scheme was involved.

The 2005 Finance Act amended the provision regarding stock options and residence subject to a commencement order which at the time of publication had not been issued. Income tax will be charge in cases where the recepient was not resident in the State when the option was granted.

Returns by employers

Employers must provide certain information to the Revenue Commissioners about the stock options granted and exercised by employees.

Stock Options and Self-Assessment

If you receive stock options from your employer, you are liable to tax under self-assessment in respect of the profit arising from the stock options. Under self-assessment you must pay your preliminary tax by the due date and also submit your income tax return by the relevant filing date. For the tax year 2006 the return filing date is 31st October 2007.

If you don't adhere to these dates, surcharges and interest will apply. The onus lies with the taxpayer to submit their tax return and to pay their tax on time.

However, with effect from 30th June 2003 income tax is payable 30 days from the date of exercised of any stock options. The amount payable is 42% of the net cheque received i.e. 42% of the difference between the sale price of the shares less the option price.

Relief for new shares purchased by employees/share subscription schemes

When an employee or director of a company subscribes for new shares in a company, they are entitled to a deduction from their total income, up to a maximum lifetime deduction of €6,350, provided certain conditions are met.

- The individual subscribes for new ordinary shares in the company.

- The deduction is granted for the tax year in which the shares are issued.

- The company in which the shares are issued must be resident and incorporated in Ireland and must be a trading or a holding company.

- If the employee sells the shares within three years of the date of acquiring the shares any income tax relief granted is withdrawn by reference to the tax year in which it was originally given.

- The relief will not be withdrawn where the employee ceases employment with the particular company, or where the employee ceases to be a resident for tax purposes or ceases to be a full time employee.

- When the shares are sold the amount of the tax deduction granted is excluded from the base cost of the shares when calculating the Capital Gains Tax liability on the sale of the shares.

Save as you earn scheme (SAYE)

Under a SAYE scheme a company grants options over shares to its employees. The share options are granted at a price which is fixed by the directors at the time of the grant. This may be at the full market price value or at a discount of up to 25% on the market value.

SAYE schemes operate by allowing the employee to save between €12 - €320 per month out of their net income for a three or five year period in order to finance the purchase of the shares. The employee must save in a special savings scheme which has been set up for SAYE schemes, with a qualifying savings institution. Any interest or bonus paid on the savings contract will be exempt from tax including deposit interest retention tax.

5 Years Saving Contract	€
Monthly savings	€50.00
Share price at grant	€3.33
Discounted option price (75% of market value)	€2.50
Savings on maturity	€3,000
Interest on maturity	€250
Total savings & interest	€3,250
Options granted for 1,300 shares	

Normally when an employee exercises a share option, a charge to income tax will arise based on the excess value of the shares over the option price regardless of whether or not the shares are retained. However, options granted through a SAYE scheme approved by the Revenue Commissioners will not be liable to income tax on either grant or exercise provided the option is not exercised before the third anniversary of the grant. After this time any disposal of the shares will trigger a charge to capital gains tax based on the excess of the net sales proceeds over the actual option price.

Example

As part of a Share Incentive Scheme, you save €200 per month from January to June 2006. At the end of 6 months you have saved €1,200.

Shares in your employer's company are €10 per share at June 2006. You buy 140 shares at 30th June 2006 at €8.50, at 15% discount, total cost of €1,190. You keep the shares until November 2006 when you sell them for €2,100.

	€
Income Tax Liability at 30th June 2006 - (Date Shares Acquired)	
Market Value of Shares Acquired (140 x €10)	€1,400
Price Paid (140 x €8.50)	€1,190
Taxable Benefit	**€210**

A liability to Capital Gains Tax may arise when the shares are sold in November 2006, if the market rate at the time of sale exceeds €1,400.

As Share Incentive Schemes are designed to encourage employees to invest in their employer's business, many schemes prohibit the sale of shares immediately after they are acquired. Where the employee is prohibited from disposing of the shares for a number of years, the Revenue will allow an abatement in the income tax charge depending on the number of years of the prohibition on the disposal.

The abatement is as follows:

No. of Years	Abatement
1 Year	10%
2 Years	20%
3 Years	30%
4 Years	40%
5 Years	50%
Over 5 Years	55%

Share incentive schemes/employee share purchase plans (ESPP)

These are schemes whereby a fixed amount is deducted from your salary every month. After the end of a fixed period, say six months, you purchase shares in your employer's company at a discounted price.

This discount is a taxable benefit for you and is liable to income tax. If you sell the shares immediately on acquiring them no further liability to tax arises. However, Capital Gains Tax may be payable if you keep the shares and sell them at a profit at a later stage.

Other Benefits

Where shares in a company are given to staff free of charge, or at a discounted price or under a share scheme the employee is liable to tax on the benefit provided to them. However, PAYE and PRSI does not apply. Instead the details should be included on the employees income tax return, and the tax must be paid over by the employee directly to the Collector General. PRSI will not apply on benefits received by way of shares.

For stock options income tax is payable within 30 days of the exercise of the stock option.

"Whatever business you are in, we make it our business to solve your payroll needs."

At TAB Payroll Services, we believe that outsourcing your payroll can provide a more flexible and cost-effective solution to your payroll needs while allowing you to dedicate resources to your core business.

Our Service includes:

➤ Running of payroll

➤ Employee payslips

➤ Payments through EBB

➤ P60's, P45's

➤ P30's, P35's

➤ Secure email of all payslips / reports

➤ Provision of back-up service to include dealing with all staff payroll queries

➤ Provision of stationery

➤ Postage of all payslips and/or reports to your office (Swift post and courier charges are additional)

Our basic fees are calculated as a "single figure" depending on your average number of employees. Unlike other payroll companies we do not have additional charges for P45s, P60s, payroll reruns, etc.

For further information please contact
Pam or Philip at 01-676 8638 or email info@tabpayroll.ie

tab payroll services

Eagle House, Wentworth, Eblana Villas, Dublin 2. Tel: 01-676 8638 Fax: 01-676 8641

13

Maximising your redundancy options

Redundancy payments are regulated by the 1967-2003 Redundancy Acts.

As an employee, you are covered under these Acts if you meet the following requirements.

- You are between the ages of 16 and 66.

- You have at least 2 years continuous service (104 weeks)

- You must be in employment which is insurable under the Social Welfare Acts.

- You must have been made redundant as a result of genuine redundancy situation i.e. your job no longer exists and you are not replaced.

When does redundancy arise?

As a general rule, a redundancy situation exists where

- An employer requires fewer employees to do work of a particular kind,

- A company goes into liquidation/receivership,

- It is decided to rationalise/reorganise a company or, of course,

- A company simply closes down.

Other examples would include partial closing down of a company, a decrease in an employer's requirements for workers of a particular kind and skills/qualifications or an employer's requirements for fewer employees due to an economic recession.

Voluntary redundancy

Voluntary redundancy occurs when an employer requires a smaller work force and asks for volunteers for redundancy. The person or persons who volunteer for redundancy are also entitled to the statutory lump sum payment, provided they fulfil the normal conditions.

Notice of redundancy

An employer who, because of redundancy, intends to dismiss an employee who has at least 104 weeks continuous service with the firm must give notice in writing to the employee of the proposed dismissal. The employer can do so by giving part A (notification of redundancy) of Form RP5O to the employee.

Effects of change of ownership of a business on a redundancy lump sum payment

Where there is a change in the ownership of a business and you continue, by arrangement, to work for the new owner with no break in your employment, you are not entitled to any redundancy payments at the time of the change of ownership. Your continuity of employment is also preserved for the purpose of the redundancy payments in the event of your dismissal or redundancy by the new employer at any future date. You are not entitled to a redundancy payment if an offer of employment by the new owner is unreasonably refused by you.

If the new owner merely buys the premises in which you were employed, this will not constitute a change of ownership of the business and your former employer will be liable to pay any redundancy payment which may be due to you.

Calculation of statutory redundancy lump sum payments

The amount of the lump sum payment which a qualified redundant employee is entitled to receive from their employer is calculated as follows:

- Two week's pay for each year of employment continuous and reckonable between the ages of 16 and 66.

    and

- In addition, the equivalent of one week's normal pay.

For the purpose of calculating statutory redundancy, a week's pay is limited to a maximum of €600.

If the total amount of the reckonable service is not an exact number of years, the excess days are credited as a portion of a year.

Time limit on redundancy claims

A dismissed employee will not be entitled to a lump sum unless within 52 weeks after the date of termination of employment:

- The payment has been agreed and paid

  or

- The employee has given a written claim to the employer

  or

A question as to the right of the employee to the payment or its amount, has been referred to the Employment Appeals Tribunal.

The Employment Appeals Tribunal has discretion to extend the 52 week time limit, provided that it receives the necessary claim within 104 weeks of the date of dismissal and it is satisfied that the delay by the employee in making the claim was reasonable.

Lump sum payments to employees from the social insurance fund

- If an employee claims that their employer is liable to pay a lump sum

  and

- The employee has taken all reasonable steps, including a written application (Form RP77 may be used for this purpose) but excluding legal proceedings, to obtain the payment and the employer refuses or fails to pay the whole or part of the lump sum

  or

- The employer is insolvent and the whole or part of the lump sum remains unpaid,

or

- The employer has died and the lump sum cannot be paid to the employee until the employer's affairs have been settled, the employee can apply to the Minister for Enterprise, Trade and Employment, Davitt House, Adelaide Road, Dublin 2 for the lump sum payment from the Social Insurance Fund.

For further information or relevant forms, contact the Department of Enterprise, Trade and Employment, Davitt House, Adelaide Road, Dublin 2 or FÁS, at any of their offices throughout the country.

Taxation of lump sum redundancy payments

Lump sums such as redundancy payments, ex-gratia payments or compensation payments may or may not be liable to tax. Payments can be:

- Totally exempt from tax.

- Relieved from tax.

- Subject to tax.

Totally exempt from tax

- Payments made under the Redundancy Payments Acts 1967-2003.

- Payments made on account of an injury or disability.

- A lump sum payment from an approved pension scheme but excluding a refund of an employee's contributions to that pension scheme.

Relieved from tax

If you receive a lump sum payment from your employer which is not exempt from tax, you may be entitled to claim an extra tax-free amount. The amount is the highest of the following three exemptions:

Basic exemption

The basic exemption is €10,160 together with an additional €765 for each complete year of service.

Increased exemption

The basic exemption may be increased by €10,000 to a maximum of €20,160 plus €765 for each complete year of service provided:

- You have not made a claim for the increased exemption amount in the previous 10 tax years.

  and

- No tax-free lump sum has been received or is receivable under an approved pension scheme. If a tax-free amount is received or receivable and is less than €10,000 then the increased exemption amount will be €20,160 plus €765 for each complete year of service less the tax-free amount received or receivable from your pension scheme.

Standard capital superannuation benefit (S.C.S.B.)

The third exemption is the Standard Capital Superannuation Benefit. This is arrived at using the following formula:

$$\frac{A \times B}{15} - C$$

A = Average yearly remuneration from the employment for the last 36 months ending on the date of termination.

B = Number of complete years of service.

C = The value of any tax-free lump sums received or receivable under an approved pension scheme.

For the purpose of calculating the increased exemption and the S.C.S.B. amount, the tax-free lump sum receivable from the pension scheme is the present day value of any deferred tax-free lump sum receivable at retirement from the existing pension scheme. A refund of pension contributions which were subject to tax at 25% are excluded.

If you sign a waiver letter i.e. a letter confirming you will not avail of any tax-free lump sum from your current pension scheme now or at retirement, the value of any deferred tax-free lump sum receivable will be Nil. (See C above).

Example

You commenced employment with company XYZ Ltd. on 1st December 1984.

You opted for early retirement on 1st November 2006 and you received a lump sum of €60,000 (excluding statutory redundancy).

You received a tax free lump sum of €15,000 from your pension scheme.

The tax-free amount of this €60,000 is the highest of the following:

Basic exemption

$$€10,160 + (€765 \times 21) = €26,225$$

Only complete years count for the purpose of the additional €765. So even though you had 21 years 11 months service, you only receive €765 x 21.

Increased exemption

As you received a tax-free lump sum from the pension scheme in excess of €10,000, the increased exemption would not apply to you.

Standard capital superannuation benefit (SCSB)

Assuming your salary for the last 36 months was as follows:

	€	
01/01/06 - 31/10/06	€42,000	(10 months)
01/01/05 - 31/12/05	€50,000	(12 months)
01/01/04 - 31/12/04	€45,000	(12 months)
01/11/03 - 31/12/03	€7,000	(2 months)
Total salary for 36 months	€144,000	
Average for 12 months	**€48,000**	

Calculation of SCSB

$$\frac{A \times B}{15} \text{ less } C = \frac{€48,000}{15} \times 21 \text{ less } €15,000 = €52,200$$

The highest of the above three exemptions is the SCSB amount of €52,200. This is the amount which you can receive tax-free.

A summary of your position, assuming you pay tax at 42%, is as follows:

		€
	Gross Lump Sum	€65,000
Less:	SCSB Amount	€52,200
	Taxable	€12,800
	Tax @ 42%	€ 5,376
	Levies @ 2%	€ 256
	Net Lump Sum	**€59,368**

Foreign Service and Redundancy

Your redundancy lump sum may be completely tax free provided;

- 75% or more of your entire period of employment, ending on the date of termination was foreign service.

    or

- Your period of service exceeded 10 years but the whole of the last 10 years was foreign service.

    or

- One half of your period of service including any ten of the last twenty years was foreign service, provided your period of service exceeded 20 years.

Foreign service is defined as a period of employment the emoluments of which were not chargeable to Irish tax, or if chargeable to Irish tax were chargeable on the remittance basis.

Foreign service not sufficient to exempt

If you have foreign service but don't qualify for full exemption from income tax your redundancy payment, as reduced by the basic/increased or SCSB exemption may be further reduced by the following formula;

$$\underline{P \times FS}$$

$$TS$$

P   =   Gross Lump Sum Payment (as reduced by SCSB or basic / exemption) (€12,800)

FS =   No of years of foreign service (6)

TS =   No of years of total service (21)

Example

Using the example on page 271 and assuming that you had spent 6 years working in the U.S. Foreign Service relief would be;

$$\underline{€12,800 \times 6} = \qquad €3,657$$
$$21$$

Your taxable lump sum is now reduced by foreign service relief of €3,657

		€
	Gross Lump Sum	€65,000
Less:	SCSB Amount	€52,200
		€12,800
Less:	Relief for foreign service	€3,657
	Taxable	€ 9,143
	Tax @ 42%	€ 3,840
	Levies @ 2%	€ 183
Net Lump Sum		€60,977

Top Slicing Relief

This relief is available after the end of the tax year in which you received a lump sum. Top slicing relief works by calculating your average rate of tax for the three years prior to the tax year in which you received a lump sum. If this average rate is lower than the rate of tax which you paid on your lump sum, the tax will be recalculated at the lower rate and you are entitled to a refund of the difference.

The amount of the relief due to you is calculated by the following formula:

$A-(P \times T/I)$

Where

A = The tax which you paid on your lump sum.

P = The taxable lump sum after deducting the exempt amount.

T = The aggregate of tax payable in respect of the total income of the payee for the three preceding years of assessment.

I = The aggregate of the taxable incomes of the payee for the three preceding years of assessment.

Example

Your taxable income and tax paid for the last 3 years was as follows;

	Taxable income €	Tax paid €
2003	€26,000	€9,100
2004	€28,000	€9,500
2005	€30,000	€9,000
	€84,000	**€27,600**

Assuming you received a lump sum in November 2006, the taxable lump sum was €12,800 and you paid tax @ 42% on this, amounting to €5,376. Your top slicing relief would work out as follows;

	€
A = Tax paid on lump sum	€5,376
P = Taxable lump sum	€12,800
T = Total of tax paid in the last 3 years	€27,600
I = Total of your taxable income for the last 3 years	€84,000

Top Slicing Relief due to you;

$$€5,376 - (€12,800 \times \frac{€27,600}{€84,000}) = €1,170$$

You would have to wait until the end of the 2006 tax year (i.e. the tax year in which you received the lump sum) in order to claim the Top Slicing Relief

14

Self assessment & the self-employed

If you are self-employed or if you are in PAYE employment but have non-PAYE income the tax on which cannot be recovered by restricting your tax credits under the PAYE system you will be regarded as a "chargeable person" and liable to self assessment. For the tax year 2005 when deciding whether to tax your non PAYE income through the PAYE system, the Revenue Commissioners may look at the amount of income for the current year or a previous year before any deductions, losses or reliefs.

Proprietary directors are also subject to the self assessment system even if all their income is taxed under PAYE. A proprietary director is one who holds more than 15% of the share capital of the company.

Under the self-assessment system, you are required to ;

- Pay your preliminary tax on the due date in the year of assessment e.g. your preliminary tax for 2007 is due on the 31 October 2007.

- Submit your completed Income Tax Return - (Form 11) to your Inspector of Taxes on/before the 31st October following the year of assessment e.g. your 2006 tax return must be submitted on/before the 31st October 2007.

Preliminary tax

Preliminary tax is your estimate of income tax payable for the year. It is payable by the 31st October in the year of assessment e.g. on 31st October 2006 you pay your Preliminary Tax for 2007.

The amount payable is the lower of;

- 90% of your final liability for the current year, **or**

- 100% of your liability for the previous year

Payment by direct debit

If you choose to pay your preliminary tax by direct debit, your payments will be based on 105% of your final tax liability for non PAYE income in the pre-preceding year e.g. if your final tax liability for non PAYE income in 2005 was €8,000 - your 2007 preliminary tax liability can be paid by 12 monthly instalments of €700 (€8,000 x 105% ÷ 12).

Surcharge

If you don't submit your tax return by the 31st October, a surcharge will be added to your tax bill. The amount of the surcharge will depend on when your tax return is eventually submitted.

A surcharge of 5% of the total tax due (up to a maximum of €12,695) is added where your tax return is submitted before the 31st December following the year of assessment or 10% (up to a maximum of €63,485) where the return is submitted after the 31st December following the year of assessment.

Pay Preliminary Tax	-	31st October in year of assessment e.g. 31st October 2007 pay preliminary tax for tax year 2007.
File Tax Return	-	31st October following the end of the tax year e.g. tax return for 2007 (year ended 31st December 2007) must be filed by the 31st October 2008.
Pay Balance of Tax	-	31st October following the return filing date. Balance of tax due for 2007 (year ended 31st December 2007) must be paid by 31st October 2008.

ROS

For the last number of years if you pay your income tax and file your tax return using Revenue Online Service (ROS) you can avail of an extension to the 31st October deadline. In 2006 ROS filers had until 16th November 2006 to file their returns and pay their tax.

Contract of service Vs contract for service

If you work for an employer for more than eight hours a week you are entitled to a contract of employment. This contract gives you the benefit of protective legislation, including the Holiday's Act 1973, the Unfair Dismissal Acts 1977 and 1993, the Minimum Notice and Terms of Employment Act 1973 and many others. As an employee you pay PAYE and PRSI.

As a contractor you have an independent business and your contract for work is a contract for services so you are not protected under the employment legislation mentioned earlier.

Setting up as a contractor

There are a number of issues you must face as a contractor. These include, do you operate as a Sole Trader / Partnership or Limited Company, VAT is also another consideration.

Limited company

Limited companies prepare audited accounts annually, which may be more costly than preparing accounts as a sole trader.

Corporation tax charged on non-manufacturing company's profits is 12.5%. The taxable profit is computed in the same way as the taxable profit for a sole trader. Preliminary tax is payable in two instalments. The first instalment is due 31 days before the end of the accounting period. The second instalment is due within six months following the end of the accounting period. A companies tax return form CT1 should be submitted to the Inspector of Taxes within nine months of the company's year end.

If you operate as a company, you can decide the level of salary you will receive under the PAYE system.

From a pension point of view, a company can make more generous pension contributions to your retirement fund and have these contributions offset against its taxable profits.

If a director owns a car and pays their own car insurance, motor tax and petrol costs, they can claim a mileage allowance for any business miles they travel on behalf of the company in accordance with the civil service mileage rates (see page 251) and have this cost offset against profits.

Sole trader

As a sole trader you are liable to income tax at 20% or 42% (41% in 2007) on the profits earned by the business in each year, regardless of the actual cash you withdraw from the business. Tax is due for payment on 31st October each year.

Cars

As a sole trader the cost of running a car can be apportioned between your business and private use on a basis agreed with your Tax Inspector.

VAT

If you provide a service and your sales are in excess of €27,500 p.a. you must register for VAT. If you provide goods this VAT limit is increased to €55,000.

The implications of VAT registration are as follows;

- VAT must be charged on all invoices.

- VAT on business expenses (other than entertainment and motor expenses can be reclaimed).

- Proper VAT records must be kept and returns completed every two months.

Budget 2007: From 1st March 2007 the VAT registration threshold for small businesses are increased to €35,000 in the case of services and €70,000 in the case of goods.

Insurance

If you are operating a business from your own home , you need to be aware your home is also now a business premises and can be treated as such for insurance purposes.

Insurance companies have become increasingly aware of the dual use of private homes and expect clients to inform them when their home is being used for business purposes. This may not necessarily result in a higher annual insurance premium, but it may affect your right to make a successful claim if equipment is stolen or damaged or if somebody is injured on your premises.

Capital Gains Tax (CGT)

Using your house for business purposes means you can claim some of the running costs against your annual income tax bill. These can include electricity, gas, telephone, insurance, etc. However, a drawback could occur on the sale of your home and you may face a CGT bill for that part in respect of which you were claiming tax reliefs.

Calculation of your profit

Income tax is charged on taxable profits. Taxable profits are your gross income less expenses which are allowed for income tax purposes.

The following expenses are specifically disallowed:

- Any expenses which are not wholly and exclusively made for the purpose of the trade.

- Entertainment expenses - this would include the provision of accommodation, food or drink or any other hospitality for clients. Entertainment provided for staff within reason would be an allowable expense.

- Personal expenses.

- Capital expenditure incurred on improvements to the business premises.

- Any debt except bad debts and doubtful debts that are not expected to be recouped.

- Where the car is leased and the list price of the car exceeds €23,000 a portion of the lease expenses is disallowed. The disallowed lease expense is calculated as follows:

$$\frac{\text{Leasing charges x List price of car limit}}{\text{List price of car}}$$

Capital allowances

Depreciation, as such, is not allowable for tax purposes but Capital Allowances in the form of Wear and Tear Allowances are allowed for plant and machinery, fixtures and fittings and motor vehicles which are used for the trade or profession. The rate of Wear and Tear allowance for plant and machinery and motor vehicles bought after 4th December 2002 is 12.5% for eight years. For taxi's and short term hire vehicles the annual rate of Wear and Tear is 40% each year.

Capital allowances on business cars can only be claimed on an amount up to €23,000. If the business car costs in excess of this amount, the capital allowances can only be claimed on €23,000.

Budget 2007: For expenditure incurred in the basis period for the tax year 2007 the car value threshold for business cars is increased to €24,000.

Withholding tax on payments for professional services

Tax at the standard rate - is deducted by Government Departments, State Bodies, Health Boards, etc. from payments made for professional services.

The tax deducted can be claimed in the year in which it is withheld, i.e. tax withheld in 2006 can be offset against your tax liabilities for 2006 and any excess can be reclaimed.

Basis of assessment - new business

First Year

Actual profits from commencement to following 31st December.

Second Year

(i)   If there is one set of accounts made up to a date within that tax year and these accounts are for 12 months, these accounts will form the basis period for the second year of assessment.

(ii)   If the accounts are for less than one year or if there is more than one set of accounts ending within the tax year, then the basis of assessment is the full amount of the profits for the 12 months ending on the latest of these dates.

(iii)   In all other cases, the actual profits for the tax year.

If the actual profits of the second year are less than the profits for the first 12 months of trading the difference can be used to reduce the income for the third year of assessment.

Third and following years

Profits for accounts for 12 months ending in the actual tax year.

Basis of assessment - cessation of business

Final	Actual profits from the 1st January to date of cessation.
Penultimate (2nd last)	Where the actual profits (1st January to 31st December) of the penultimate tax year exceed the profits assessed for that tax year, the assessment will be increased to the amount of the actual profits.

Partnership

A partner is assessed on the share of the partnership profits as adjusted for tax purposes, by reference to the profit sharing ratio in force during the period.

Capital allowances on plant and equipment are split between the partners according to their profit sharing ratio in the tax period.

The profits of a trade or profession carried on by a partnership are not assessed for income tax on the partnership as such, but each partner is deemed to be carrying on a separate trade and, thus, each is assessed for tax individually.

Relevant period

For trades or professions carried on by a partnership, there is what is referred to as the "relevant period". This begins when two or more persons commence to carry on a trade or profession in partnership, continue as partners or join or leave the partnership, provided at least one person who is a partner before a change in the partnership remains on after the change. The relevant period ceases only in any of the following circumstances:

- The cessation of a trade.

- Where all the partners but one retire.

- Where a completely new group of partners replaces the old partners.

When the relevant period commences, the partners are assessed on the basis that they have set up new trades and each partner is assessed for tax under the commencement rules for Cases I and II. For the duration of the relevant periods, the partners are treated as continuing these separate trades and are assessed for tax accordingly.

The self-employed and PRSI

With few exceptions, all self-employed people between the ages of 16 and 66 must pay PRSI contributions on their reckonable income, if their gross income exceed €3,174 in a year. Reckonable income can be both earned and unearned and includes the following:

- Income from a trade or profession.

- Income from which tax has been deducted at source such as annuities, bank interest or building society interest and dividends.

- Irish rents and income from foreign property.

However, the following are excluded for PRSI purposes:

- Any sum received by way of benefit, pension allowance or supplement from the Department of Social and Family Affairs.

- Any sums received from FÁS for training courses.

- Any payments received by way of occupational pension, also income continuance plans payable in the event of loss of employment due to ill health where the scheme has been approved by the Revenue Commissioners.

- Redundancy payments (either statutory or non-statutory), "golden handshake" type payments and early retirement gratuities. However redundancy payments with the exception of statutory redundancy are liable to health levies.

- Health Board payments by way of Infectious Diseases Maintenance Allowance or Mobility Allowance.

- Payments received by a person in respect of the following offices; income related to a member of the Dáil, An Seanad or the European Parliament, the judiciary, public offices under the State such as Labour Court members, the Comptroller and Auditor General, Harbour Commissioners etc.

- Prescribed relatives i.e. certain relatives on low income who help out a self-employed person in the running of a family business, assuming they are not partners in the business.

Self-employed individuals including propriety company directors pay PRSI under Class S.

The PRSI & Levies contribution

Class S rate of PRSI & Levies is 3% of all earnings or the sum of €253, whichever is the greater. If your annual reckonable income exceeds €22,880 you are also liable to pay a Health Contribution Levy of 2% on your reckonable income.

If you enter insurance for the first time after the prescribed age (56) and if you will not be entitled to a Contributory or Non-Contributory Old Age Pension, you may be entitled to a refund of the pension element of the PRSI contribution paid by you.

Budget 2007: From January 2007, the annual reckonable income for the payment of the Health Levy increases to €24,960. If you income exceed €100,000 the Health Levy increases to 2½

Self-employed PRSI (S1) Rate

2007

Self employed PRSI contributions	Health levy
3% of all income Minimum contribution €253	2% (not payable where income for the year is €24,960 or less)

2006

Self employed PRSI contributions	Health levy
3% of all income Minimum contribution €253	2% (not payable where income for the year is €22,880 or less)

Budget 2007: From 1st January 2007 the Health Levy is increased to 2½% on income exceeding €1,925 per week. (€100,000 per annum)

Paying PRSI

If you pay income tax directly to the Collector General, you also pay your PRSI contributions to the Collector General.

Class "S" benefits

Self-employed people paying Class "S" PRSI will generally be entitled to the following benefits, assuming they have paid the minimum qualifying contributions:

- Old Age Contributory Pension (after 10 years contributions).
- Contributory Widow's/Widower's Pension (after 3 years contributions).
- Orphan's contributory allowance (after contributions for 26 weeks).
- Maternity and Adoptive Benefits.
- Bereavement Grant.

15

Calculating your capital gains tax

Capital Gains Tax (CGT) is a tax on gains arising from the disposal of capital assets. It was first introduced in 1974.

Persons chargeable

All persons resident in the State for tax purposes are liable to Capital Gains Tax (CGT). Individuals who are resident and domiciled in Ireland are chargeable on all gains wherever arising, while those who are resident and non-domiciled are liable in respect of all Irish and UK gains and other gains to the extent that the gains are remitted to Ireland.

Non-Irish residents are liable only in respect of gains made on the disposal of assets related to Irish property, or mining/exploration rights.

Chargeable assets

All forms of property are assets for CGT purposes including options, debts and foreign currencies, except those specifically exempted.

Disposal

A disposal for CGT takes place whenever the ownership of an asset changes. This includes a part-disposal and also even where no payment is received e.g. a gift or exchange. An exception to this latter rule is on death. In the case of death, no chargeable disposal takes place and the person who receives the asset is treated as acquiring it at the market value at the date of the death.

Married couples

Transfers between spouses do not give rise to a CGT charge - the spouse who received the asset is deemed to have acquired it on the date and at the cost at which the other spouse acquired it.

Capital gains tax rates

A single rate of 20% applies to most chargeable gains including gains from the sale of development land.

Payment Date

Up to 31st December 2002 CGT was payable on 31st October in respect of gains made in the previous tax year. However for disposals made after 1st January 2003 a preliminary payment will be required to be made by 31st October in relation to disposals made on or before 30 September in the tax year. For disposals made in the period from 1st October to 31st December payment is due by 31st January in the following tax year.

Exemptions and reliefs

Annual allowance

The first €1,270 of chargeable gains arising to an individual in each tax year is exempt. This is an individual allowance and is not transferable between spouses.

Principal private residence (PPR)

No CGT arises on the disposal of your main residence and grounds of up to one acre, provided it has been occupied by you throughout the entire period of ownership. You are still deemed to occupy the residence where you are absent for any period of employment abroad or during absence imposed by conditions of your employment, provided you live in the house before and after the period(s) spent abroad. If your house was not your principal private residence for the entire period of ownership e.g. if you rented the house for a period, any gain arising on the sale of the house will be apportioned between the period when it was your principal private residence (PPR) and the period when it was not. The gain when it was your PPR is exempt and the balance of the gain is liable to CGT @ 20%.

Tangible moveable assets

A gain arising to an individual on such assets is exempt if the total consideration received does not exceed €2,540.

Life assurance policies/deferred annuities

Disposals of these contracts are exempt from CGT in the hands of the original beneficial owner. A chargeable gain can arise on the disposal of such contracts by a person who is not the original beneficial owner if they acquire them for a consideration of money or money's worth. A rate of 40% applies on disposal of certain foreign life assurance annuitised offshore funds.

Irish government securities

Exempt.

Site from parent to child

From 6th December 2002 Capital Gains Tax no longer applies on the transfer of a site from a parent to a child provided it is for the construction of the child's principal private residence and the market value of the site does not exceed €254,000. A parent can transfer one site to each child for the purpose of this exemption.

However, if the child subsequently disposes of the site without having occupied a principal private residence on the site for at least three years, then the capital gains which would have accrued to the parent on the initial transfer will accrue to the child. However, the gain will not accrue to the child where they transfer an interest in the site to his or her spouse.

Retirement relief

Where an individual aged over 55, having owned a farm or business for more than 10 years, disposes of a farm or business for a consideration of less than €500,000, the disposal is ignored for CGT. Where the proceeds exceed €500,000 the CGT arising is restricted to the lower of, half of the difference between the proceeds and €500,000, or the CGT as computed in the normal way.

Complete exemptions can be claimed by an individual meeting the above conditions if they dispose of their farm/business to their child (or nephew/niece working in the business). However, this exemption is lost if the recipient disposes of the farm/business within six years.

Budget 2007: With effect from 1st January 2007 the threshold for retirement relief is increased from €500,000 to €750,000.

Roll-over relief

A person could defer the payment of CGT arising on the disposal of certain assets used solely for business purposes, if the proceeds arising were reinvested in similar assets and used solely for business purposes. The assets which qualified for this relief were plant and machinery, land, buildings, goodwill and in certain circumstances, shares in private companies.

Roll over Relief was abolished on CGT arising from disposals on or after 4th December 2002.

However, any capital gains arising on disposal's which have been deferred before 4th December 2002 can continue to be deferred so long as the consideration for the disposal of the "new assets" continues to be re-invested in other permitted assets. The gain on the disposal of the "new assets" themselves cannot, however, be deferred.

Disposal on emigration

Irish non-residents normally pay Irish Capital Gains Tax on disposals relating to Irish property or mineral/exploration rights only.

So, if you are emigrating and wish to dispose of certain assets before you become non-resident any chargeable gain on such disposals e.g. shares in a company will be liable to Irish Capital Gains Tax.

Capital Gains Tax on such disposals can be reduced if the disposal takes place after you become non-resident for Irish tax purposes. It is also important to note that the date of disposal for Capital Gains Tax purposes is the date of contract.

Computation of gains and losses

Basically, this is done by deducting from the proceeds received, the cost of the disposed asset and, where the asset is held for more than 12 months, "indexation relief" as measured by the increase in the consumer price index. This is done by multiplying the cost of the asset by the indexation factor relative to the tax year in which the purchase took place.

Payment of CGT

The due date for payment of CGT is;

- For disposals occurring between 1st January - 30th September , CGT is due to be paid by the 31st October in the same year.

- For disposals occurring between 1st October - 31st December, CGT is due to be paid by 31st January in the following year.

Indexation relief

When you sell an asset, the original cost and enhancement expenditure may be increased by indexation before any CGT liability is calculated.

Where an asset is acquired prior to 6th April 1974, the "cost" to be indexed is the market value at 6th April 1974, rather than the original cost. Indexation relief does not apply to Development Land.

Indexation relief will only apply for the period of ownership up to 31st December 2002.

Capital gains tax indexation factors

Year of purchase	Year of Disposal								
	98/99	99/00	00/01	2001	2002	2003	2004	2005	2006
1974/75	6.215	6.313	6.582	6.930	7.180	7.528	7.528	7.528	7.528
1975/76	5.020	5.099	5.316	5.597	5.799	6.080	6.080	6.080	6.080
1976/77	4.325	4.393	4.580	4.822	4.996	5.238	5.238	5.238	5.238
1977/78	3.707	3.766	3.926	4.133	4.283	4.490	4.490	4.490	4.490
1978/79	3.425	3.479	3.627	3.819	3.956	4.148	4.148	4.148	4.148
1979/80	3.090	3.139	3.272	3.445	3.570	3.742	3.742	3.742	3.742
1980/81	2.675	2.718	2.833	2.983	3.091	3.240	3.240	3.240	3.240
1981/82	2.211	2.246	2.342	2.465	2.554	2.678	2.678	2.678	2.678
1982/83	1.860	1.890	1.970	2.074	2.149	2.253	2.253	2.253	2.253
1983/84	1.654	1.680	1.752	1.844	1.911	2.003	2.003	2.003	2.003
1984/85	1.502	1.525	1.590	1.674	1.735	1.819	1.819	1.819	1.819
1985/86	1.414	1.436	1.497	1.577	1.633	1.713	1.713	1.713	1.713
1986/87	1.352	1.373	1.432	1.507	1.562	1.637	1.637	1.637	1.637
1987/88	1.307	1.328	1.384	1.457	1.510	1.583	1.583	1.583	1.583
1988/89	1.282	1.303	1.358	1.430	1.481	1.553	1.553	1.553	1.553
1989/90	1.241	1.261	1.314	1.384	1.434	1.503	1.503	1.503	1.503
1990/91	1.191	1.210	1.261	1.328	1.376	1.442	1.442	1.442	1.442
1991/92	1.161	1.179	1.229	1.294	1.341	1.406	1.406	1.406	1.406
1992/93	1.120	1.138	1.186	1.249	1.294	1.356	1.356	1.356	1.356
1993/94	1.099	1.177	1.164	1.226	1.270	1.331	1.331	1.331	1.331
1994/95	1.081	1.098	1.144	1.205	1.248	1.309	1.309	1.309	1.309
1995/96	1.54	1.071	1.116	1.175	1.218	1.277	1.277	1.277	1.277
1996/97	1.033	1.050	1.094	1.152	1.194	1.251	1.251	1.251	1.251
1997/98	1.017	1.033	1.077	1.134	1.175	1.232	1.232	1.232	1.232
1998/99	-	1.016	1.059	1.115	1.156	1.212	1.212	1.212	1.212
1999/00	-	-	1.043	1.098	1.138	1.193	1.193	1.193	1.193
2000/01	-	-	-	1.053	1.091	1.144	1.144	1.144	1.144
2001	-	-	-	-	1.037	1.087	1.087	1.087	1.087
2002	-	-	-	-	-	1.049	1.049	1.049	1.049
2003	-	-	-	-	-	-	1.000	1.000	1.000
2004	-	-	-	-	-	-	1.000	1.000	1.000
2005	-	-	-	-	-	-	-	1.000	1.000
2006	-	-	-	-	-	-	-	-	1.000

Computation of liability on sale of investment property

In August 2006, a married couple sold a house for €500,000. Sales costs amounted to €5,000. They had bought the house in August 1973 for €30,000. The market value of the house at 6th April 1974 was €32,000. The couple had added an extension costing €20,000 to the house in March 1989.

The house was not their principal residence and they had no other chargeable gains in the tax year 2006.

Capital Gains Tax computation 2006

			€
	Sales Price		€500,000
Less:	Selling Costs		€5,000
			€495,000
Deduct:	Value on 6th April 1974 adjusted for inflation: i.e. €32,000 x 7.528	€240,896	
	1988/89 Expenditure, adjusted for inflation: i.e. €20,000 x 1.553	€31,060	€271,956
	Capital Gain		€223,044
Less:	Exemption (House in Joint Name)		€2,540
	Taxable @ 20%		€220,504
	Tax Payable		**€44,100**

Note: The Capital Gains Tax of €44,100 will be payable on 31st October 2006.

16

Foreign income - bringing it home

Generally, your liability to Irish Income Tax on foreign income depends on:

- Whether you are resident in Ireland.

- Whether you are ordinarily resident in Ireland.

- Whether you are domiciled in Ireland.

Residence

You will be regarded as being resident here for tax purposes in the current tax year:

- If you spend 183 days or more here

  or

- If the combined number of days you spend here in the current tax year and the number of days you spent here in the last tax year exceeds 280. In applying this two year test, a period of less than 30 days spent in Ireland in a tax year will be ignored.

Your presence in Ireland for a day, means your presence at midnight.

Electing to be resident

If you come to Ireland and are not regarded as resident here for tax purposes but you can show that you intend to remain and be resident here next year, you may elect to be treated as resident for tax purposes from the date of your arrival.

Electing to be non-resident

This is not possible in any circumstances.

Ordinarily residence

The term "ordinarily resident" as distinct from "resident", relates to your normal pattern of life and denotes residence in a country with some degree of continuity.

When does ordinary residence begin?

If you have been resident here for three consecutive tax years, you become ordinarily resident from the beginning of the fourth tax year.

When does ordinary residence cease?

If you have been ordinarily resident here, you will cease to be ordinarily resident at the end of the third consecutive year in which you are not resident. For example, if you are resident and ordinarily resident here in 2003 and leave the State in that year, you will remain ordinarily resident up to the end of the tax year 2006.

Domicile

Domicile is a complex legal concept. It is generally the country which you consider to be your natural home. When you are born, you obtain a domicile of origin which is normally the domicile of your father.

Tax summary

Individual	Liability To Irish Income Tax
Resident and domiciled in Ireland	On worldwide income from all sources.
Resident but not domiciled or ordinarily resident in Ireland	On all Irish and UK income and foreign income remitted to Ireland.
Ordinarily resident but not resident here in the relevant tax year.	On worldwide income. However, employment or income from an employment trade or profession which is exercised wholly abroad or income from other sources which does not exceed €3,810 will be ignored for tax purposes. Double taxation agreements may exempt some foreign income.
Not resident or ordinarily resident.	Taxed on income arising from Irish sources.

Remittance basis of Taxation

From 1st January 2006 the remittance basis of taxation is discontinued in respect of employment income if the employment is exercised in Ireland.

With effect from 31st March 2006, where a payment or emoluments is made by an intermediary on behalf of an employer, the employer is to be treated for the purposes of the PAYE regulations as having made the payment if the intermediary does not operate PAYE.

Where an employee works for someone based in Ireland (the relevant person), but is employed by a non- resident employer and PAYE is not applied by the employer (or a non-resident intermediary), the relevant person will be liable to account for PAYE on the amount that the employee receives, grossed up where the employee is entitled to a net sum, free of tax.

Where only part of an employee's earnings are chargeable to tax under Schedule E , and the part which is not chargeable is unknown at the time, Revenue may, on application from the employer, give a direction as to the proportion of pay on which PAYE is operated. In the absence of a direction, the employer must operate PAYE on the whole amount.

Double taxation

Generally, Irish residents are liable to Irish income tax on worldwide income and non-residents are liable to Irish income tax on income arising in Ireland. As similar provisions apply to residents of other countries, this can give rise to double taxation. The purpose of Double Taxation Agreements is to prevent this double taxation of income. This may be achieved either by:

- Exempting certain income from tax in one country

  or

- By offsetting the tax paid on income in one country against the tax liability arising on that same income in another country.

Full personal tax credits and reliefs

- If you are a resident here, you are entitled to full personal tax credits and full tax reliefs.

- If you are not resident here but are resident in another Member State of the European Union and 75% or more of your worldwide income is taxable here, you will also be entitled to full personal tax credits and full tax reliefs here.

Partial personal tax credits and reliefs

- If you are a citizen of Ireland or a citizen, subject or national of another Member State of the European Union

  or

- If you are a former resident of the State who is now resident outside of this country because of your health or because of the health of a member of your family resident with you,

  or

- If you are a resident or national of a country with which Ireland has a Double Taxation Agreement which provides for such allowances.

If any of the above applies and you are non-resident here for tax purposes you will be entitled to a certain proportion of personal tax credits and tax reliefs. The exact proportion of these allowances is determined by the relationship between your income which is subject to Irish tax and your income from all other sources.

Example

In 2006 a single man who is an Irish citizen not resident here, had the following sources of income:

	€
Rental income in Ireland	€10,000
US Dividends	€3,000
Rental Income in UK	€4,000
Total Income	€17,000

As the individual is not resident here, they are liable to Irish tax only on income arising in Ireland and entitled to partial personal tax credits as follows;

	2006 €
Irish Income	€10,000
Taxable	
€10,000 @ 20%	€2,000
Less: Tax Credits $€1,630 \times \dfrac{€10,000}{€17,000}$	€959
Net tax payable	€1,041

Year of arrival/return

If you return to Ireland but you are not already resident here for tax purposes and if you can show that you intend to remain here and to be resident here for tax purposes next year, you may elect to be treated as a resident here for income tax purposes from the date of your arrival and your tax position will work out as follows:

Example

You returned to Ireland on 1st September 2006 after spending 3 years abroad. Your earnings in Ireland from 1st September 2006 to 31st December 2006 were €18,500.

	2006 €
Irish Income	€18,500
Tax Payable	
€18,500 @ 20%	€ 3,700
Less: Tax Credits	
Personal (€1,580)	(€1,630)
PAYE	(€1,490)
	(€3,120)
Net tax payable	€ 580

You will be liable to Irish tax on any foreign income which may accrue to you after the date of your return, subject to any relevant double taxation agreement.

Year of departure

If you are resident in Ireland during the tax year you leave and you will be non resident for the following tax year you will be deemed to be non resident from the date of departure. This means that your employment income will be exempt from Irish tax from that date. In order to avail of this arrangement *(known as split year treatment)* it is necessary that you satisfy your local tax office of your intention **not** to be resident in Ireland for the tax year following your departure.

Example

You leave Ireland on the 30th September 2006 to take up a 2 year contract in the USA. From the 1st January 2006 to the date of departure you earn €35,000 in Ireland and pay PAYE of €7,080. Your income in the USA from 1st October 2006 to 31st December 2006 will be €21,000. Your position in 2006 will be as follows:

	Split year treatment €
Salary - Ireland (up to Sept 06)	€35,000
Taxable	€35,000
Tax Payable	
€ 32,000 @ 20%	€6,400
€ 3,000 @ 42%	€600
	€7,000
Less: Tax Credit	
Personal Credit	(€1,630)
PAYE Credit	(€1,490)
Tax Liability	€3,880
Less: PAYE Paid	(€7,080)
Refund Due	(€3,200)

299

Seafarer's allowance

An allowance of €6,350 is available for seafarers. This allowance can be offset against the seafaring employment. It is conditional on the seafarer being at sea on a voyage for at least 161 days in a tax year.

Spouses

Your spouse's resident status is not governed by your residence status. If the residence status of your spouse differs from yours, you may choose to be treated as single people for tax purposes if it is to your advantage to do so.

Right of appeal

If you disagree with your Tax Inspector's decision relating to your taxation in the year of your arrival or departure or to the special tax relief's applicable to foreign assignments, you have a right to appeal the decision to the Appeal Commissioners.

Renting while abroad

Many homeowners going abroad for a limited period will rent their homes while they are abroad. This income is taxable in Ireland regardless of residence status.

Example

You rent your home for €1,000 p.m. while you work abroad. You have a mortgage of €85,000, mortgage interest of €4,800 p.a. and outgoings (agency fees, insurance, repairs etc.) of €1,600.

		€
	Gross Rental Income	€12,000
Less:	Mortgage Interest	(€4,800)
	Outgoings	(€1,600)
	Taxable Income	**€5,600**

Note: From 1st January 2006 in order to claim mortgage interest relief as a rental expense it will be necessary to register with the Private Residential Tenancies Board (PRTB).

Capital gains tax (CGT)

When you sell your main private residence it is normally exempt from CGT. However, if you have rented your main private residence for a number of years, at the date of sale, the CGT exemption will be restricted on a time basis.

For CGT purposes, certain periods of absence are regarded as periods of occupation e.g.

- The last 12 months of ownership.

- Any period of absence throughout which you worked in a foreign employment or any period of absence not exceeding 4 years during which you were prevented from occupying the residence because of employment, provided you occupy the residence before and after the period of absence.

Example

You bought your home in January 1994 for €150,000. You rented it out from 1st January 2002 to 31st December 2005 while you worked abroad. You sold it in December 2006 for €500,000. Your CGT liability will be calculated as follows:

Period of Ownership:	
1st January '94 - 31st December '01	8 Years Principal Private Residence (PPR)
1st January '02 - 31st December '05	4 Years Rented
1st January '06 - 31st December '06	1 Year Deemed PPR - last 12 months of ownership
Total Period of ownership	13 Years
Non Principal Private Residence	4 Years

		Your position €
	Sale Price	€500,000
Less:	Selling Costs	(€12,000)
		€488,000
	Purchase Price Jan 94	€150,000
	Indexation @ 1.331	€49,600
	Indexed Purchase Price	€199,650
	Capital Gain	€288,350
Less:	Capital Gains Exemption	(€1,270)
	Taxable Gain	€287,080
	Tax @ 20%	**€57,416**

However, you may claim CGT exemption for the eight years while the property was your main private residence, together with the last 12 months of ownership which is deemed to be your Principal Private Residence. So, your CGT liability will be €17,666 (4/13 x €57,416).

You could also claim total exemption from total CGT, provided you returned and lived in your former home for a period before you sold it.

Tenants tax obligations

If you work abroad and rent your home, your tenant is obliged to deduct tax at the standard rate from the rental income and pay this tax over to the Revenue Commissioners. When you complete your Irish tax return, you will get credit for this tax.

This obligation on your tenant to deduct tax from your rental income is removed if you appoint an agent to look after your tax affairs here in Ireland while working abroad.

Coming to live in Ireland

If you become a resident in Ireland, you will only be liable to Irish income tax from the date of your arrival, provided you were non-resident here in the previous year. Even though you will only be taxed in Ireland on income for part of the year, you will receive a full year's tax credits. If you arrive in Ireland and are not resident here for tax purposes, any income arising in Ireland will be liable to Irish tax. However, you will only receive tax credits for the portion of the year that you are actually here.

Emergency tax

If your employer does not receive either a certificate of tax credits and standard rate cut off point or a P45 for you, they will be obliged to deduct tax on an emergency basis from your salary. Under emergency tax, a temporary tax credit is given for the first month of employment. See page 135 for more details. In order to get a tax credit and standard rate cut off point certificate you must first get a Personal Public Service Number (PPS).

Obtaining a PPS Number

In order to obtain a PPS number, you must present yourself at your local social welfare office together with some form of ID e.g. your passport and they will issue you with a PPS Number. You must then complete a Form 12a which is available in any tax office. When your employer receives a tax credit and standard rate cut off point certificate for you, you will receive a refund of any tax which you may have overpaid.

You can expect to pay tax on all income, which may include:

- Gross salary.

- Bonuses and commissions.

- Cash allowances for housing, school fees, cost of living , etc.

- Benefit-In-Kind (BIK).

- Share incentives, though various rules apply depending on the scheme.

If you have earnings from other sources, such as rental income, share dividends and/or deposit interest, it will also be subject to tax, whether it has been earned here or abroad, however in the case of UK income special rules may apply. Income earned outside of Ireland or the UK may only be taxable in Ireland if it is brought into this country.

On the plus side, business and relocation expenses, pension contributions, shares taken as part of an approved profit sharing scheme and even severance payments can result in important tax reliefs and opportunities to reduce your overall tax bill.

Capital gains tax (CGT)

Once you are resident here, any assets you still hold abroad, but dispose of could be subject to Irish Capital Gains Tax (currently 20%), though this would not include your principal private residence. An annual CGT exemption of €1,270 applies in Ireland. The amount of tax you will have to pay will also be affected by whether or not you are legally domiciled here and by how much, if any, of the gain from assets outside of Ireland and the UK is brought into Ireland.

Leaving Ireland

When you leave Ireland, providing you had been resident here for tax purposes, you will be taxed on your income up to the date of your departure, though you can offset a full years tax credits against this income. Depending on when you leave Ireland you may be entitled to a refund upon departure.

In order to claim a refund, you must complete a Form 12, and submit it to your tax office together with your P45 and details of all your tax credits, e.g. home carers allowances, service charges etc.

Relief for trans border workers

This allowance is aimed mainly at Irish residents who commute to work in Northern Ireland. However, it also applies to individuals who travel to the UK and elsewhere to work and return to Ireland at the weekends. It applies to individuals who commute daily or at weekends to work outside Ireland, to a country with which Ireland has a Double Taxation Agreement.

The relief means that such residents will not pay tax in Ireland on income from the foreign employment. Tax however, may be payable in the foreign country in which the individual is working.

To claim this relief you must comply with the following conditions;

- The work must be outside the State in a country with which Ireland has a double tax treaty.

- Employment must be held for a continuous period of 13 weeks.

- The duties of the employment must be performed wholly outside the State.

- The income must be taxed in the other country.

- The employee must be at least one day per week in the State.

- The employment must not be with the Government or an authority set up by the State.

The final amount of the tax payable is calculated using the following formula;

$$\frac{A \times B}{C}$$

Where

A   =   The tax payable without this relief and before any credit for foreign tax paid.

B   =   Your income for the year excluding any income for a qualifying employment.

C   =   Total income for the year.

Example

An individual who is single and living in Donegal, went to work in Derry in September 2006 and his income from Northern Ireland in the 2006 tax year is Stg. £15,000. He also earned €28,000 in Ireland from 6th April 2006 to 30th August 2006.

The tax payable in the UK is as follows;

2006/07 Northern Ireland		Stg. £	€
	Salary	£15,000	€21,936
Less:	Single Allowance	£5,035	€7,363
	Taxable	£9,965	€14,573
	£2,150 @ 10%	£215	€314
	£7,815 @ 22%	£1,719	€2,514
UK Tax Payable		£1,934	€2,828
Exchange Rate: €1 = .6838p Stg.			

If he did not qualify for Trans Border Relief his tax would be calculated as follows;

2006/07 Northern Ireland	€
Income from Employment - Northern Ireland	€21,936
Income from Employment - Ireland	€28,000
Taxable	€49,936
Tax Payable	
€32,000 @ 20% €6,400	
€17,936 @ 42% €7,533	
	€13,933
Less: Tax Credits	
Personal	(€1,630)
PAYE	(€1,490)
Total tax due without Cross Border Relief	**€10,813**

Cross Border Relief would reduce this tax bill to €8,811 (€2,828 in Northern Ireland + €6,063 here). Calculated as follows;

*   A = €10,813 $\underline{\text{€10,813 x €18,000}}$ = €6,063

        B = €28,000   €49,936

        C = €49,936

UK employment income

Unfortunately, many of the benefits applicable to foreign employment income as outlined earlier are not applicable to U.K. employment income. We outline here the general principles applicable to income earned in the U.K. while you are treated as resident here for tax purposes.

Paid by UK company while working and living in Ireland

If you are resident in Ireland and are employed by a UK resident company, you are normally liable to tax in Ireland on this income, under the Self Assessment System.   Usually, the UK company will pay you gross, less a PRSI deduction.

Paid by an Irish company while working and living in the UK

If you are working short-term in the UK and paid from Ireland then there is normally no UK income tax payable and your tax position will be effectively ignored by the UK tax authorities.

PAYE in the UK

When you commence work in the UK you will be asked to complete a Residence Enquiry Form P86 and a Tax Coding Form P15. How you will be taxed on your employment income in the UK will to a large extent be determined by your own personal plans: for example, how long you intend to stay or work in the UK?

If it is your intention to work and take up short-term residence in the UK, your UK employment income will normally be taxed under PAYE on a "week one" basis. However, if it is your intention to work and take up long-term residence in the UK you may be taxed on a PAYE cumulative basis i.e. the UK tax authorities will issue you a tax-free allowance from the 6th of April preceding your arrival.

UK-personal income tax summary tax allowances

	2004/05	2005/06	2006/07
	Stg. £	Stg. £	Stg. £
Personal Allowance			
Under 65	£4,745	£4,895	£5,035
65 to 74 Note 1	£6,830	£7,090	£7,280
75 and over Note 1	£6,950	£7,220	£7,420
*Married Couple's Allowance - Note 3 minimum amount	£2,210	£2,280	£2,350
65 and 74 Note 1 + 3	£5,725	£5,905	£6,065
75 and over Note 1 + 3	£5,795	£5,975	£6,135
Blind Person's Allowance	£1,560	£1,610	£1,660
Income Limit for Age-Related Allowances	£18,900	£19,500	£20,100

Note 1   The higher personal allowances for taxpayers aged 65 and over are reduced by £1 for every £2 of income above the income limit (£20,100). However, they cannot be reduced below the basic level of the personal allowance (£5,035) available to those aged under 65.

Note 2   The married couple's allowances are only available to taxpayers born before 6 April 1935 and are reduced by £1 for every £2 of income above the income limit (£20,100). However, they cannot be reduced below the minimum amount of £2,350. The higher levels of personal allowance are reduced before the higher levels of married couple's allowance.

Note 3   These allowances, unlike the personal allowance, are not income you can receive without having to pay tax. Instead, they give relief at a set rate of 10% of the allowance you are entitled to. For example, those receiving the married couple's allowance of £6,135 will have their tax bill reduced by up to £613.50 (10% of £6,135).

U.K. tax rates

2005/06	2006/07
10% on first £2,090	10% on first £2,150
22% on next £30,310	22% on next £31,150
40% over £32,400	40% over £33,300

Average rates of exchange between Ireland and the U.K.

Tax Year Ending	€
31/12/05	Stg. £0.6838

If you are a student in the UK for the summer, you will normally be taxed under PAYE on a week one basis. On your return to college here, you will probably be due a tax refund. In order to get this refund from the UK tax authorities, you should complete the following:

- Tax repayment form P50.
- Residence enquiry form P85.

and send both together with your UK P45 to your tax inspector (address available from your UK employer).

It is also advisable to provide some evidence of your imminent return to college here on a full-time basis if you wish your UK tax inspector to speed up your tax refund. Normally, refunds of PAYE tax will only be made after the 5th April.

17

Marriage matters

Tax and financial issues arising from marriage are spread throughout our tax and financial system. To make everything as simple and as straight forward as possible, we shall look at marriage under a number of different headings:

- Legal Impact

- Income Tax

- Capital Gains Tax

- Capital Acquisition Tax

- Stamp Duty

- Probate Tax

- Social Welfare

Legal impact

Marriage changes the legal status of two people from a couple to spouses, with many consequential and financial implications. For example, a surviving spouse's legal entitlements under the 1965 Succession Act are as follows:

If there is a Will	(Irrespective of what's in it, the minimum legal entitlements of a surviving spouse are;)
Spouse and No Issue	One-half of estate to the surviving Spouse
Spouse and Issue	One-third of estate to the surviving Spouse
No Will in Existence	
Spouse and No Issue	Whole estate to the surviving Spouse

| Spouse and Issue | Two-thirds to the surviving Spouse, one-third to issue in equal shares. |

Succession Act rights may be voluntarily renounced by a prenuptial agreement.

Income tax

A marriage ceremony in itself does not give rise to any income tax advantage. To obtain these benefits, a couple must be married and "living together".

Under the income tax rules, a married couple are deemed to be "living together" unless

- They are separated under an order of a Court of competent jurisdiction or by Deed of Separation,

  or

- They are in fact separated in such circumstances that the separation is likely to be permanent.

A married couple living together may choose to be taxed jointly, separately or as single people.

The significant tax advantages for a married couple living together and claiming joint assessment under Income Tax rules are as follows:

- A married tax credit which is double the single person tax credit.

- Home carer's tax credit.

- Double a single person's mortgage interest relief available for a principal private residence.

- Trading losses incurred by one spouse can be set against income of the other spouse.

- Double the age tax credit even though only one spouse may be over the age of 65 years.

- Medical expenses incurred or defrayed by one spouse can be claimed by the assessable spouse.

- Increased blind person's tax credit where both spouses are blind.

- Tax relief can be obtained by one spouse in respect of a person employed to take care of the incapacitated other spouse.

Individualisation

Prior to the introduction of individualisation the married rate tax band was double that of a single person. This applied regardless of whether one or both spouses worked. For the tax year 2006 the standard rate tax band for a married couple is €41,000. Where both spouses have income this can be increased by the lower of ;

- €23,000

    or

- the income of the lower earning spouse.

To gain the maximum benefit from the new 'individual' band increases for a two income couple, each spouse must have a minimum 'individual' income of €23,000 in the year 2006.

For example, a two income couple where one spouse earns €45,000 in the tax year 2006 and the other earns €8,000, the maximum married couple standard rate band of €41,000 can be utilised by the higher earning spouse but only €8,000 of the 20% band can be utilised by the lower earning spouse. The balance of €15,000 is left unused. (see page 107 for 2007 notes)

Year of marriage

In the year of marriage, you and your spouse are treated as two single people for income tax purposes for the entire tax year. However, if you pay more tax than that which would have been payable as a married couple, you can claim a refund. This refund will be the excess of the tax paid as two single people over the tax payable as a married couple jointly assessed, reduced in proportion to the part of the tax year in which you were not married.

Example

A married couple have income of €60,000 and €25,000 respectively. Their date of marriage was 1st July 2006. Their tax liability for 2006 will be as follows:

	€		€
Salary	€60,000		€25,000
Tax Payable			
€32,000 @ 20%	€6,400	€25,000 @ 20%	€5,000
€28,000 @ 42%	€11,760		
Less: Tax Credits	€18,160		
Personal	(€1,630)		(€1,630)
PAYE	(€1,490)		(€1,490)
Net Tax	€15,040		€1,880
Total tax as single people			**€16,920**

At the end of the year, they may apply for a reduction in their tax liability on the basis of joint assessment as illustrated:

	2006 €
Total Salaries	€85,000
Tax Payable	
€64,000 @ 20% (see note)	€12,800
€21,000 @ 42% €672	€8,820
	€21,620
Less: Tax Credits	
Personal	(€3,260)
PAYE	(€2,980)
Net Tax	€15,380
Less: Tax Paid (See above)	(€16,920)
Excess of single over joint basis of assessment.	€1,540
Restriction for Pre Married Period €1,540 x 6/12	€770
Tax Refund Due	**€770**

The tax refund due to each spouse will be in proportion to the amount of tax each has paid.

Married couples/income tax options

After the year of marriage, you have three options as to how you are taxed.

Joint assessment

Joint assessment is automatic, unless either spouse gives notice of election for separate or single assessment to the Revenue Commissioners.

The assessable spouse is the spouse with the higher income and will continue to be so unless you jointly elect to change it.

Repayments made are allocated between each spouse according to the amount of tax they paid in the year.

Separate assessment

A claim may be made for separate assessment of income tax liability where the joint assessment basis applies. The claim must be before the 1st April in the year of assessment, or before 1st April in the following year in the case of marriage. Where separate assessment is claimed the tax credits are divided between the spouses. If at the end of the tax year, the total tax payable under separate assessments is greater than the amount payable if an application for separate assessment had not been made, you can apply for a tax refund.

Single assessment/(separate treatment)

As a married couple, you may each elect for single assessment. Each spouse is treated as a single person with no right of transfer of allowances or relief's between spouses. Single assessment is normally only beneficial where one spouse has foreign employment income.

Capital gains tax (CGT)

A couple must be married and "living together" in order to maximise their benefits under Capital Gains Tax which include:

Entitlement to dispose of assets to each other without being subject to CGT.

Capital losses available to one spouse can be used by the other spouse.

Capital acquisitions tax (CAT)

The "living together" rules do not apply to CAT and all gifts and inheritance given by one legally married spouse to the other are exempt from CAT regardless of their "living together" status.

Pensions benefits

Section 56 of the CAT Act 1976 provides that any pension benefit taken by a person, other than the pension member, will be treated as a gift or inheritance for tax purposes.

However, the spouse exemption from CAT means any lump sum death benefit or dependent's pension benefit received by your spouse from a pension scheme of which you were a member will be exempt from tax.

Life assurance policies

Section 32 of the CAT Act 1976 provides that an interest in possession in life assurance policies is only deemed to occur when a benefit becomes payable under the policy. So if you effect a Life Assurance policy on your own life for the benefit of someone else, no gift or inheritance tax will arise until the benefit becomes payable under that policy. Any sums received by you or your spouse from a life assurance policy, of which you or your spouse were the original beneficial owners, will be exempt from tax.

Stamp duty

Tranfer of all assets between spouses is exempt from stamp duty. This exemption includes a direct transfer of assets from one spouse to another or a transfer from one spouse into joint names.

Social Welfare

Social welfare Widow(er)'s Contributory Pension is payable to the widow(er) following the death of their spouse, for as long as the widow(er) does not remarry or cohabit with someone else as man and wife. A spouse may qualify for this pension either on their own PRSI contribution record, or on that of the other spouse.

A Non-Contributory Social Welfare Widow(er)'s Pension is payable to a widow(er) as long as they do not remarry or cohabit with someone else as man and wife.

Tax options -

Example: 2006

A couple are married with two children, with salaries of €50,000 and €25,000 respectively. The higher earning spouse pays pension contributions of €5,400 in the 2006 tax year.. Their tax options are illustrated on page 318.

Method of assessment	Joint Assessment		Separate Assessment				Single Assessment			
€	€	€	€	€	€	€	€	€	€	€
Salary	€75,000		€50,000		€25,000		€50,000		€25,000	
Less: Pension	(€5,400)		(€5,400)				(€5,400)			
Taxable Income	€69,600		€44,600		€25,000		€44,600		€25,000	
Tax Payable	**Amount**	**Tax**	**Amount**	**Tax**	**Amount**	**Tax**	**Amount**	**Tax**	**Amount**	**Tax**
20%	€64,000	€12,800	€32,000	€6,400	€25,000	€5,000	€32,000	€6,400	€25,000	€5,000
42%	€5,600	€2,352	€12,600	€5,292			€12,600	€5,292		
Total		€15,152		€11,692		€5,000		€11,692		€5,000
Less: Tax Credits										
Personal		(€3,260)		(€1,630)		(€1,630)		(€1,630)		(€1,630)
PAYE		(€2,980)		(€1,490)		(€1,490)		(€1,490)		(€1,490)
				€ 8,572		€ 1,880		€ 8,572		€ 1,880
Total Payable	**€8,912**		**€10,452**				**€10,452**			

Note: Separate assessment results in an additional tax bill of €1,504 which can be reclaimed at the end of the tax year. Single assessments result in the same additional bill. However under single assessment this amount could not be reclaimed back at the end of the year.

18

Separation and divorce

To make everything in this section as simple as possible, we will look at each of the issues relating to "Separation and Divorce" under the same headings as those used in the previous chapter entitled "Marriage Matters". To get a better understanding of the tax implications of "Separation and Divorce", we advise you to first read the previous chapter outlining the tax issues arising on marriage.

Marriage breakdown is a major and traumatic event for couples and it is best approached in a logical and non-confrontational manner. A brief checklist of points to consider in relation to separation and divorce is included at the end of this section.

When a married couple decide to separate, they will normally go about it in one of the following ways:

- They decide to live apart.

- They seek a Legal Separation.

- They seek a Judicial Separation.

Living apart

Legal impact

Living apart does not change the legal status of your marriage.

Succession rights

There is no automatic loss of your Succession Act entitlements if you live apart from your spouse. However:

- A spouse who is guilty of desertion, which continues for two years or more up to the death of the other spouse, is precluded under the

Succession Act from taking any share in the estate of the deceased, either as a legal right or on intestacy.

- If a surviving spouse is deemed to be "guilty of conduct which justified the deceased separating and living apart", then the surviving spouse could be deemed to be guilty of desertion and hence precluded under the Succession Act from taking a share in the deceased spouse's estate. For example where a wife leaves home because of violent behaviour on the part of her husband, he could be found guilty of desertion and lose his Succession Act rights to her estate while, conversely, she could in fact, retain her rights to his estate.

- Any spouse who has been found guilty of a serious offence against the deceased spouse or against a child of the deceased spouse, is also precluded, under the Succession Act, from taking any legal right under the estate of the deceased.

Income tax

A couple's Income Tax position following separation is determined by three main factors:

- Whether the separation is likely to be permanent.

- Whether maintenance payments are being made by one spouse to the other.

- If maintenance payments are being made, whether these payments are *legally enforceable*.

If the separation is not likely to be permanent, there is no change in the Income Tax position and you can elect for Joint, Separate or Single Assessment.

If the separation is likely to be permanent and if there are no legally enforceable maintenance payments, the spouses are assessed for Income Tax under Single Assessment. Any Voluntary maintenance payments are ignored for income tax purposes.

If the separation is likely to be permanent and if there are legally enforceable maintenance payments being made, then the couple may generally opt for either Single Assessment or if both spouses remain resident in Ireland, Separate Assessment. If Single Assessment applies, maintenance payments are tax-deductible for the payer and are taxable in the hands of the recipient. Under Separate Assessment, maintenance payments are ignored for income tax purposes.

Capital Gains Tax (CGT)

If the separation is not likely to be permanent, there is no change in the spouse's status for CGT purposes.

If the separation is likely to be permanent, the spouses are treated as two unconnected persons for CGT purposes:

- Transfers between spouses are no longer exempt from CGT. However, any transfer by virtue of, or in consequence of, the Separation will not trigger a CGT liability.

- No transfer of unused CGT losses is permitted between spouses.

Capital Acquisition Tax (CAT)

Spouse's exemption from Capital Acquisitions Tax will continue to apply.

Pensions/death-in-service benefit

If a member of a pension scheme dies while still working for an employer, Death in Service Benefits may be paid to the member's dependants. Many pension schemes give discretion to the pension trustees as to how these death-in-service benefits may be paid e.g. the pension rules may require a spouse to be living with, or ordinarily residing with, their spouse at the date of death.

Life assurance

The proceeds are normally exempt from tax, provided you or your spouse were the original beneficial owners of the relevant policy.

Stamp duty

Exemption from Stamp Duty will continue to apply on relevant property transactions.

Social welfare

The Contributory Widow(er)'s Pension is payable to the widow(er), following the death of their spouse, for as long as the widow(er) does not remarry and does not cohabit with someone else as man and wife. A widow(er) may qualify for this pension either on their own PRSI contribution record or that of their late spouse.

Qualifying adult dependent payment

A qualifying adult dependent payment is generally payable to a claimant who is separated, provided their spouse is wholly or mainly maintained by the claimant.

Legal separation

Under a Legal Separation, both spouses voluntarily enter into a legal agreement. This legal agreement is often referred to as a "Deed of Separation".

A Deed of Separation will usually include:

- An agreement to permanently live apart.

- Arrangements for custody of, and access to, children.

- Provision for maintenance to be paid by one spouse for the benefit of the other spouse and/or children.

- Succession Act rights: one spouse may voluntarily renounce rights to the other's estate, etc.

Legal impact

A Deed of Separation will not change the legal status of your marriage.

Succession rights

- There is no automatic loss of your entitlements under the Succession Act.

- Your entitlements under the Succession Act may be voluntarily renounced under a Deed of Separation

- Any specific bequest in your Will to your spouse will stand until you make a new Will or change your existing Will.

Income tax

A couple's Income Tax position following separation is determined by three main factors:

- Whether the separation is likely to be permanent.

- Whether maintenance payments are being made by one spouse to the other.

- If maintenance payments are being made, whether these payments are *legally enforceable.*

If the separation is not likely to be permanent, there is no change in the Income Tax position and you can elect for Joint, Separate or Single Assessment.

If the separation is likely to be permanent and if there are no legally enforceable maintenance payments, the spouses are assessed for Income Tax under Single Assessment. Any Voluntary maintenance payments are ignored for income tax purposes.

If the separation is likely to be permanent and if there are legally enforceable maintenance payments being made, then the couple may generally opt for either Single Assessment or if both spouses remain resident in Ireland, Separate Assessment. If Single Assessment applies, maintenance payments are tax deductible for the payer and taxable in the hands of the recipient. Under Separate Assessment, maintenance payments are ignored for income tax purposes.

Assessable spouse

The spouse with the greater income in the year of marriage will generally be deemed to be the assessable spouse from year to year.

The assessable spouse may be changed provided both spouses elect jointly for an alternative option. The assessable spouse is generally responsible for submitting the annual return and paying any tax due.

Year of separation

The Married Tax Credit and Double Rate Tax Band can be claimed for the year of separation by the assessable spouse providing:

- Separation does not occur on the first day of that tax year.

  or

- The non-assessable spouse has not submitted a claim for single assessment prior to separation.

The assessable spouse is liable to Income Tax for the tax year of separation on their own income under joint assessment if they were previously taxed jointly for the full year, and on the other spouse's income up to the date of separation. A tax deduction will be available for legally enforceable maintenance payments.

Example

A married couple separated on 1st October 2006 on a basis that is likely to be permanent. In the tax year 2006 their tax position will work out as follows:

We assume no maintenance is payable. In the interest of simplicity, we are using the same figures in this example as were illustrated in Chapter 17 Marriage Matters.

	€
Assessable Spouse's Income	€50,000
Non- Assessable Spouse's Income to 1st October 2006	€25,000
	€75,000
Non-Assessable Spouses income from 2nd October 2006	€6,250

	Assessable Spouse's Income €	Non-Assessable Spouse's Income €
Assessable Spouse' Salary	€50,000	
Non-Assessable Spouse's Salary	€18,750	€6,250
	€68,750	€6,250
Less: Allowances		
Pension	€5,400	-
Taxable	€63,350	€6,250
Tax Payable		
€63,350/€6,250 @ 20%	€ 12,670	€1,250
Less: Tax Credits		
Personal	(€3,260)	(€1,630)
PAYE	(€1,490)	(€1,490)
Tax Payable	€7,920	€ Nil
After Tax Income	€60,830	€6,250

Note: The total tax bill in 2006, the year of separation, worked out at €7,920 compared to €8,912 as a married couple under joint assessment (see page 318).

Year of separation/Single assessment

If the couple in the previous example were paying tax under Single Assessment before the separation, each spouse would have been responsible for submitting their own tax returns and paying their own tax. No change in their status for income tax purposes would have occurred on separation and they would pay the same tax bill as illustrated on page 330 under Single Assessment.

Subsequent tax years

How you will be taxed in subsequent tax years will depend on a number of factors e.g.

- Voluntary Maintenance Payments.
- Legally Enforceable Maintenance Payments.
- Single Parent Credits.
- Mortgage Repayments etc.

Maintenance payments

Tax is not deducted at source from legally enforceable maintenance payments from one spouse to the other. Such payments may be allowed for tax purposes as a deduction against the income of the payer and may be chargeable to income tax, in the hands of the recipient. A spouse will not be entitled to the marriage credit where he/she claims a deduction for maintenance payments made.

Where maintenance is received for the benefit of a child:

- The payment is to be made without deduction of income tax,
- The amount is to continue to be treated as the income of the payer,

  and

- The payer's income tax liability is calculated without any allowance for the payments made.

PRSI & levies

If you are legally separated and you receive maintenance payments from your spouse, PRSI & levies will be payable on the maintenance received if you are taxed as a single person. If you have opted for separate assessment, maintenance payments are ignored for income tax purposes and PRSI and levies are not payable on the maintenance.

The PRSI payable would be the Class S1 rate, which in 2006 is 3% of the gross income.

Health levies of 2% are also payable on the maintenance you receive. However, an exemption from these levies is given if your total gross income, including maintenance, is below €22,880 in 2006 and €24,960 in 2007. If the paying spouse has already paid PRSI/levies on the maintenance, there is an element of double taxation. However, the paying spouse may be entitled to a refund of these levies. If the spouse receiving the maintenance pays PRSI as an employee, no PRSI is payable in respect of the maintenance. However, if they are self- employed then PRSI will be payable on all maintenance payments received.

Voluntary maintenance payments

If you wholly or mainly maintain your spouse by voluntary maintenance payments, you will be entitled to the married couple's tax credit. The Revenue generally accepts that you wholly or mainly maintain your spouse if the voluntary maintenance paid to him/her exceeds his/her earned income.

Example

> You and your spouse agree to separate.
>
> - Your income is €50,000 p.a. for the tax year 2006. Your spouse has no income.
>
> - You agree to pay your spouse €200 per week.
>
> The arrangement is informal and nothing is legally enforceable.

Your tax position

	2006	
	Joint assessment married	**Single assessment separated**
	€	€
Salary	€50,000	€50,000
Tax Payable		
€41,000 @ 20%	€8,200	
€32,000 @ 20%		€6,400
€ 9,000 @ 42%	€3,780	
€18,000 @ 42%		€7,560
	€11,980	€13,960
Less: Tax Credits		
Personal	(€3,260)	(€3,260)
PAYE	(€1,490)	(€1,490)
	€7,230	€9,210

The €200 p.w. maintenance which you pay is not tax deductible. Your additional tax payable as a separated person under single assessment is **€1,980**

Notes:

- The marriage tax credit will be granted because your spouse is wholly or mainly maintained by you. You are not entitled to deduct the maintenance payments as these are voluntary and not legally enforceable.

- Your spouse is not living with you and you are not entitled to the benefit of the double tax bands because the maintenance payments are not enforceable.

Legally enforceable maintenance payments

Legally enforceable maintenance payments are tax-deductible from the income of the paying spouse and are taxable in the hands of the receiving spouse.

Example

You and your spouse agree to separate. Your spouse works in the home.

- Your salary is €56,000 p.a. in the 2006 tax year.

- You agrees to pay your spouse €200 per week and the arrangement is legally enforceable.

Your Tax Position

	2006	
	Joint assessment married €	Single assessment separated €
Salary	€56,000	€56,000
Maintenance paid	€0	€10,400
Taxable	€56,000	€45,600
Tax Payable		
€41,000/€32,000 @ 20%	€8,200	€6,400
€15,000/€13,600 @ 42%	€6,300	€5,712
	€14,500	€12,112
Less: Tax Credits	(€3,260)	(€3,260)
Personal	(€1,490)	(€1,490)
PAYE		
	€9,750	€7,362

As legally enforceable maintenance payments are tax-deductible, reduction in tax payable under single assessment is €2,388.

Capital gains tax (CGT)

Normally, under a legal separation the spouses are treated as two unconnected persons for CGT purposes:

- Transfers between spouses are no longer exempt from CGT. However, any transfer by virtue of, or in consequence of, the Deed of Separation will not trigger a CGT liability.

- No transfer is permitted between spouses of unused CGT losses.

Capital acquisition tax (CAT)

Spouse's exemption from Capital Acquisitions Tax will continue to apply.

Pension benefits

Pension rights negotiated under a Deed of Separation may not be enforceable, unless the agreement is backed up by a formal court order.

Life assurance

Specific rights obtained under a Deed of Separation in relation to life assurance policies may not be legally enforceable - to avoid problems make sure that your interest in a life assurance policy is backed up by a relevant court order e.g. Financial Compensation Order, under the Family Law Act 1995.

Stamp duty

Exemption from Stamp Duty will continue to apply on relevant property transactions.

Social welfare

The Social Welfare Contributory Widow(er)'s Pension is payable to the widow(er) following the death of their spouse, for as long as the widow(er) does not remarry and does not cohabit with someone else as man and wife. The surviving spouse may qualify for a Widow(er)'s Pension either on their own PRSI contribution record, or that of their late spouse.

- A Qualified Adult Dependent supplement may not be payable to a claimant if that claimant's spouse is no longer wholly or mainly maintained by the claimant.

Judicial separation

A decree of judicial separation can be obtained by a spouse applying to the courts under the Judicial Separation and Family Law Reform Act 1989. The application may be made on one or more of the following grounds:

- The other spouse has committed adultery.

- That the other spouse has behaved in such a way that the applicant spouse cannot reasonably be expected to live with the other spouse.

- That the other spouse has deserted the applicant spouse for a continuous period of at least one year immediately preceding the application and that the spouses have lived apart from one another for a continuous period of at least one year immediately preceding the application and that the other spouse consents to a decree being granted.

- That the spouses have lived apart from one another for a continuous period of at least three years immediately preceding the application and that the marriage has broken down to the extent that the court is satisfied in all circumstances that a normal marital relationship has not existed between the spouses for at least one year immediately preceding the application.

Ancillary orders

On the granting of, or following, a decree of Judicial Separation, the Circuit or High Court can make a number of orders relating to maintenance or specific assets. These orders are known as Ancillary Orders.

Under a Judicial Separation either spouse, or, in some cases, a person acting on behalf of a dependent child, can apply to the courts to have one or more Ancillary Orders made in relation to:

- Maintenance.
- The family home.
- Property.
- Pension benefits.

- Life assurance policies.

- Succession rights etc.

While the Courts retain the discretion to grant an Ancillary Order sought by a spouse, or a person acting on behalf of a dependent child, the Family Law Act 1995 does provide specific factors which the Court is obliged to take into account before making a decision.

- The income, earning capacity, property and other financial resources which each of the spouses has, or is likely to have in the foreseeable future. The financial needs, obligations and responsibilities which each of the spouses has or is likely to have in the foreseeable future (whether in the case of remarriage of the spouse or otherwise).

- The standard of living enjoyed by the family concerned before the proceedings were instituted or before the spouses separated, as the case may be.

- The age of each of the spouses and the length of time during which the spouses lived together.

- Any physical or mental disability of either of the spouses.

- The contributions which each of the spouses has made or is likely in the foreseeable future to make to the welfare of the family, including any contribution made by each of them to the income, earning capacity, property and financial resources of the other spouse and any contribution made by either of them by looking after the home or caring for the family.

- The effect on the earning capacity of each of the spouses of the marital responsibilities assumed by each during the period when they lived together and, in particular, the degree to which the future earning capacity of a spouse is impaired by reason of that spouse having relinquished or foregone the opportunity of remunerative activity in order to look after the home or care for the family.

- Any income or benefits to which either of the spouses is entitled by or under statute.

- The conduct of each of the spouses, if that conduct is such that in the opinion of the court it would in all the circumstances of the case be unjust to disregard it.

- The accommodation needs of either of the spouses

- The value to each of the spouses of any benefit (for example, a benefit under a pension scheme) which by reason of the decree of judicial separation that spouse will forfeit the opportunity or possibility of acquiring.

- The rights of any other person, other than the spouses but including a person to whom either spouse is remarried.

Enforcing maintenance orders

Experience has shown a relatively high rate of defaulting on regular maintenance payments; a court can enforce these payments in one of two ways:

- *Secured Payments.* Here the periodic payments are secured on some capital asset or investment. For example, the court could order the sale of an investment property to generate the necessary funds.

- *Attachment of earnings order* where the court may order an employer to deduct the periodic payments from the earnings of one spouse and pay it to the other spouse.

Payments orders will normally specify the period, or periods, during which the payments are to be made, which can be a fixed number of years, or for the lifetime of either spouse. However, payment orders will generally cease on:

- The death of either spouse.

- The date of remarriage of the applicant spouse.

Legal impact

A Judicial Separation does not change the legal status of your marriage.

Succession rights

- There is no automatic loss of entitlements under the Succession Act.

- Your entitlements under the Succession Act may be voluntarily renounced under a Judicial Separation.

- Any specific bequest in your Will to your spouse will stand until you make a new Will or change your existing Will.

Income tax

If there are no legally enforceable maintenance payments being made, the spouses are assessed for Income Tax under Single Assessment. Any voluntary maintenance payments are not tax-deductible for the paying spouse and are not taxable in the hands of the receiving spouse.

If there are legally enforceable maintenance payments being made, then the couple can generally either opt for Single Assessment or if both spouses remain resident in Ireland, Separate Assessment. If Single Assessment applies, maintenance payments made for the benefit of the spouse are tax deductible for the payer and taxable in the hands of the recipient. Under Separate Assessment, maintenance payments are ignored for tax purposes.

If you have a Judicial Separation, your income tax position is the same as under a Legal Separation.

Capital gains tax (CGT)

Normally, under a judicial separation the spouses are treated as two unconnected persons for CGT purpose:

- Transfers between spouses are no longer exempt from CGT. However, any transfer by virtue of, or in consequence of, a decree of Judicial Separation will not trigger a CGT liability.

- No transfer of unused losses is permitted between spouses.

Capital acquisitions tax (CAT)

Spouse's exemption from Capital Acquisitions Tax will continue to apply.

Pension benefits

The Family Law Act 1995 envisages a number of ways in which a spouse's pension benefits might be taken into account in the event of a judicial separation:

- **Earmarking.**

- **Pension Splitting.**

- **Offsetting.**

Earmarking	-	A charge is set against a spouse's pension benefits, so that when they become payable a designated part of these benefits are payable to the other spouse.
Pension Splitting	-	The relevant pension benefits are split on an agreed basis between both spouses.
Offsetting	-	If proper financial provision can be made by other orders (e.g. a financial compensation order), or a property adjustment order the court may decide to offset these benefits against any relevant pension rights rather than "splitting everything down the middle".

Life assurance

Once a decree of Judicial Separation is granted, a spouse or a person acting on behalf of a dependent child may seek a Financial Compensation Order which can compel either or both spouses to:

- Effect a policy of life insurance for the benefit of the applicant or the dependent child.

- Assign the whole or a specified part of the interest in a life insurance policy effected by either, or both, spouses to the applicant or for the benefit of a dependent child.

- Make or continue to make the payments which either, or both, of the spouses is, or are, required to make under the terms of the policy.

A Financial Compensation Order will generally cease on the death or remarriage of an applicant spouse.

Stamp duty

Exemption from Stamp Duty will continue to apply on relevant property transactions.

Social welfare

The Social Welfare Contributory Widow(er)'s Pension is payable to the widow(er) following the death of their spouse for as long as the widow(er) does not remarry or does not cohabit with someone else as man and wife. The surviving spouse may qualify for a Widow(er)'s Pension either on their own PRSI contribution record, or that of their late spouse.

An Adult Dependent Supplement may not be payable to a claimant if that claimant's spouse is no longer wholly or mainly maintained by the claimant.

Divorce

The grounds on which a court may grant an application for a decree of divorce are those set out in Article 41.3.2 of the Constitution:

At the date of the institution of the proceeding, the spouses must have lived apart from one another for a period of, or periods amounting to, at least four years during the previous five years.

- There is no reasonable prospect of a reconciliation between the spouses

  and

- Such provisions as the court considers proper, having regard to the circumstances that exist, will be made for the spouses, any children of either or both of them and any person prescribed by law

  and

- Any further conditions prescribed by law are complied with.

Ancillary orders

The courts, on application by either spouse or by someone acting on behalf of a dependent child, can issue one or more of a number of Ancillary Orders including the following:

- Periodical payments and secured periodical payments order.
- Lump sum payments order.
- Property adjustment order.
- Order regarding occupation or sale of family home.

- Order regarding title of property.

- Variation of benefit of either spouse, or any dependent family member, of any pre or post nuptial agreement.

- Order regarding partition of property.

- Financial compensation orders.

- Pension adjustment orders.

- Order extinguishing succession rights.

- Order for sale of property, except the family home where a remarried spouse ordinarily resides with their spouse.

- Maintenance Pending Relief Order.

- Order for provision for one spouse out of the estate of the other spouse.

Legal impact

Divorce legally dissolves the marriage and each spouse may legally remarry after the decree.

Succession rights

Each spouse's succession rights are automatically extinguished by the decree of divorce. Any specific bequest in a Will to a former spouse will stand until a new Will is made or an existing Will is changed.

Income tax

If there are legally enforceable maintenance payments being made then the couple can generally either opt for Single Assessment or if both spouses remain resident in Ireland, Separate Assessment. If Single Assessment applies, maintenance payments for the benefit of the spouse are tax-deductible for the payer and are taxable in the hands of the recipient. Under Separate Assessment, maintenance payments are ignored for Income Tax purposes.

If you are divorced, your income tax position is the same as that under legal separation.

Capital gains tax

Divorced spouses are treated as two unconnected persons for CGT purposes:

- Transfers between spouses are no longer exempt from CGT. However, transfers by virtues of, or in consequence of, the divorce will not trigger a CGT liability.

- No transfer of unused losses between spouses.

Foreign divorce

If you obtain a foreign divorce which is not legally recognised in Ireland and you remarry, this marriage will not be legal in Ireland. However, it is current Revenue practice that when a marriage certificate is produced to accept it at face value from an Income Tax or Capital Gains Tax point of view.

Capital Acquisitions Tax

After divorce, you are no longer legal spouses and the spouse exemption ceases to apply in respect of any future gifts or inheritances for CAT purposes. The "stranger threshold" will apply for CAT purposes after the divorce. However, property transfers between former spouses on foot of a court order governing a decree of divorce will be exempt from Capital Acquisition Tax.

Pensions

The Family Law (divorce) Act 1996 envisages a number of ways in which a spouse's pension scheme benefits might be taken into account in the event of a decree of divorce:

> **Earmarking.**
>
> **Pension Splitting.**
>
> **Offsetting.**

Earmarking   A charge is set against a spouse's pension benefits, so that when they become payable a designated part of these benefits is payable to the other spouse.

Pension Splitting	The relevant pension benefits are split on an agreed basis between both spouses.
Offsetting	If proper financial provision can be made by other orders, e.g. financial compensation order or property adjustment order, the court may decide to offset these benefits against the relevant pension rights rather than "splitting everything down the middle".

Life assurance

After the granting of the decree of divorce, a spouse, or a person acting on behalf of a dependent child, may seek a financial compensation order which can compel either or both spouses to:

- Effect a policy of life insurance for the benefit of the applicant or the dependant child.

- Assign the whole or a specified part of the interest in a life insurance policy, effected by either or both spouses, to the applicant or for the benefit of a dependent child.

- Make or continue to make the payments which either, or both, of the spouses is, or are, required to make under the terms of the policy.

Such an order will cease on the death or remarriage of an applicant's spouse.

Social welfare

There is no change in either spouse's entitlement to a Social Welfare Widow(er)'s Pension following a decree of divorce provided that the other spouse has not remarried or is not cohabiting with someone else as man and wife.

If the deceased spouse had remarried both their current spouse and their ex-spouse are entitled to claim a Widow(er)'s pension if they meet the normal qualifying conditions.

19

Death - what to do about taxes

Chapter 19

While tax and financial matters are not the foremost consideration when somebody dies, they are nevertheless areas that must be sorted out before a deceased person's estate can be finalised.

Before looking at the tax consequences arising on a death it might be helpful to look briefly at some key terms, at the ways in which property passes on a death to the beneficiaries and at certain procedures that must be gone through before assets are handed over to the beneficiaries.

What is an "estate"?

A deceased's estate consists of whatever assets (e.g. bank accounts, stocks and shares, house, land, livestock, jewellery, car, etc.) which can be passed on to beneficiaries following the deceased's death.

How does the estate pass on to the beneficiaries?

The assets, which make up the deceased's estate, can be passed on in a number of ways. Assets left by Will pass to the beneficiaries in accordance with the terms of the Will. If there is no Will (a situation known as intestacy), assets that would otherwise have passed by Will pass instead under special rules laid down by law. In addition, assets can also pass outside of the Will or intestacy.

Examples of assets which pass under the Will or intestacy

- Assets owned in the deceased's sole name.

- Assets owned by the deceased but placed in the name of another person for convenience or some similar reason.

- Assets placed by the deceased in the joint names of the deceased and another person without the intention of benefiting that other person.

Examples of assets which pass outside of the Will or intestacy

- Assets passing by nomination, e.g. the deceased may have instructed An Post to pay Saving Certificates on his or her death to a particular person, called the nominee.

- Death benefits passing under a life insurance policy or pension scheme where the beneficiaries are particular family members named in the policy or scheme.

- Assets passing in which the deceased had an interest for his or her life only.

- Assets placed by the deceased in the joint names of the deceased and another person with the intention of benefiting that other person on the deceased's death.

The Personal Representative

The **Personal Representative** is the person who is responsible for finalising the deceased's affairs. He or she must, within a reasonable time, collect the assets passing under the **Will** or **intestacy**, pay any debts and distribute the surplus assets to the beneficiaries entitled to them.

If there is a Will, it is likely that the Personal Representative has been appointed by being named in the Will as its executor and has taken on the responsibility, because he or she is the deceased's spouse or one of the next-of-kin. A Personal Representative who has not been appointed by Will is known as an **administrator**.

Beneficiary

A **Beneficiary** is a person who inherits either the whole or part of the deceased's estate whether passing under the Will or intestacy or outside of the Will or intestacy.

Trustee

Instead of providing for property to be given directly to the beneficiary, the deceased's Will may provide that, for a specified period, the property is to be held in trust on behalf of the beneficiary by **trustees** named in the Will. Such trusts may arise because the beneficiary concerned is very young, or because the deceased wishes the property to be held for the benefit of one person for life and, on the death of that person, to be transferred to another beneficiary. The trustees will take over the management of the trust property only after the estate has been administered by the personal representative. The trust will then continue until the time specified in the Will for the ultimate handling over of the property.

Note: The same person can have more than one role; for example, a Personal Representative can also be a Beneficiary.

Assets passing outside of the Will or intestacy

Before assets are handed over to the beneficiaries certain procedures must be gone through. Broadly, these are as follows:

Before assets are handed over to the beneficiaries

In the case of an asset passing outside of the Will or intestacy, production of a death certificate by the beneficiary is often all that is required to establish the beneficiary's entitlement to receive the asset in question.

Assets passing under the Will or intestacy

In order to get legal confirmation of his or her appointment, the Personal Representative must apply to the Probate Office of the High Court for a document known as a Grant of Representation. The Grant of Representation acts as an assurance to financial institutions (e.g. banks, building societies, credit union, etc.) and to others that they can safely place the deceased's assets in the hands of the person named as Personal Representative in the grant. The Grant of Representation is also known as a Grant of Probate (where there is a Will) or Letters of Administration (where there is no Will).

The application for the **Grant of Representation** will normally be made by a solicitor acting on behalf of the Personal Representative. In straightforward cases, it may be possible to make a personal application for the grant through the Personal Application Section of the Probate Office.

Special additional procedure relating to money in joint names

In the absence of a letter of clearance from the Revenue Commissioners, banks, building societies and other financial institutions are prohibited by law from releasing monies (other than current accounts) lodged or deposited in the joint names of the deceased and another person or persons. This applies if, at the date of death, the total of all the amounts standing with the institution in the joint names of the deceased and that other person or persons exceeds €6,350. It does not apply, however, to monies which have only been held in the joint names of the deceased and his or her surviving spouse.

Applications for letters of clearance for production to financial institutions should be made to the Capital Taxes Office of the Revenue Commissioners.

If you are a Personal Representative

In summary this is what you should do about tax and when you should do it.

Sorting out the deceased's pre-death tax affairs

As Personal Representative, you are responsible for settling any outstanding tax matters for the period up to the date of death. Depending on the circumstances, you may need to pay additional taxes or claim a repayment.

Notifying the tax office

The deceased's tax office should be advised as soon as possible of the date of death and the name and address of the Personal Representative. This will ensure that correspondence will be addressed to the Personal Representative until such time as the administration of the estate is finalised.

The address of the deceased's tax office can be found on any correspondence from that office to the deceased. If you are in any doubt as to which tax office to contact, get in touch with your local tax office.

Remember that:

- If you distribute the estate without paying any outstanding tax liabilities, you may have to pay the tax out of your own pocket.

- If you fail to claim a tax rebate due to the estate, you may have to make good the loss to the estate.

If the deceased was *self-employed*, you will most likely get the deceased's accountant to file any outstanding Income Tax returns and business accounts with the deceased's tax office. As well as Income Tax, you will also need to ensure that any outstanding VAT, employer's PAYE/PRSI, or other taxes in respect of the period up to the date of death are fully paid.

If the deceased was an employee, there may be a PAYE tax rebate due, as the deceased's tax credits for the year of death may not have been fully used up. The deceased's employer will send Form P45 to the tax office which dealt with the deceased's tax affairs. Any tax rebate will form part of the deceased's estate. As Personal Representative, it is your responsibility to file any outstanding tax returns on behalf of the deceased.

Completing the Revenue Affidavit

The Revenue Affidavit is an account of the deceased's estate that has to be completed and sworn by the personal representative in order to get a Grant of Representation from the Probate Office. Before being presented to the Probate Office it must be submitted to the Capital Taxes Office for certification.

What information is looked for in the Affidavit?

The Revenue Affidavit looks for:

- A full account of the deceased's assets and liabilities at the date of death;

- Information on, among other things, assets passing outside of the Will or intestacy.

  and

- Details of the beneficiaries and of the value of the benefits taken.

To complete the Affidavit for gifts/inheritance taxes on or after 5th December 2001, you will need to establish whether the beneficiaries have received any other gifts or inheritances - either from the deceased or from any other person - at any time on or after 5th December 1991.

What happens to the Affidavit?

The Capital Taxes Office having examined the Affidavit will certify it once satisfied that Inheritance Tax due by the beneficiaries will be paid. A copy of the certified Affidavit will then be returned to your solicitor or - if you are making a personal application for the Grant of Representation - to the Probate Office or to the appropriate District Probate Registry. The certified Affidavit is part of the documentation required by the Probate Office when processing the application for the Grant of Representation.

Income and capital gains during the administration period

It may take the Personal Representative some time to administer the estate during which time income may be earned or capital gains may be made. Broadly the position is as follows.

Income tax

- The Personal Representative is liable to pay Income Tax at the standard rate on income earned during the administration period. There is no entitlement to personal tax credits or to any of the reliefs otherwise available to individual taxpayers.

- In certain circumstances, the tax office may concessionally agree to treat the beneficiary as succeeding to the inheritance from the date of death. In such circumstances, the beneficiary will take full responsibility for paying Income Tax on the post-death income as if he or she had been entitled to the asset - and the income - from the date of death.

Capital gains tax (CGT)

- Death does not give rise to a Capital Gains Tax liability. For example, if the deceased bought shares for €10,000 and they were worth €15,000 at the date of death, the €5,000 capital gain is not taxable.

If the Personal Representative sells any property during the administration period, there may be a liability to Capital Gains Tax - but only to the extent that the value of the property in question has increased between the date of death and the date of sale. Following on from the example above, if the Personal Representative sells the shares during the administration period for €16,000, the relevant capital gain is €1,000 and is taxable. The distribution of property by the personal representative to the beneficiaries does not give rise to a Capital Gains Tax liability.

You should be aware that, in addition, the Personal Representative has secondary liability for the payment of any Inheritance Tax due by the beneficiaries in respect of the benefits they take under the Will or intestacy. This means that if a beneficiary should fail to pay, the personal representative will have to do so.

If you are a surviving spouse

This section gives an outline of the main tax exemption and reliefs specifically for surviving spouses.

Main tax exemptions reliefs for surviving spouses

In summary these are covered under the following headings;

- Inheritance Tax;
- Income Tax;

Inheritance tax

If you take an inheritance from your late spouse you don't have to pay Inheritance Tax. The exemption is unlimited - it doesn't matter how much you inherit, it is entirely exempt. There is no necessity to claim this exemption and you don't have to fill in any Inheritance Tax forms.

Income tax - for the year in which your spouse has died

Your Income Tax treatment for the tax year (i.e. the year to 31st December) in which your spouse has died will depend on how you and your spouse were treated before your bereavement.

Your tax office will help you to do the calculations and make sure you have the right tax credits. Broadly, the position is as follows:

- If your late spouse was the "assessable spouse", i.e. the person responsible for making a joint tax return on behalf of both of you, then you will be entitled to a special increased widowed person's credit from the date of your spouse's death up to the following 31st December. The single person's rate bands will apply for this period.
- If you yourself were the "assessable spouse", you will continue to get the married person's credit and rate bands for the remainder of the tax year.

You will be taxable on your own income for the full tax year and your spouse's income from 1st January to date of death.

- If you were both taxed as single persons, you will get the special increased widowed person's credit and single rate bands for the year.

Special credit for surviving spouse with a dependent child

If you have any dependent children you may be entitled to a special Income Tax credit (called "widowed parent's credit") for the 5 tax years after the year of your spouse's death. You may also be entitled to the "one-parent family credit" for as long as you have any dependent children.

Widowed person's tax credit

A widowed person whose spouse has died in a given tax year is entitled to the widowed person's bereaved credit, for that year only. This credit is the same as the married person's credit but is not available to a surviving spouse who is the subject of a joint assessment for the same year. A widowed person with dependent children is also entitled to;

- The One Parent Family Credit

  and

- Widowed Parent Credit

Widowed parent tax credit

This credit is available for the five years following the year of death. For the 2006 tax year the amount of the credit are as follows; (see page 107 for 2007 rates)

€3,100	in first tax year after death.
€2,600	in second tax year after death.
€2,100	in third tax year after death.
€1,600	fourth tax year after death
€1,100	in fifth tax year after death.

Widow(er) in year of bereavement

The tax treatment for individuals in the year of death depends on whether they were taxed under joint or separate assessment and whether it was the assessable spouse who died.

- If your late spouse was the assessable spouse, i.e. the person responsible for making the joint tax return on behalf of both of you, then you will be entitled to a special increased widowed person's credit from the date of your spouse's death up to the following 31st December. The single person's rate bands will apply for this period.

- If your late spouse was not the "assessable spouse", you will continue to get the married person's credit and rate bands for the remainder of the tax year. You will be taxable on your own income for the full tax year in which your spouse died plus your late spouse's income from 1st January to the date of death.

- If you were both taxed as single persons, you will get the special increased widowed person's credit and single rate bands for the year.

See example on page 351

Note: The surviving spouse can elect for joint assessment for the year of death before the end of that tax year.

Widow(er) in subsequent tax years

The tax position of a widow or widower in subsequent tax years is as follows;

- A reduced Personal Tax Credit.

- A single person's Tax Band.

- A single person's PAYE Tax Credit.

- Reduced Mortgage Interest Tax Credit, if applicable.

- Single Parent Tax Credit.

- Widowed Parent Tax Credit (for 5 years following bereavement).

Example

A married Couple/Widow(er) with one dependent child and a salary of €40,000 p.a. (only one spouse working).

Widow(er) in subsequent year

	2006			
	Married €		**Widow(er)** €	
Gross Salary	€45,000		€45,000	
Taxable Income	**Tax**		**Tax**	
Taxable @ 20%	€41,000	€8,200	€36,000	€7,200
@ 42%	€ 4,000	€1,680	€ 9,000	€3,780
Total Tax Payable		**€9,880**		**€10,980**
Less: Tax Credits				
Married Person		(€3,260)		
PAYE		(€1,490)		(€1,490)
Widowed Person		(n/a)		(€1,630)
Single Parent		(n/a)		(€1,630)
Net tax payable		**€5,130**		**€6,230**

350

Income tax for the year in which your spouse has died

A married couple have annual earnings of €25,00 p.a. each. The assessable spouse, dies on 30th September 2006. The surviving spouse is entitled to a widow's pension of €9,000 p.a. from 1st October 2006

	Assessable Spouse	Non - Assessable Spouse
	€	€
	(9 months)	(3 months)
Salary - Assessable Spouse (to date of death)	€18,750	
Salary - Non Assessable Spouse	€18,750	€6,250
Pension		€2,250
Taxable Income	€37,500	€8,500
€37,500 / €8,500 @ 20%	€7,500	€1,700
Less: Tax Credit		
Personal	(€3,260)	
PAYE	(€2,980)	(€1,490)
Net Tax payable	€1,260	€210

At the end of the tax year the surviving spouse could apply for a refund if the total amount of tax paid for the full year exceeds €1,980

A married couple had annual earnings of €25,000 p.a. each. The non-assessable spouse dies on 30th September 2006. The surviving spouse is entitled to a widow's pension of €6,000 p.a. or €500 p.m. from 1st October 2006

	Assessable Spouse	Non - Assessable Spouse
	€	€
	(12 months)	(9 months)
Salary - Assessable Spouse (to date of death)	€25,000	
Salary - Non Assessable Spouse	€18,750	n/a
Pension	€2,250	n/a
Taxable Income	€46,000	n/a
€46,000 @ 20%	€9,200	n/a
Less: Tax Credit		
Personal	(€3,260)	n/a
PAYE	(€1,490)	
Net Tax payable	€4,450	NIL

Any unused allowances which the non assessable spouse had at the date of their date could be transferred to the assessable spouse before the end of the tax year.

Let yours be a Willing heart...

... to make the world a healthier place for our children and grandchildren to inherit.

The Irish Heart Foundation is working to reduce premature death and disability from heart disease and stroke. Please remember us in your will and let your personal legacy to the next generation be one of generosity, care and far-reaching compassion.

If you have already made a will, it's easy to amend it to include a gift to the Irish Heart Foundation. Minor changes like this do not require a new will, as an existing will can be amended by completing a codicil, which your solicitor will help you draw up. **Legacies to charity are exempt from tax.** So by leaving a gift to The Irish Heart Foundation, you could substantially reduce the amount of tax payable on your estate.

Ask us to send you our free information booklet titled:

Leave a Legacy and Save a Life

Contact:
The Irish Heart Foundation
4 Clyde Road, Ballsbridge, Dublin 4
Tel: +353 1 - 668 5001   Fax +353 1 - 668 5896
Email: Info@irishheart.ie   Or visit our website www.irishheart.ie

Where there's a Will there's a relative!

This old proverb is never out of date. It has also been said that nothing is more inevitable than death and taxes. While, good financial planning cannot lessen your sense of loss on the death of a loved one, it can reduce your tax bill.

Issues that need to be considered when you have assets to pass on, include:

- Making a Will.

- Testate and Intestacy.

- The Succession Acts.

- Capital Acquisition Tax.

- Probate.

Anyone who owns property or other assets such as a life assurance policy, savings plan or even a simple deposit account, should make a Will. A Will not only ensures that you can distribute your wealth as you wish, but it also means that your family and beneficiaries are spared the expense and distress of a complicated and drawn-out administration of your estate, as set out by the Succession Act 1965.

Wills should be drawn up with the assistance of a solicitor. The simpler the terms of the Will, the less work involved and the lower the fee. However, it will be money well spent.

Many people do not realise that a Will is revoked on marriage unless it is clearly made with the marriage in mind. An important time to make a Will, if you haven't done so already, or to review an existing one, is when you have children. This is in order that you name a legal guardian for the child(ren) in the unlikely event that both you and your spouse should die together, or soon after each other.

When you make a Will you will have to name an executor, someone who has the responsibility of seeing that your wishes are carried out and your assets distributed. Married couples often name each other, or an adult child or a family advisor - a solicitor or accountant - to act as executor. Others choose a business partner, bank manager or friend. Even if you, as a spouse, are named as Executor, your family advisor can assist with the various procedures involved.

Planning ahead

Before you meet your solicitor, gather up a list of your assets and the names and addresses of the people whom you wish to be beneficiaries and make sure your Executor consents to being named in your Will.

- A Will must be in writing - verbal ones are not valid.

- A Will must be witnessed by two people, neither of whom can be beneficiaries.

- You cannot disinherit your spouse.

- Your Will will remain in force until death or marriage unless it is clearly made with the marriage in mind. If a new Will is made, it automatically revokes any previous Wills you may have made.

- You should always keep a copy of your Will in a safe place - a strongbox or bank safety deposit facility. Let your Executor and family know where it is and where your other valuable papers are kept.

Dying "intestate"

If you die without making a Will, this is known as dying "intestate" and all your property will be distributed according to the 1965 Succession Act. (See page 356).

Since there is no official Executor, the Personal Representative of the deceased - who can be a spouse, relative or even friend, will need to obtain what is known as a grant of Letters of Administration, in order to distribute the proceeds of your estate to your beneficiaries.

Death and taxes

Capital Acquisition Tax (CAT) is the State levy on a deceased person's estate.

Inheritance tax

If after your death the beneficiaries of your estate receive sums in excess of the Thresholds for Capital Acquisitions Tax (CAT) purposes Inheritance Tax will be payable.

Gift tax

A liability to gift tax arises when a person receives a benefit liable to capital acquisitions tax other than on a death.

Tax-free threshold for CAT

There are three tax free thresholds which apply for CAT purposes. From 1st January 2006 these threshold amounts were as follows:

Group 1   €478,155 where the recipient is a child, or minor grandchild of the benefactor, if the parent is dead. In some cases this threshold can also apply to a parent, niece or nephew who have worked in a family business for a period of time.

Group 2   €47,815 where the recipient is a brother, sister, niece, nephew or linear ancestor/descendent of the benefactor or where the gift is made by the child to the parent.

Group 3   €23,908 in all other cases.

From April 2000 Group 1 Threshold applies to gifts/inheritance taken from a foster parent to a foster child provided the foster child was cared for and maintained from a young age up to the age of eighteen for a period of 5 years. The foster child must also have lived with the foster parent for the period.

SUCCESSION ACT 1965

Relatives surviving	Distribution of estate where the deceased dies intestate
Spouse and Issue	2/3rds to spouse, 1/3rd to issue in equal shares. Children of a deceased son or daughter take their parent's share.
Spouse and no Issue	Whole estate to spouse.
Issue and no Spouse	Whole estate to Issue in equal shares Children of a deceased son or daughter take their parent's share.
Father, mother, brothers and sisters	1/2 to each parent.
Parent, brothers and sisters	Whole estate to parent.
Brothers and sisters	All take equal shares. Children of a deceased brother or sister take their parent's share.
Nephews and nieces	All take equal shares.
Remoter next-of-kin	All take equal shares.

Legal rights of spouse under a Will

Irrespective of what the deceased leaves to his Spouse, the Spouse has a legal entitlement as follows:

Relatives surviving	Spouse's share by legal right
Spouse and Issue	One-third of estate
Spouse and no issue	One-half of estate

CAT rates

Amount	Rate
Below Threshold	Nil
Balance	20%

Some benefits are not subject to CAT:

- Any inheritance or gifts made between spouses;

- The first €3,000 of all gifts received from a benefactor in any calendar year;

- Any inheritance received from a deceased child which had been given to that child as a Gift by the parent;

- Irish Government stock given to a non-Irish domiciled beneficiary, so long as it had been held by the beneficiary for at least three years previously, extended to six years for gifts and inheritance taxes after 15th February 2001.

- After 1st December 1999, a family home, provided the following conditions are met;

    - It is the principal private residence of the disponer and/or the recipient;

    - The recipient had been living in the home for the three years prior to the transfer;

    - The recipient does not have an interest in any other residential property;

The relief will be withdrawn if the recipient disposes of the home within six years of the transfer.

Business relief

Relief from CAT is available where business property is acquired under a gift or inheritance. This relief works by reducing the value of the qualifying asset which pass under a gift or inheritance by 90%.

The following condition apply to this relief;

- The qualifying business assets must have been owned by the disponer for at least 5 years in the case of a gift or at least 2 years in the case of an inheritance.
- Qualifying business assets;
    - Unquoted shares or securities of an Irish company.
    - Land, buildings, machinery or plant owned by the disponer but used by a company controlled by the disponer.
    - Quoted shares or securities of an Irish company which were owned by the disponer prior to them being quoted.

The relief will be clawed back is the assets are disposed of within 6 years of the gift/inheritance.

Agricultural land

Agricultural lands which are passed on as part of an inheritance enjoy some additional CAT relief's. Instead of the land being assessed for CAT purposes at its full market value, it is assessed at 10% of its value. The relief will be disallowed, however, if the property is disposed of within six years of the inheritance (or gift) and partly disallowed if disposed of within six to ten years.

CAT payments

As a recipient of a gift or inheritance you are obliged to file a return within four months of the valuation date (date of benefit) where 80% of your threshold amount is exceeded.

Inheritance/gift from a child to a parent

If a "child" gives a gift to a parent the Group 2 threshold of €47,815 applies. However, the Group 1 threshold of €478,155 applies if a parent receives an inheritance from "a child".

Section 60 policy

CAT can be avoided by a beneficiary if a Section 60 life assurance policy was taken out for the purpose of paying CAT. Policies like these appeal to people who are leaving large estates to their families or other beneficiaries.

Since Capital Acquisitions Tax in the form of an Inheritance or Gift are subject to aggregation - a rolling up of benefits from various sources - the relevant thresholds can be affected. The calculations can be very complicated and you should always consult your financial or tax advisor.

Foreign Inheritance

If you receive an inheritance or gift from another jurisdiction there may be a tax liability to be met in that country and here. However, you may be entitled to a tax credit on the tax paid abroad to ensure you don't pay double tax. The credit will not exceed the Irish rate of tax payable.

Death - capital gains tax

A liability to Capital Gains Tax does not arise on death. When you inherit an asset you are treated for Capital Gains Tax purposes as receiving the asset at the date of death at the market value at that time.

Useful References

The Pensions Board, Verschoyle House, 28/30 Lower Mount Street, Dublin 2. Tel: 01 6131900 www.pensionsboard.ie pb@pensionsboard.ie	The Irish Credit Bureau ICB House, Newsteed, Clonskeagh, Dublin 14 Tel: (01) 260 0388. http://oasis.gov.ie/personal_finance/irish_credit_bureau.html
Revenue Commissioners www.revenue.ie	Department of Social & Family Affairs, Information Services, Aras Mac Dhiarmada, Store Street, Dublin 1. Tel: 01 8748444 www.welfare.ie
Department of Social & Family Affairs, Pension Services Office College Road, Sligo. Tel: 071 9169800 Locall: 1890 500 000 www.welfare.ie	The Ombudsman's Office, 52 St. Stephen's Green, Dublin 2. Tel: 01 678 5222 ombudsman@ombudsman.gov.ie
Office of the Pensions Ombudsman, 36 Upper Mount Street, Dublin 2. Tel: 01 647 1650 www.pensionsombudsman.ie	Irish Financial Services Regulatory Authority (IFSRA) PO Box 9138, College Green, Dublin 2. Locall: 1890 777 777 www.ifsra.ie consumerinfo@ifsra.ie

Glossary of Terms

APR

This stands for annual percentage rate - the annual rate of interest charged on a loan. It takes account of all the costs involved over the full term of the loan, such as any setup charges and the interest rate. It provides one of the best means of comparing the cost of different types of credit.

Bridging Loan

This is a short-term loan given by a lending institution to 'bridge' a time difference between buying a new home and selling your existing home. This loan is then paid off when the current property is sold.

Collateral

Property or some other asset used as security for a loan

Conveyancing

Technical term for the legal process of buying, selling and mortgaging a property.

Current Account Mortgage

A current account mortgage is a mortgage linked to your current account which allows you to vary your monthly payments. By over-paying each month you can save yourself a substantial amount of interest

Deeds

The legal document by which legal title to freehold and leasehold property is transferred from the seller to the buyer.

Default

Failure to pay some or all installments due on a mortgage or other loan.

Deposit

The amount, usually around 10% of the house purchase price.

Equity

Net value of your home calculated by subtracting the outstanding mortgage owing from the current market value.

Equity Release

Equity is the difference between the amount of money a person owes on their mortgage and the current value of their home. Equity Release allows you to borrow up to 90% of the current value of you home, for a number of different purposes.

Freehold

The owner of the property owns the property without payment of any rent and without a limit in time.

Ground Rent

A sum of money, usually paid annually, by leaseholders to the owner of the freehold.

Guarantor

A person who agrees to pay the borrowers debt if the mortgage holder defaults (fails to pay).

HB47

The Home Bond Scheme Certificate provided by your builder). The aim of this scheme is to protect new houses against structural defects and to ensure that property standards are maintained in the house building industry.

Indemnity Bond

An insurance policy, in favour of your lender, to cover any shortfall that might arise between the amount owing and the value of your home if you default. An indemnity bond is usually required when you are borrowing more than a certain percentage of the purchase price - e.g. 75%. Many lenders waive this fee for first-time buyers.

Irish Credit Bureau

A credit reference agency that maintains a database of individual credit histories and ratings. You can obtain a copy of your own details for a small fee by contacting the ICB on (01) 260 0388 or download a form from www.oasis.gov.ie.

Irish Financial Services Regulatory Authority (IFSRA)

The Irish Financial Services Regulatory Authority (IFSRA), now called the Financial Regulator, is in charge of 'regulating' the Irish financial services market - including advisers, banks, building societies, credit unions, and insurance companies.

Land Registry

A Government body that records ownership of property.

Legal Charge

A legal document conferring legal ownership of the mortgagor's (borrowers) estate to the lender, while allowing the mortgagor to remain in possession and to use the property with the right to redeem legal ownership, which is called equity of redemption.

Leasehold Property

The purchaser owns the property buy pays ground rent annually and is subject to the terms of the lease.

Letter of Offer

Also called the 'offer of advance' this is a formal statement by the lender of the amount they are prepared to lend you.

Loan-to-Value (LTV)

This is a percentage size of the loan based on the value of the property. E.g. If you owe €50,000 and you home is worth €200,000, your LTV is 25%.

Mortgage Protection

This is a term life insurance product, which lenders are legally obliged (except in limited circumstances) to ensure you have in place. It pays off the outstanding amount due on your mortgage if you die. You are free to shop around for the best rates and do not have to accept the lenders' product or recommendation.

Mortgage protection insurance should not be confused with mortgage repayment protection, which provides cover for a certain number of installments in the event that you fall ill, have an accident or become unemployed.

Mortgage Repayment Cover

This ensures that your mortgage repayments are met for a period of up to 12 months, following an accident, sickness or redundancy.

Negative Equity

This occurs when the amount owing on your house is higher than the market value.

Net Worth

In order to calculate your net worth you add up the value of all your assets and then deducting the total of all your debts. This is what you are really worth.

Rate of Return

This is the amount of money you make from an investment. It is worked out by adding together any capital appreciation and any income you have received. The rate of return is expressed as a percentage.

Redemption

The word used to describe a mortgage when it is repaid.

Remortgage

A mortgage which is a replacement loan for another mortgage

Retention

A condition of a mortgage whereby the lender holds back a portion of the advance, pending work to be carried out by the mortgagor.

Searches

Your solicitor will undertake searches to confirm that the seller of a property can pass ownership to you and that there are no outstanding judgments or liens (outstanding debt) against the property.

Structural Survey

A comprehensive and detailed assessment of the condition of the property, which is carried out by a qualified surveyor. It can identify defects that would not be evident from a valuation.

Surety

Another name for a guarantor.

Split Rate (Mix & Match)

Here you can set a part of your mortgage at a fixed rate and the remainder at a variable rate. If rates fall, the repayments on the variable part of your mortgage will reduce, and if rates rise you have the security of knowing that only the variable payment is affected.

Term

The number of years over which the mortgage loan is arranged.

Tied Agent

Sales people selling products and services on behalf of one company. Their financial advice is neither impartial nor independent.

Title

The legal right to ownership of the property.

Title Deeds

The documents showing the ownership of the property.

Undertaking

A condition of a mortgage where the borrower is obliged to carry out certain works within a specific period of time following completion of the mortgage.

Unsecured Loan

A loan that is not supported by an asset to guarantee repayment of the loan.

Variable Rate

With a variable rate, your monthly repayments may rise or fall from time to time, in line with general market interest rates. If rates fall your monthly repayment reduces, but if rates rise you pay more.

Index

Are You Paying Too Much Tax?

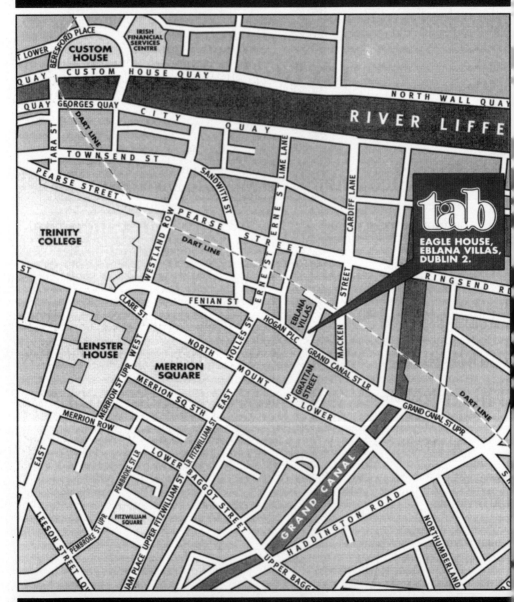

Let TAB Map out Your Financial Options For You!